Loving
Letters from
Ogden Nash

Loving
Letters from
Ogden Nash

A Family Album

Introduced and Selected by
Linell Nash Smith

Little, Brown and Company
BOSTON TORONTO LONDON

FIRST EDITION

Frontispiece: Ogden Nash with daughter Linell (*standing*) and
Frances Leonard Nash, fall 1950.
Photo by Robert W. Kelley, *Life* magazine © Time Inc.

LIBRARY OF CONGRESS CATALOGING-IN-PUBLICATION DATA

Nash, Ogden, 1902–1971.
Loving letters from Ogden Nash: a family album/introduced and
selected by Linell Nash Smith. — 1st ed.
p.   cm.
ISBN 0-316-59835-6
1. Nash, Ogden, 1902–1971 — Correspondence.   2. Nash, Ogden,
1902–1971 — Biography — Family.   3. Poets, American — 20th century —
Correspondence.   I. Smith, Linell Nash.   II. Title.
PS3527.A637Z48   1990
[B]
89-14009
CIP

10 9 8 7 6 5 4 3 2 1

F G

Published simultaneously in Canada
by Little, Brown & Company (Canada) Limited

PRINTED IN THE UNITED STATES OF AMERICA

Then, now, and always,
for F.L.N.
*"With that extra five minutes at the
end of always"*

Preface

IN THE early summer of 1988, I visited the Harry Ransom Center at the University of Texas at Austin to choose letters for this book from the vast collection of Ogden Nash work and memorabilia that has been housed there since the university acquired it from my father in 1967. The enormity of my task soon became apparent when I realized that there were almost seven hundred letters that fitted the profile of the family album I had in mind. At home in Maryland, I had borrowed and collected about four hundred others from family members, and so was working with a combined total of over a thousand personal letters, a treasury of insight into the private world of Ogden Nash. Clearly this book is not the definitive collected letters of Ogden Nash, for it only includes family correspondence. It is not even the definitive collected family letters of Ogden Nash, since, through much heart-wrenching editing, only a tenth of the available material is to be found here.

However, these letters to his family span sixty years of my father's life and seem to tell their own unique story of that life. The bulk of correspondence on these pages is addressed to my mother, and on reading my father's courtship letters one feels a certain sense of frustration at not being able to read the replies to his suit. It's rather like watching someone play tennis against a backboard. However, my mother's sense of privacy is something that one cannot help but understand. After all, *she* wasn't the public personality, and her responses to the tumultuous siege of communications from New York were meant for the recipient's eyes only.

When negotiations with the University of Texas for my father's papers began in 1965, she was put in a miserable position. She knew that his love letters were the linchpin of the collection, and that no matter how she might feel about strangers reading what he had written her, there could be no question about their inclusion in the package. But hers to him were another matter. She had never been a public figure; the love, the doubts, the fears, the joys that she had expressed in her letters were a private matter, shared only with him. And so while she sadly agreed to give up his letters, which she had carefully preserved and cherished since November of 1928, it was only on the condition that my father destroy those she had written him. A costly bargain for both parties — but it was struck and faithfully kept.

I would like to note here that my mother's letters to my grandparents and to my sister and me were awaited as eagerly as those from my father. Her observations, descriptions, and anecdotes rivaled his and always made us feel as if we were with her instead of miles — sometimes oceans — apart. So her letters to my father must have been delightful, and while he chided her occasionally for lack of quantity, the quality could never have been in question.

In one of his letters to her, he noted he had formed a "lopsided attachment . . . for a young female with a pleasant voice and symmetrical features and the modest hesitant shyness of a Jane Austen heroine without the ability of a Jane Austen heroine to carry on a voluminous and agreeable correspondence." To have matched him letter for letter would have been a Herculean task, since between November 1928 and March 1931 Daddy bombarded her with almost 350 letters. However, a count of his acknowledgments of her replies totals roughly 150, which means he wrote on the average a letter every two and a half days; she, a letter every five and a half days. A modest, hesitant, shy Jane Austen heroine would not have produced more without losing her modifying adjectives.

Except for explanatory passages here and there, the following book is by Ogden Nash. The reader will find in it the private side of the man, the one his family knew and loved. The heart of the work is the torrent of letters, poems, notes, and cards to my mother. And this is as it should be, for the love that they shared was the most important thing in his life. It was born the day they met and ended only with his death in 1971. His last words were "I love you, Frances."

Acknowledgments

I WOULD LIKE to thank Cathy Henderson and other staff members of the Harry Ransom Humanities Research Center of the University of Texas at Austin for their generous assistance to me during the preparation of this book. Also, my heartfelt thanks to George William Crandell, whose meticulous *Catalogue of Correspondence* of the Nash material at Texas was an indispensible aid. The dedicated work of my father's friend and racing buddy, David F. Woods, in collecting reminiscences of Ogden Nash from friends and family during the 1970s proved to be invaluable and I would like to acknowledge it here. My thanks go also to my agent, Perry Knowlton, for believing in the book, to my editor, Kit Ward, for guiding me through what seemed to be an impossible number of agonizing choices that had to be made because of the mass of material that was involved, and to editorial assistant Kelly Aherne for leading me through the maze of getting a book ready for publication.

But most of all I would like to thank my family — Mother, Isabel, Freddy, Johnny, and all the children, especially my after-hours typist, Francie. Their contributions and their support have made this book what it should be — a family effort. My father would have approved of that.

As the Twig Is Bent . . .

OVERLEAF:
Frederick Ogden Nash at five.

IN THE FALL of 1943, the musical comedy *One Touch of Venus* opened in New York to rave reviews. Its lyricist and coauthor was also making his Broadway debut, though his name had already become a household word in America because of his unique light verse. That man was Ogden Nash.

I remember the night I first saw a performance of *Venus*, and I can still feel the special thrill of listening to Mary Martin singing songs that I had heard in the making. The next morning, when I carefully pasted the program into my theater scrapbook, I wrote beside it in my very best hand, "This is my favorite play. I went with Mummy and Daddy and Minnie and Isabel and Mrs. Longwell." And then I added, in parentheses, "This is *Daddy's* play!"

I was eleven at the time; Ogden Nash was just "Daddy" to me — and only in that sense a household word. My ignorance of my father's place in the world of American letters was appalling but it stood testimony to the gentle, unassuming nature of the man himself. Until *Venus* blazed its success across the serene skies of my own small world, I had no idea that Daddy was an important part of a much, much larger one.

As children, my sister Isabel and I basked in the secure knowledge that, second only to being our mother's husband, being our father was the most important thing in his life. We knew that he wrote funny poems that appeared in books and magazines and that sometimes he would be asked to read them on the radio. To us, though, these were just things he did on the side. Being "Daddy" was what he *really* did. We felt ourselves at the center of his universe.

But when *Speak Low* made the Lucky Strike Hit Parade and stayed on it for months, we began to acknowledge reluctantly the larger world of Ogden Nash. We didn't like it much, for we were jealous of his place in our own, and afraid that the magic circle we shared as a family would be broken. We were especially discomfited by the increasingly posed question, often delivered in a rather arch manner, "Now tell me, dear, *what* is it like to be the daughter of Ogden Nash?" I would usually squirm in misery and manage an inarticulate "Uh . . . well . . . neat, I guess," and flee, but Isabel would take on the interrogator in her own inimitable way. Her blue eyes wide and innocent, she would respond, "I have no basis for comparison. You see, I've never been anyone else's daughter." This logical answer, delivered with the addition of a sunny smile, would leave the tormentor to murmur in confusion, "Why, how *clever* of you, dear. I never thought of that."

Each of us, in her own way, was guarding the secret place where Ogden Nash was only "Daddy," the place that he had created for us and was himself most careful to preserve. Once, when pressed for personal anecdotes in the course of an interview, he said, "I have no private life and no personality." In 1966 he served fair warning to all future biographers in the verse "The Non-Biography of a Nobody." I'm sure that he would have smiled in satisfaction when one would-be chronicler, after months of dogged investigation, abandoned the project in disgust with the comment, "There's no money in *this* stuff — it reads like something for *Reader's Digest*." But the quiet, decent, private life that evoked the frustration of a biographer was the catalyst for a family's happiness. Our existence was untouched by artistic temperament in our home, or by headlines in a scandal sheet on a corner newsstand.

Humor was an important part of the magic that was Daddy. He once called it "Hope's companion-in-arms," and he urged its use in times of trouble as "a shield, a weapon, a survival kit." He also taught us to laugh at ourselves, an indispensible lesson for coming to terms with life.

Recollected scenes from the Eden that was my childhood sustain me still. When gathering material for this book, one memento in particular validated my memories of Daddy. It was a little diary, all pages blank save one. On that, written in my mother's hand, is a question-and-answer game, the heading for which reads

Baltimore, June 15, 1940 — Ogden

My father's answers to five of the questions that followed drew my especial attention, and seemed to form an incisive portrait of the man I remember.

What is your favorite occupation?

Writing verse.

What trait of character do you admire most in a man?

Fortitude.

What is your idea of happiness?

To know what you want.

What is your idea of misery?

Aimlessness.

The last question and response on the page was this:

As the Twig Is Bent . . .

What is your dream?

> To have my children glad that I'm
> their father.

Half a century later, if I could tell him that his dream had always been reality, I would hope that he might respond with the closing lines he wrote for *Venus:* "You don't have to tell me. I know."

On looking back at my father's life, I came to realize that the key to understanding Ogden Nash the man was to learn what nourished and shaped the boy. And I found that from his earliest days, the central theme and touchstone of his life was family.

In today's world, the definition of "family" is open to interpretation. Often it consists of only two or three people, and almost always it includes merely the so-called "nuclear unit." But the world into which my father was born viewed the word "family" very differently. Children were familiar with the distinctions between first cousins once removed and second cousins, between second cousins once removed and third cousins and, moreover, accepted them all as members of the working family roster. This large and sometimes far-flung network kept in constant touch by letter, recording births, deaths, and marriages and sharing hopes and heartaches.

Within an individual household, a religious, moral, and disciplinary structure gave a certain feeling of safe harbor to the children that, while frowned on as restrictive by today's sociologists, has yet to find an effective substitute in terms of a secure and protected childhood. My father's parents each brought this strong tradition to their marriage, and to it they added the shining example of an enduring romantic love.

My grandfather Edmund Strudwick Nash was the youngest child of a respected North Carolina lawyer who could claim the Revolutionary governor of that state as his grandfather and the chief justice of its supreme court as his father. Grandfather was only seven when the Civil War shattered the tranquil existence that was antebellum Hillsborough. When the war was over, all was gone; the world had forever changed. My grandfather completed a local education and then set forth in 1875 for the commercial capital of the country, New York City, armed only with his looks, his heritage, and his determination to restore his family's fortunes.

His was a success story often repeated in that boisterous, swashbuckling era. By dint of talent, dedication, and long hours of hard work, he moved from clerk to junior partner in the respected naval-stores firm of Paterson, Downing and Company, spending much of his time in Europe on company business.

At this point in his career, well-situated enough to consider marriage, he met my grandmother Mattie Chenault. He found the dark-eyed young woman from Louisville entrancing. She was undeniably a beauty, but more than that, she had an air about her that drew attention. Her Huguenot blood ran close to the surface, characterized by a sparkling presence, a quick wit, and a spirit of restlessness that men found intriguing.

She was the eldest of the three daughters of a much-revered Louisville educator. While the girls were noted for their good looks and were designated "belles" in the language of the day, they were also often stigmatized by the dreaded term "bluestocking." Their father was a devout feminist and insisted on teaching them side by side with the young scions of Louisville society at his own renowned prep school, preparing them for entrance to august Eastern colleges, even though their sex would deny them that entrance. At any rate, she did go East to college — to Wellesley — which did her cause no good with the majority of young Southern gentlemen seeking brides. But at this point in her life, she was no more enamored of the local beaux than they of her. She longed for a world beyond Louisville, the one she had studied and learned to love. Then she met Edmund.

My grandfather Nash at thirty-four was a man to turn a woman's head. Well over six feet tall, he carried himself with an ease and grace that bespoke a gentleman. His bearing was confident but never arrogant. His features were strong and rather hawklike, but this impression was softened somewhat by a quick and engaging smile. To my grandmother, he seemed almost god-like — a Greek hero come to life, or a Plantagenet king. His knowledge of the world enthralled her. She listened in wonder to his tales of the czar's court at Saint Petersburg and the way of life in other countries. The hard-to-please young lady who had become increasingly scornful of the men she met was suddenly a woman in love. It was an all-consuming passion, matched only by Edmund's for her, and one that would last for a lifetime. They were married in 1889.

At the time of my father's birth in 1902, Grandfather was forty-eight; Grandmother thirty-five. He and his brother Aubrey were distinct afterthoughts. The oldest child, Gwen, was already twelve; next came ten-year-old Eleanor, and then Ted, who was six. They lived in almost idyllic circumstances, afforded by Grandfather's spectacular success in the naval-

Ogden Nash's first formal portrait.

stores trade. The family's existence was punctuated by summers in Rye, New York, winters in Savannah, Georgia, and trips abroad.

Family letters were an important part of my father's upbringing, and he soon began writing them himself.

The earliest letter of my father's found in the family archives was written to his beloved sister Gwen when she was on a grand tour of Europe that culminated in a trip to Egypt. He would have been eight at the time, his schooling a product of his mother's input and perhaps an occasional lesson from the older children's tutor.

Savannah, Georgia
January 2, 1911

Dear Gwen,

Are you in Egypt yet? for if you are I hope you like it and when you come home bring me some queer old Egyption [sic] things like a piece of the Spinx [sic] or a whole pyramid (excuse my spelling but I have no one to correct it just now) or something like that. I hope you have a nice trip. Aubrey is writing to Eleanor. I hope everybody is well. Mother got your telegram this morning. Yesterday I went to Tom's and had a fine time. We got together and made mudballs to soak him with.

> *With Love To All,*
> *Your Teasing Brother,*
> Ogden

Gwen held a hallowed place in the Nash family. She was adored by her younger sister and brothers. She was her father's darling and her mother's strong right arm, and her role as touchstone and comforter was to continue after her marriage (she met her future husband, Douglas Gorman, on the Egyptian trip), throughout her years of motherhood and widowhood, and end only with her death in 1966. Gwen was safe haven. Sunnybrook, her home in a quiet valley outside Baltimore, sheltered every member of her family at one time or another during difficult periods in their lives. My father's devotion to her was unfailing.

Gwen was also the subject of his first recorded poetic attempt. On the occasion of her wedding in January 1912, her small brother, clad in his page-boy costume, declaimed at the reception, "Beautiful spring at last is here! And has taken my sister, I sadly fear." As he remarked in later years, to call January "spring," even in Savannah, was distinct poetic license and "exhibited an early talent for inaccuracies which have distinguished my later work." Little did the smiling guests realize that these less-than-immortal lines would presage a successful career in the craft.

My father's experience with formal schooling began at Mr. and Mrs. Shaw's school, known as Red House, located in Groton, Massachusetts, where boys where prepped for Groton itself. My uncle Ted was already at Groton, and Grandmother felt that he could keep an eye on my father. Grandmother had very little regard for most schools. She felt that they were inadequate and unimaginative. The daughter of an innovative and respected educator, she had been brought up to believe that a good classical education was the quintessential ingredient for a productive and useful life.

My father's schooling in particular had been a problem to Grandmother. When he was seven, he contracted a serious eye infection — so severe that his doctors despaired of his sight. For many months he was kept in a darkened room, forbidden to use his eyes. Thus Grandmother herself took on the task of educating him. He would often say later that he had received his most valuable education at that time. His love of the classics, of history, of languages, of words, of learning itself — all of these were nurtured by his mother, who must have been an extraordinary teacher.

———————

Groton, Massachusetts
Thursday
October 24, 1912

Mother Darling,

I have been terribly homesick for you, and Father, and Jane, and Eleanor, and Aub, and Rye. I am thirty pages ahead in arithmetic and 6 lessons ahead in latin. I got your letter telling me not to do evening study, so I am not, but it is very inconvenient, for I have to take the time out of history. It is not bad for my eyes at all. When I told Mr. and Mrs. Shaw, they said that my eyes have not changed a bit. I am *way* ahead in lessons; Mr. Shaw says that at recitation time the other boys let me do all the reciting. As for football, I am as good as any of the other boys. Mr. and Mrs. Shaw are very kind, and everything is great, but for all that I would rather be at home with you. Tell Aub he ought to see some of the hills I go up. Why, Rye is nothing but a level piece of land, compared with Groton, Mass. Mr. Shaw has just told me to tell you that I have been working in the evening for a month, and my blinking has gone. By the way, please send me two or three more spectacles. These are broken, but I can wear them. Also a round head-guard, 6 7/8.

> *Love,*
> Ogden

Another letter to Gwen, in 1914, with a rather facetious enclosure to his newest nephew, demonstrates his closeness to his oldest sister in that he felt comfortable sending her his poems. (Ordinarily he kept them quite secret, showing them only to his parents.)

Rye, New York
July 31, 1914

Darling Momma Number Two,

It was bad enough to be one uncle, but two — well it is unspeakable. Really, Gwennie, it was quite thoughtless of you to get another baby. However, let us try to look on the bright side of life.

Little Douglas will have a playmate, and the minister will get a job when he is christened.

We are having wonderful weather here now — just cool enough, and just warm enough. I send you my two latest poems. Here they are.

> *The Song of the Wanderer*
>
> The purple hills are calling me,
> Where e'er I chance to stray,
> The wanderlust has got me,
> And *no where* can I stay.

"... *And has taken my sister, I sadly fear*"
Daddy (*right*) and Uncle Aubrey flank a bevy of girl cousins
in this formal portrait of the young attendants at
Aunt Gwen's wedding,
1912.

Over the hills I wander,
Through forest, field and plain,
There's always something calling me,
From every grassy lane.
And when the tall pines whisper,
As I lay me down to sleep,
It's a lullaby to my weary soul,
And my sleep is long and deep.

And when I hear some bright brook babbling,
Over its hard round stones,
I realize how vile man is,
And something within me groans.

I must wander, I must wander,
Through forest, field and plain,
And not until I leave this earth,
Can I ever rest again.

The Devil

The devil is a bad man,
He has horns both sharp and strong,
The devil is a red man,
And his tail is very long.
Some people call him Satan,
And some Mephistophelese [sic],
But I think that "the devil,"
Is pronounced with the greatest ease.

I went to see the devil,
And the devil said to me,
"Be bad, young Tommy Simpson,
Or I'll lay you cross my knee."

I replied, "you red old devil,
I will do no such thing,"
And started to talk back at him,
But then — I woke up — "Bing."

Love to all,
Uncle Og

[ENCLOSURE]

July 27, 1914

Dear Nephew Teddy,

Permit your old uncle to congratulate you upon your arrival in this world. It is a cold and cruel old world sometimes, but at others it is hot and kind.

But don't you think it was rather — well, rather selfish, one might say, to break your brother's nose so soon?

And listen, my boy, if ever they treat you badly down there, just come to your lonesome old Uncle and live with him. By the way, what do you look like? And please tell your grandmother that her grandson's uncles and aunt and gran'pa want her a good deal more than her grandson does.

> *So long, old top,*
> *Your Uncle,*
> Ogden Nash

———————————

I suppose "The Devil" is the first extant example of my father's turn toward humor in his writing. In a rather lackadaisical attempt at keeping a diary when he was thirteen, the pages were often taken up with jokes and puns. In the following verse, written in his hostess's guest book when one of his many childhood indispositions overtook him during a visit to family friends the Coopers, he continued the trend.

> If I'm fated to be sick I've already made my pick
> As to where I'm going to go and convalesce
> For if Mrs. Cooper'll stand me and the doctors will unhand me
> I'm going to settle here for more or less.
> For if comfort you desire and a jolly blazing fire
> And companions and whole bubbleful of mirth —
> Then just come right here and stay 'til the final judgment day
> For there's no place more like heaven on the earth.
> > Ogden Nash May 30–June 17, 1917
> > "remember the hot water bottle"

But the Nashes' luxurious world dissolved when, in March 1913, Grandfather lost everything, the victim of an unscrupulous business partner's speculation with funds. While others in the company declared bankruptcy, he alone dedicated himself to repaying company debts.

The ensuing years were very difficult. Grandfather struggled heroically to find another livelihood, and in the meantime possessions were sold at auction and the younger boys' schooling was suspended. But throughout these financial reversals my father saw and was part of the constancy and love that surrounded Grandfather until the day he died, and of which Grandfather himself was well aware. In an over-the-years letter he left his children, he recounted his victories and defeats and the abiding faith and love that had sustained him.

In 1917, Grandfather at sixty-three was successful in his quest and for the next four years he brilliantly built up the naval-stores firm that had hired him to do just that. My father's three years at St. George's School in Newport, Rhode Island, were made possible by those efforts. He must have felt great pressure to make good, both to justify his parents' faith in him and to satisfy his own strong need to excel. His academic achievements during his three years at St. George's stand testimony to his deep commitment: honor roll every year, winner of the French Prize, the Latin Prize, and, in his senior year, the Binney Cup, which was the school's highest award for scholarship. But it wasn't all work and no play, for he also made the baseball team, the football squad, the glee club, and the choir, served on the boards of both *The Dragon* (the school paper) and *The Lance* (the yearbook), and was president of the civics club.

Friends and teachers recalled a carefree boy with ready wit who never seemed chained to the pursuit of honors, but their picture of him had been carefully painted by the subject himself. He had come to learn that if he could make it appear he was casual about succeeding, then he would be better able to deal with private failures when they came; but the devastation he felt when those failures were public ones was almost too painful to bear.

This protective covering, crafted in boyhood, gave rise to the kind of verse that would make him famous. He once admitted that his unique form was "a sort of mask that I can operate behind without really revealing myself. This concealment enables me to express myself without self-consciousness."

During his years at school, he made many contributions to *The Dragon*. Most were on the order of "November":

> The gray sea reaches out to grasp the shore
> Shuddering back before the icy touch,

The tumbling breakers add their hollow roar
And vainly strive to make secure their clutch
Upon the dreary sands the flying spray
Drenches the beach, then futile melts away.

But one, "The Syncopated Classics," was first produced as a sight translation in Latin class. The Latin master submitted it to the paper forthwith.

The Syncopated Classics

*Being a rather far-fetched rendering
of Ovid, Metam vii 429–459,
set down in Profane Flippancy.*

When the ships had dropped anchor
Atrides was present,
The ocean was calm,
And the breezes were pleasant,
Here suddenly, just
As in life was his custom
Achilles rose up
And threatened to bust 'em.

It looked like the old days,
When armed with a sword
He gave Agamemnon
The fear of the Lord.
He shouted in wrath
Would you give us the slip,
And toddle away
In your elegant ship?
Would you really leave me
In this comfortless fix?
Did our valor die with me?
O nix, cat, nix!

Polyxena's a peach,
From arctics to lashes —
Oh, slaughter her here,
To comfort my ashes.
The sailors bow down

To the powerful spirit
And promise to do
Anything that will cheer it.
From her sorrowing mother
They snatch the poor maiden,
And in anticipation
Start digging and spading.

And now she could see
The ill omened altars,
The priests standing round
With their hymnals and psalters,
And brave Neoptolemus
Clad in a grin
Sharpening his sword
On his sandpaper skin.

He got on her nerves,
The disgusting old brute,
Till she shrieked, "If you're going to
For heaven's sake shoot.
Remember, remember,
I'm somebody's daughter."

But he only sneered
As a good villain oughter.
When her last supplications
Had failed to enthuse 'em.
She played her last card
By unveiling her bosom.
But nothing was gained
By this play to the gallery —
With a masterly stroke
The priest earned his salary.
A neat little mound
On the verdant arena
Was all that remained
Of poor Polyxena.

In later years, my father would often explain the evolution of his form
of verse in the following way: "I made up my mind long ago that I'd

rather be a great bad poet than a bad good poet. . . . As a small boy, I wanted to be a serious poet, a Keats or a Shelley, but my serious poems were very, very bad. My humorous verses are really a mocking of those early attempts. I thought I'd better laugh at myself before everyone laughed at me."

He must have preferred the Ovid translation to "November."

Frederick Ogden Nash entered Harvard in the fall of 1920 having achieved "top twenty" in the college-board exams. But Grandfather's fortunes once again took a plunge, and this time they never recovered. The company, for which the elderly man had made millions in four years, accepted a lucrative buyout offer. There were no "golden parachutes" in those days, and, at sixty-nine, E. S. Nash was without a job and in failing health.

My father dropped out of college and returned to St. George's to teach fourth-form French — a formidable assignment, one would think, for someone who had just turned nineteen. He would later comment wryly that he lost his entire nervous system carving lamb for a table of fourteen-year-olds. The experience was enough to persuade him to try his hand at another way of earning a living, and for the next few years my father became a job-jumper.

First he tried the stock market. This entailed working in the mail room at Dillon Reed at eighteen dollars a week. His sojourn there lasted a year and a half, during which time he managed to sell one bond — to his godmother. Then followed a very brief stint as a salesman for F. S. Smithers on a commission basis. There were few commissions. Evidently his forte was not in sales. He moved on to Barron G. Collier to write streetcar advertising copy. In an address he gave in 1970 at the meeting of the Friends of the Columbia Libraries on "Reminiscences of Dan Longwell — from Doubleday to *Life*," my father described how he was rescued by Dan from that job.

> I was grateful to Dan first of all because in March of 1925 he rescued me from the lowest stratum of a decaying empire, that of Barron G. Collier, the king of streetcar advertising. I had been working there for 2 years. I was told later that both Scott Fitzgerald and John Held, Jr., had served a term there too, but I did not know it at that time and I did not have their example to cheer me. I was rather lost, and at the end of 2 years there I was making $100.00 a month and not having much fun.
>
> Fortunately, there were 6 of us, 6 young men living together in a cold water flat on 3rd Avenue. With one of these roommates (Joe Alger) I wrote a

children's book, a very bad one, called "The Cricket of Carador." It was a miserable combination of "Alice" and "The Wizard of Oz," but at any rate Doubleday saw fit to publish it. And through that I met Dan.

Longwell, as advertising manager at Doubleday, offered the young author a position as an assistant. It paid $90.00 a month, and, my father noted, "In addition to taking the loss in salary, I had to buy a commutation ticket, because I was living in New York whereas Doubleday was in Garden City. Anyway, it worked out not too badly ... I got into a very exciting world."

Uncle Aubrey remembered the cold-water flat with fondness. It was known affectionately as "The Rabbit Warren." The landlord was Jim Moriarity, of speakeasy fame. Aubrey visited his older brother there whenever there was an empty bed. He describes the life-style as "very simple": "We had double-decker beds; we had all our meals out; we were bulging at the seams. It was not the highest quality building."

High quality or not, the inhabitants of "The Rabbit Warren" led a stimulating and happy-go-lucky existence at the height of the Jazz Age. My father had moved there when the Barron G. Collier job came along. The senior Nashes had consolidated themselves in rented rooms at the Gotham and as soon as he had the wherewithal to do so, he was determined to save them the extra board. But soon after he went to work at Doubleday, his parents moved to an apartment at 119 East Eighty-fourth Street. Grandfather's health became a source of major concern, and my father moved back in with them in 1926, adding as much as he could in the way of both financial and emotional support. He would occasionally escape for weekends with Gwen or Ted or Eleanor when he could, though the work at Doubleday left very little free time. Saturdays were workdays for him and, if truth be told, his work was interesting enough to provide a very satisfactory escape from the worries at home. The authors he met, the friends he made, the projects he undertook — all these things made for an exciting world of infinite variety in which he delighted. Again from his reminiscences of Dan Longwell: "We worked all hours of the day and night. It was great. Sometimes I went home, back to New York, getting there at 11:30 or 12 o'clock, and came back again on the 7:49 the next morning, but it was like a very exciting college life. There was a team spirit."

It was on a weekend respite at Gwen's from this stimulating world that my father found his life changed forever. On November 13, 1928, at Gwen's behest, he reluctantly attended a dinner dance in Baltimore. The party was held at the venerable Elkridge Hunt Club and was later rated by connoisseurs of such parties as the most elegant and successful of the season.

The climate of the twenties had pervaded even that staid old dowager of a city. The restless energy of the Jazz Age was at its zenith. A sybaritic American youth had at last torn free from the clinging tendrils of the old order and seemed to take unholy delight in outraging the sensibilities of the older generation. The nation was flying high; money seemed as plentiful and as renewable as the bootleg liquor that flowed unchecked and seemed to teach Americans first to judge and then to scorn the law. Those who had fortunes flaunted them while those who were of modest means were possessed of great expectations. The rewards seemed to be there for those who were willing to work for them.

My father fell into the latter category, and on that November evening, had begun to feel a fish out of water amid talk of fox hunting, duck hunting, and local gossip. He contemplated making an early departure directly after dinner and was running possible excuses to his hostess through his head when his attention was suddenly riveted on a girl in a flowered dress who was entering the room. She was tall and slim and had an incandescent beauty that took his breath away. He grabbed his sister's arm. "Gwen! Who is the girl in the doorway?"

"The dark, pretty one in the flowered dress?"

"Pretty? My God, she's beautiful."

"Frances Leonard. Ogden, I'll introduce . . ."

But the young man was gone. What happened then, he told years later as follows:

At a dinner dance in November of 1928, I surreptitiously shifted my place card at the table while my hostess's back was turned so that I might sit next to a girl I had met during cocktails. Fortunately, she did not realize that I had substituted myself for her alloted companion, a rich and handsome former Princeton fullback, and I was able to attract her attention with well-phrased laudatory remarks about Al Smith and P. G. Wodehouse, remarks which changed imperceptibly into other and more personal compliments. My aim was then, as it is now, to persuade her to stay beside me for the rest of my life. In this I have so far succeeded, though there have been moments when she must have rebelled against being the major course selected for self-improvement by a perpetual undergraduate. Still here she is, here we are, and I have hope for the future, since I can now call up the fascination of grandchildren to reinforce my own fading charms.

Dear Miss Leonard —

FRANCES LEONARD was twenty-two in November 1928. She was the only child (an older brother had died in infancy) of William Wirt and Nellie Jackson Leonard. Her mother, Nellie, was in many ways her best friend, for Frances, naturally shy, had never stayed in one school long enough to make lasting friendships with other girls and had lived a very solitary existence as a child, though she was surrounded by what now would be called a large extended family. That family was headed by her grandmother Jackson, a tiny but formidable matriarch who ran her sons' and daughters' lives as she once had run the Governor's mansion in Maryland when her husband was chief executive of that state.

My mother's childhood years were full of family treks to such vacation spots as Atlantic City, New Jersey; Ocean City, Maryland; and various towns on Cape Cod, as well as numerous visits to her grandmother's home in Salisbury, Maryland, where she had been born. She lived for a time in Georgia, Florida, and Texas, and also spent months touring Europe, where she once attended school in Versailles, and at another time lived with a French family. Her American schooling included two different schools in Baltimore — Calvert School and Roland Park School — as well as a New England boarding school, Great Barrington, from which she graduated in June 1924. Vassar was her father's choice of college for her. In an effort to please him, she attended.

Frances always tried hard to please him, but felt she never managed to quite fulfill his expectations of her. Her cousin and closest girlhood friend, Isabel Jackson, seemed to her the kind of daughter Will Leonard would have wished for — pretty, outgoing, popular, and an outstanding athlete in the bargain. Frances was shy beyond words, and basically very uncertain of her own worth. Her mother's support and unlimited love were not enough to give her the self-confidence she lacked, and her father probably never realized that the girl who tried so hard to win his approval needed more recognition than perhaps he was capable of giving.

Outwardly, Frances had every reason in the world to have gained self-confidence. She had become, by any standard, a real beauty — the tall awkward child had blossomed into a radiantly lovely woman. She had a plethora of beaux and was popular, too, with her own sex. And yet, inside, she remained ever the little girl who peeped in on someone else's party. She was unsure of herself and therefore unsure of the rightness of any decision she might make. Much like Ogden, she had created a certain image to show the world that did not always correspond to the doubts and fears that inwardly beset her.

The dinner dance that fateful November evening was heralded as one of the highlights of the 1928 Baltimore social season. Frances had been looking forward to it eagerly, but by the time dinner was announced she had begun to anticipate a problem that would have to be faced at evening's end. Her escort, a young man of whom she was very fond but for whom she held no romantic attachment, was at the point of crossing the invisible Rubicon that separates "tight" from "drunk." She had no intentions of breaking her neck on a wild drive home in order to spare his feelings, but she dreaded begging a ride from someone else. And then an amusing stranger from New York appeared as if by magic. He admired both Al Smith and P. G. Wodehouse. He solved her transportation problem by asking if he could take her home, and then she found herself spending several delightful hours in his company, discussing books and politics and listening to funny stories about the strange world of publishing. She was sorry when the evening was over, for it had been great fun. It was a pity that the young man lived in New York!

———————

119 East 84th Street
New York, New York
November 21, 1928

Dear Miss Leonard —

Or is this formality necessary? I hope not. It's only fair to tell you that if two books creep to you mysteriously through the mails they are from me. Please like them. I don't want to be forgotten too soon, because I keep thinking about that evening at the Wilson's party — perfect, and only spoiled afterwards by my not being able to see you again before I left Baltimore. For the first time I found fault with the Valley for being where it is. Prejudiced of me, but very natural.

Aren't you coming to New York some time soon? It's nice now; all the policemen have put on their overcoats, the corners are covered with hot-chestnut men, and all the lights go on at half past four. Wonderful weather to have tea in, or go to the theater. Do think about this seriously, and please let me know if and when you are coming. It would do a lot to brighten a life now pitch black with the job of trying to persuade

Frances Rider Leonard,
aged one.

the public that it can make this the biggest, merriest Christmas ever by rushing into the bookstores and demanding armfuls of Doubleday Doran books. Then there are other complications, some of them of a kind you just can't foresee. For instance: my stenographer was leaving to get married. On her last day I dictated a letter to a girl who had asked for a job, saying it had been filled. I had to leave early, and asked the stenographer to sign the letter and send it out. She did, but her mind was on higher things; two days later I got an indignant letter from one of our authors asking what the devil I meant by implying that he wanted a job from us, or that if he did want one, he couldn't get it. Following that, a letter from an anti-tobacco lady, saying that since she saw a photograph of Kipling with a pipe in his mouth she has named him The Skunk-Man and burned all his books, of which she possessed a complete set, 28 volumes at $2.50 a volume. However, she didn't ask for a refund. Strange oriental letters from a gentleman named Mirza Mahmoud Khanghaphi, Page to the Mad Shah of Persia and Son of the Court Physician threatening strangulation and beheading if his book isn't advertised more sensationally; from the Warden of Sing Sing complaining bitterly because his book about life in the death house is advertised *too* sensationally; from an old whaling captain who has written his autobiography and lashes himself into a salt sea fury whenever we mention the word "whale." At such times there's nothing to do but mutter "Doubleday Doran Doubledare Doubleday Doran Doubled-dare Doubleday Doran" over and over very fast; it's quite good fun, very soothing, and has the great merit of eventually so swelling the tip of the tongue that you can't say a word till you're a gentleman again. That's the advantage of not working for Knopf or MacMillan and Company Ltd. or the Oxford University Press, whose names would be practically useless in a crisis; though Dodd Mead might have a nice profane sound.

All this is nonsense and says nothing that I want to say. What I am really writing to find out is if there is a chance of your coming up here. Perhaps I'm prejudiced about this too, but it is a wonderful idea. Anyhow I am going to try to get to Baltimore for Christmas, and I hope to see you then if I may.

Ogden Nash

Mother's shyness was in full bloom by the time
this picture was taken.

December 2, 1928

Dear Frances,

For that you got the books — and liked them — and answered my letter — in the letter that you did — and asked me to dinner and may come
to New York — praise and magnification forever!

May I wait a few days before answering about dinner, as I'm not sure
just now whether or not I'll be able to get away at that time? Or will
that throw seating arrangements or the cook or something equally important out? I feel very shy about writing "Mr. Ogden Nash hasn't got sense
enough just now to know whether or not he can accept the kind invitation of etc. etc." I'm sure that the best thing is for you to come up this
week and be told in person, sparing me the embarrassment of having to
write a note like that. Because I refuse to refuse, and I won't know until
Wednesday or Thursday for certain if I can accept. I've just taken on
some new work at the office, and I'm buried to the neck in detective
stories. You have no idea of the number of people who are writing them;
perhaps you will understand when I tell you that I've just read one —
happily to be forever unpublished — in which the mystery hangs on the
fact that while one of the characters was undergoing an emergency operation for appendicitis at midnight all the lights went out and the moon
shone into his appendix and some moonlight got sewed up inside him
leaving him thereafter a rather elfin, puck-ish sort of person, handy with
a knife. Oh well.

Please don't have changed your mind about the New York trip, as I'm
still supposedly a convalescent and the doctor assures me that any sudden
fit of rage would probably carry me off just like that.

Ogden

December 16, 1928

Dear Frances,

Do you remember that I wrote you a letter that almost burst the envelope with enthusiasm for New York? What a liar I was, even if I did
have very definite and justifiable reasons for lying. I've been back for an
hour and eighteen minutes, and New York is awful. Millions of taxis,
street cars, streets, apartments, all full of millions of people with millions
of faces like ⟨ ⟨ ⟨ ⟨⟨⟨⟨- — millions of voices like RRKOI RRKOI

Dear Miss Leonard —

RRKOI — and don't forget the millions of women wearing things on their hair like ⊙ ⊙ ⊙ , which I'm sorry I can't draw very well, not being cats sitting on fences seen from the back.

No, I'm lying again. It's wonderful in New York now; you should see it while it's this way; I'm sure a trip up would do you loads of good, particularly if you made it last more than twenty four hours.

You can have such fun coming up on the Congressional. I sat in John Adams, ate dinner in Thomas Jefferson, and smoked in James (CLUB) Madison, which suggests Al (SCARFACE) Capone. It's great. And each and every passenger receives a handsome package of after-dinner mints with the compliments of the Pennsylvania Railroad. I'll never again believe that great corporations haven't got hearts.

Did you finally go dancing last night? The dinner was such fun; I enjoyed the cigarettes and the matches and I thought the black dress was marvelous, even nicer than the flowered one at the Lord's. But the glow that was ☼ is now ● ; feared and expected, of course, but still dismal. I shouldn't have gone to Baltimore if I had known that coming back would leave me feeling like this at the beginning of a long hard winter. Yes I should. I'm afraid this is a stupid letter, but this is a stupid evening and last night wasn't. Please do something about it.

Ogden

119 East 84th Street
New York, New York
January 25, 1929

Dear Frances —

I've become a collector of some very rare items — so rare, in fact, that for a while I was afraid they had become extinct. Baltimore postmarks are my mania. Shall I catalogue my collection for you?

No. 1: BALTIMORE, MD. 3 NOV 26 3:30 P.M. 1928; first of its kind; caused huge sensation; priceless.

No. 2: BALTIMORE, MD. 3 NOV 26 3:00 P.M. 1928; not to be confused with No. 1; formal but welcome invitation; not for sale.

No. 3: BALTIMORE, MD. 3 DEC 3 11:00 P.M. 1928; mentions Roosevelt and means Savoy Plaza; slightly finger-marked from much handling, but possesses invaluable associations.

No. 4: BALTIMORE, MD. 3 DEC 24 4:00 P.M. 1928; Christmas card, and a nice one too; marked down because it wasn't a letter; marked up again because it was anything.

No. 5: BALTIMORE, MD. 3 DEC 28 3:00 P.M. 1928; very pretty note of thanks; badly worn from being re-read by recipient while awaiting No. 6.

No. 6: BALTIMORE JAN 23 4:30 P.M. 1929 MD; dictated by uneasy conscience but nevertheless delightful. Interesting item: recipient starved to death before it arrived.

A very small collection, you see, but jealously guarded. And if you knew the uncomfortable 180-second minutes that spread out like umbrellas between No. 5 and No. 6. — I'm afraid I haven't the callous disposition and iron nerves that characterize our best collectors.

You say: "According to an unspoken code of etiquette among women, this is about the proper amount of time to elapse before answering a gentleman."

Sorry; I just can't believe it. Great heavens — the trees and the grass wouldn't be able to grow through the fingernails that the gentleman had bitten off in frenzy, and the rabbits and squirrels would be smothered in the hair that the gentleman tore out in despair! Do the ladies want that? Do say no.

Have you been very gay in Baltimore? No teas, dances, or theatres? Your letter indicates that you have been doing nothing but serving Art since Dec 28 3:00 P.M.1928, but this hardly seems possible. I'd like to think so, but I can't quite.

Up here, just loads of fun, of the most dismal sort. I'm just in the middle of serving on the jury. That is, I'm supposed to be; but every time I get into the jury box some lawyer throws me out. Sometimes it's the plaintiff and sometimes it's the defendant; they just can't stand me; they challenge away like madmen. I was getting rather sensitive about it; I was beginning to avoid my friends and talk to myself; but today I got elected into the nicest jury you ever saw, and now I'm going to have one twelfth of the responsibility of deciding whether Mr. Julius Singer really was at fault when his car collided with a taxi containing Mr. Harry Sperber at 2 o'clock in the morning of a Sunday in March 1928. Thus automatically I become a good citizen. At the same time that sour musty feeling I've had about the law has been confirmed.

Hoboken is splendid. I have been eight times to see After Dark, or Neither Maid, Wife, nor Widow, which is a bigger success than anything in New York, and perhaps the most amusing thing I've ever seen. It's going to run for a long time — perhaps even until you come up again. I've got to make a speech there next week — present Morley with the first copy of his new book, between the acts. There's a large party of reviewers going over — in 1870 costumes, O God! Can you see the streets of Hoboken flowing with crinolined and gaitered book critics? It's a fearful thing to get your fingers caught in the publicity mill.

Report on people I've met: an actress who is *not* sensitive about her husband's killing himself; an actor named Bradley Cass whose real name is Fuzzy Klavoon; a stenographer who thinks Ann Arbor is an authoress; a taxi driver who went west because he had a whole boatload of fish thrown on him and policemen said things about his mother; a subway guard who showed me a gold watch he stole from a German prisoner in 1918.

The taxi driver is a little gem; I must tell you more about him later.

You say New York is impossible. I'm going to try to get to Baltimore the weekend of the 9th. Are you going to be there?

Ogden

June 28, 1929

Dear Frances —

I welcomed the purple ink — skipped like a biblical hill, in fact, at sight of it. You see, I wasn't quite sure what had become of you, and my inquiries at the Roosevelt didn't help a bit. Apparently the cards were hopelessly stacked against me.

I'm enclosing the envelope of your last letter from France. Look what happened to it. I was in Newport when it arrived — on a Friday evening. My thoughtful family forwarded it to me — and it didn't reach Newport till Monday, after I had left. Then it came back to Garden City. I read it and found that you were sailing the next day, and would be at the Roosevelt on the 19th or 20th. I immediately cabled you care of Morgan. Paris: "Will call Roosevelt nineteenth and twentieth heavens sake don't disappear." (And of course you did disappear.) But more is to come. Your letter didn't say what boat you would be on — but I read in the newspaper that a young Mr. Ryan had been removed from the Ile de France, sailing the day you were to sail. So I guessed the Ile de France. The French line told me that the Ile de France would dock on the 18th. On the afternoon of the 18th I called the Roosevelt and was told that you had registered but were not in. I called again later and they said you had left. That was so awful that I couldn't believe it. They insisted, but offered me a Mrs. Lawrence Leonard of Lynn, Mass., as a substitute. I indignantly refused her. I thought there might have been a mistake and that you were waiting till the 19th or 20th to reveal yourself, so I tried the Roosevelt again on both those days. The information clerk got quite interested in my case but outside of that nothing happened except that I felt very badly. So when you say "I heard nothing from you about New York so I suppose it didn't suit or was too vague" I feel even worse. I imagine that my cable arrived too late to get you, and God knows I'm glad that you left New York quickly if you were feeling miserable in that appalling hot spell. But do let me be selfish enough to feel slightly relieved that it was sickness that was responsible for your vanishing. Also I think I'm entitled to be annoyed when you say perhaps it didn't suit me to see you. — I'm sorry to bore you with this long story but it's been rather on my mind and it had to come off.

All sorts of things have been happening to me. There have been some big changes at the office and I now find myself sitting firmly in a job I've always wanted — elevated above the Crime Club (which is a dear old thing just the same) and nursing all kinds of reputable books. Furthermore, we've found a good producer who has courteously developed a fine enthusiasm for the play and says that at the moment he has nothing he'd rather put on this winter. Of course the whole crowd of them are liars, thieves, poltroons and parricides and his words mean nothing till signed in a contract and not much then, but it's fun to be encouraged once in a while, and I'm having my fun now before things go sour again.

Were all the geographies wrong when they taught me that the shortest line between Baltimore and Cape Cod lies through New York? Finding that it doesn't is another blow. I hate blows. But will you let me know when you are leaving, as there's just a chance I may get down to Gwen's for a day or two fairly soon, and I now know how to find Rugby Road. Go right along and then branch left at the street car station. When you see the station back up and turn right. First left and nothing remains but to be told at the door that Miss Frances is at the Roosevelt.

It couldn't happen again, says hope cheerfully. Yes it could, says experience. Let's rise superior to experience, shall we?

Ogden

July 15, 1929

Dear Frances,

Do forgive the typewriter and the paper and the general air of dinginess that hangs over this letter. It is Sunday afternoon, five o'clock, and I am in the office, all alone except for three flies that are playing cop and robber around my head and panting loudly. If it's hot enough to get the flies out of breath I think it only fair that a bit of shabbiness on my part should be overlooked.

I suppose you know that I had a good time in Baltimore. I hadn't hoped to be able to do much more than see you for half an hour at tea time, and that got me on a midsummer midnight train. Then look what I got. It was good of you, and I have forever forgotten Mrs. Lawrence Leonard of Lynn. Damn Mrs. Lawrence Leonard of Lynn.

Eleanor tells me that she has written to you about Saratoga. Please come. I'm counting on those few days as my only vacation this summer. If you don't go I won't, remarking with brotherly politeness that I can see Eleanor any time. Then you see I should have no vacation at all, and overwork would probably bring on gout or hay fever or sulkiness, perhaps destroying my entire career. Besides, you might be amused up there.

I had an interesting evening with Jim Tully, the hobo and prize fighter who has turned novelist and done it with enormous success. We dined in a bedroom of steam-heated mausoleum known as the City Club so we could talk. The temperature was 92 and he ate clam chowder, a huge steak, french fried potatoes, creamed onions, and almost a whole apple pie. He's an extraordinary fellow. He has the figure of a bureau, about five feet four high and about four feet wide; bushy red hair that some one threw at the top of his head, and big blue eyes with the tiniest pupils I've ever seen. I think they shrank from distress, because he goes around being sorry about things. He had just got back from abroad, and told me how Shaw and Kipling dislike each other so much that when they were pall bearers at Hardy's funeral they wouldn't keep step with each other and as a result nearly dropped Hardy. And how Charlie Chaplin walking through Limehouse, was asked to brighten up the miserable little urchins in the streets by telling them who he was and said "I hate children" and calls his own two egocentric little brats. And how Captain Carey of the Vestris had just taken command of her the day she sailed and had had nothing to do with the loading, and when she started to sink said "My God I'm not to blame for this," and yet threw away his life belt and drowned with her because that's the way things are done. We talked for about four hours and every half hour his wife would call up and tell him to come home, which I suppose is the most embarrassing thing that can happen to a hobo. On such gossip do we fatten in this trade.

Tell me about life on the cape. And are you now differently complected? And don't take my vacation away from me.

Ogden

July 22, 1929

Dear Frances —

Human nature being what it is — or my human nature being what it is — I'm pleased that you are sunk about not being able to get to Saratoga. Yes, Eleanor got your New London letter. I had been afraid something like that would happen, but even so I felt badly when the blow fell.

HOWEVER — things improved greatly when your Wianno letter arrived. I had been afraid I wouldn't see you again until you went back to Baltimore. No I hadn't, really, because I should have got up to the Cape by hook or crook or something equally rude and efficient before long. But it's nicer to be asked.

May I wait a while before saying when I'll come? Things have suddenly become very complicated at home. My brother and Gwen and Douglas are going abroad this week and Eleanor is leaving to comfort those desultory racehorses. Meanwhile Father has become quite ill, and Mother isn't well. I'm the only child left and I can't very well go away till things clear up. That should be in ten days or so.

Do let me know what is the best time for you to have me. As soon as things are all right at home I can take any weekend I want and shall probably steal an extra day too, taking an 'eaven when given an 'ell.

You should know that I'm a dreadful summer guest. I don't play tennis — I play very bad golf and that only occasionally — and swimming is

one of my weak points. As soon as I discover my strong ones I'll let you
know. Tell me how you amuse yourself so I can practice.

I'm interested in Wsigan Penassin. Is it a secret society, or the grave of
an Indian chief, or just a typographical error? Because if it's a summer
amusement I'm afraid it's another of my weak points. Does this paper appeal to you? I borrowed it from a man at the other end of the office who
is a devout atheist but is at present loudly whistling "Praise God from
Whom All Blessings Flow" as he tots up next month's advertising budget.
In precisely ten minutes he'll begin "This Is My Lucky Day," and he will
follow that with "Smiles." I know, because I've been through it all before.

Are you glad to hear that a new P. G. Wodehouse manuscript has just
arrived? It begins this way:

"Right ho," said Algy Crufts. "Then I shall go alone."
"Right ho," said Ambrose Wiffin. "Go alone."
"Right ho," said Algy Crufts. "I will."
"Right ho," said Ambrose Wiffin. "Do."
"Right ho, then," said Algy Crufts.
"Right ho," said Ambrose Wiffin.
"Right ho," said Algy Crufts.

That's a very nice story. When it ends the young men are still telling
each other Right ho. Then there's a nice one about the Reverent Wooing
of Archibald Mulliner, who was famous all over London for his imitation
of a hen laying an egg. At imitating a hen laying an egg he was admit-
tedly a master. "Others abide our question. Thou art free," was the verdict of London's gilded youth on Archibald when considered purely in the
light of a man who could imitate a hen laying an egg. "Mulliner", they
said to one another, "may be a pretty minus quantity in a lot of ways,
but he can imitate a hen laying an egg." Archibald conducted an emi-
nently dignified courtship and as a result was about to be given the bird
when he discovered by accident (or rather, by eavesdropping) that the
one thing beloved above others by his beloved was a really good imitation of a hen laying an egg. — Good old Wodehouse, always trustworthy.
But just in case he doesn't amuse you — did you read, "A Meeting of the
Endorser's Club" when it appeared in the New Yorker? If not, I recom-
mend it and enclose it.

Now I've been as funny as I can — or I've collected all the fun I
can — and that really wasn't at all what I had in mind.

Please don't cut me off with a post card because I can't accept your invitation now. You know it's the one thing I want to do. Will later be all right? Do answer soon, because my friends will find me unbearable until I hear.

Ogden

August 7, 1929

Dear Frances —

Am I still invited? If so, may I come up next week-end, or rather a week from next week-end — that is, the week-end of the 17th? Eleanor will be back from Saratoga then and I can safely leave the family.

Is there any possibility of your leaving the Cape on August 23rd and staying away till August 26th? I've got a real reason for wanting to know. Two friends of mine, George Elliman and Charlie Duell, are spending the summer alone in the Elliman house at Bayside, Long Island. They are tired of themselves and want to give a party — a house party — a roving house party. This is the plan: Christopher Morley and his wife have already promised to attend as chaperones. The party is to consist of four men, four girls and the Morleys. (If anything happens to the Morleys between now and then Eleanor and Culver will preside.) It begins with dinner at Bayside Friday night the 23rd, followed by dancing. Saturday to be spent on The Sound in one motor boat and one sail boat. But instead of coming back to Long Island we land in Westchester and go to the Duells' over on the Hudson for Saturday night. Nobody has thought about Sunday yet. Does it sound at all amusing and can you come? If you can, do say so; if you can't, don't say anything until I talk to you about it and think of some convincing arguments.

Garden City is dreadful now; bugs have eaten all the maple leaves and maples are the only trees we have so there is no shade, and the books are piling up, and the hot weather is getting on the nerves of all the authors and the glue that goes on the backs of the books in the bindery just under my desk pollutes what air there is — So you'd better come on the 23rd.

Ogden

August 21, 1929

Dear Frances,

Please don't mind the drunken Portuguese air about this letter. It's the
first I ever wrote on a train and I'm not up on the fine points, particularly as this one seems to be running on the ties instead of the rails. I
don't like sending you such a disreputable looking thing, but I want to
talk, so I'm hoping you will let it into the house. I have now passed
through Sandwich, Sagamore, Buzzard's Bay, Wareham, Marion, Matta-
poisett, Fairhaven, New Bedford, Acushnet, Providence, Wickford Junc-
tion, Kingston and Westerly — and just then Groton, which means that
there's nothing but a drawbridge between me and New London — and at
every one of them and in between I have been thinking of the last five
days. I suppose you know I had a nice time — I did everything to show it
except wag my tail and purr. "Nice" is a mild word and not the one I
want, but for the present it will have to do. We're in New London now;
the train has stopped (hence the improved writing) and for a moment at
least the journey away has stopped also. My disappointment shortly after
noon — 12:19 I think it was (yes, it was; that's the time my watch still
points to, as it broke down at the exact second you said "I don't think
I'd better come") — has left me grateful for even such small favors. I
daresay there are those who do well on less, but that's thin comfort; as a
child I never enjoyed my spinach any the better for being reminded of the
poor little boys in the gutter who didn't have any. I don't want spinach; I
want the weekend I thought I was going to get; you must forgive me if I
beat the table with my fists and splash milk on nurse. Of course there's
still the telegram to come; I shan't be comfortable till it arrives, but I
don't much want to open it, if *that* jack-in-the-box turns out to have an
ugly face — oh well —

The trip has been a good one so far, even containing an adventure. I
sat in the next to last seat in the bus; and put my bag in the last seat,
next to the emergency door. About ten minutes after I left you the door
flew open and my bag tumbled out onto the King's Highway. Great excitement. I recovered it, dusty but undamaged and put it in a safer place.
The same door kept flying open from time to time, and as I was the only
one near it, public opinion created me door man. I was deep in thoughts
pleasant and unpleasant, so I didn't notice things. There was a girl sitting
a couple of seats in front of me; a small white headed boy of the kind
that I think puts itch powder on his sister's friends' collars and wears a

coca-cola cap as he rides his bicycle on a crowded sidewalk — was in front of her. She was quite pretty and very rural. Apparently she had a wholesome fear of city fellers. Whenever the door flew open her mouth would fly open too; she'd cast a frightened look at me, start to speak, then remember mother's advice and lean forward and whisper to the boy, who was harmless if obnoxious. He would turn around and squeak "Hey mister, door's open," in a voice like a peanut roaster; I'd get up, struggle with the door and sit down again; everything quiet till the next performance two miles later.

The road was good and the countryside worth looking at; we went for about five miles along the canal and passed a fine three-master under tow. The drawbridge outside of New Bedford was open and, we sat still while a tug went through. The railing was lined with fishermen, and I played a depressing game with myself as I watched them. I told myself that if one of them caught a fish before the bus started it would be a sign that you would come down on Friday. None of them got a bite. Am I to meet defeat even in my superstitions?

Now. Just in case you should decide to come, and don't want to go to Boston and don't want to leave till Friday morning. I've been looking at bus and train schedules. The way I did it is really easy and pleasant. Honestly, I'm not selfish enough to advise an uncomfortable trip for you. There's a bus leaving West Barnstable at 8:57. It gets to New Bedford at 10:45. The Providence bus leaves New Bedford at 11 and goes direct to the Providence railroad station, where you have half an hour to catch the Knickerbocker Limited at 1, a fast train reaching New York at 5; time to be met and go to the country and dress for dinner. All the times I have mentioned are *Standard, not* Daylight Saving. The New Bedford change is a simple one; just tell the Hyannis driver you want the Providence bus and he stops half a block away from it, at the New Bedford hotel, where you can get either a taxi or a porter to take your luggage over.

It's now dark outside. I have the American Mercury, the Atlantic, Life, and the Red Book. I've tried to read all of them. No luck. I can't read any of them. All lifeless. When I look out the window I see nothing but the reflection of my own face. What am I to do? This is New Haven and New York is an hour and three quarters away. I'm afraid that hour and three quarters will be longer than the five days I had on The Cape. Five days! Good Lord! Your family are all saints. I came for a weekend and stayed five days and they made me feel it was all right. Do thank them for me; I shall write your grandmother tomorrow.

Once more — do come!

Ogden

Sunday night
August 25, 1929

Frances darling,

Have you heard that I love you? I'm not sure that I made it clear to you, and I don't want to have any misunderstanding. It's such a young love yet — just nine and a half months old, born November 13th 1928 at about nine o'clock in the evening. But it's big for its age, and seems much older. I do hope you're going to like it, I'm sending you some now for you to try; but if it's not satisfactory, don't ever let me know.

This is a peculiarly gifted and intelligent pen. Look what it's writing now: I love you. That's a phrase I can't get out of my head — but I don't want to. I've wanted to try it out for a long time; I like the look of it and the sound of it and the meaning of it.

It's past one now and I've got to have some sleep before I face Nelson Doubleday tomorrow. But tell me something before I leave. I was told tonight on what seemed to me the best authority that you are fond of me. Can you confirm this rumor?

Then there's another problem. As long as I'm thinking about you I can't go to sleep; and I'd rather think about you than go to sleep; how am I to sleep?

Oh Frances, do tell me that everything really happened, that it wasn't just something that I wanted so much that it crystalized in my imagination.

Good night. I've just sent St. Joseph off to watch you on the train; he has promised that he will do his duty like an honest saint.

I do love you.
Ogden

August 25, 1929

Dear Mrs. Leonard,

By the time you get this letter Frances will have told you what happened this weekend. I haven't quite been able to realize it yet, it's the one thing I've thought of ever since I met her, but I have only dared hope for it about one minute out of every month. And now I'm sorry to be incoherent and I hope you will understand. I'm naturally anxious to know your verdict on me. She is yours and I am asking you for her; I don't see how you could ever let her go, but one impossibility has already happened, perhaps this will too. I am encouraged by the fact that it must have been obvious from the first that I was deeply in love, and you allowed me to keep on seeing her; but perhaps it was only that you had as small regard for my chances as I had until yesterday.

I have so much in my heart tonight that it's very difficult for me to write. I do want to talk to you.

I am going to write to Mr. Leonard tomorrow when my brain has cleared; my first thought was of you.

As I expect to be in the country this week a letter addressed to me care of Doubleday Doran, Garden City, is the best way to reach me.

I beg that you will tell me soon what you feel, as I cannot rest until I know.

I sign this with an affection that I pray you are willing to accept.

Ogden Nash

Doubleday, Doran and Company, Inc.
Publishers
Garden City, New York
August 26, 1929

Dear Mr. Leonard:

Ever since I met Frances last fall I have been completely in love with her. I saw her this weekend and I couldn't keep it to myself any longer. I had to tell her, then she said she cares for me and is willing to marry me.

May I talk to you some time soon? I could come to Baltimore next Saturday, Sunday or Monday, and I could say then the things that are so

Mother, in her early teens
(curls courtesy of Minnie).

difficult to compress into a letter. I wrote to Mrs. Leonard last night, and I shall be waiting anxiously to hear from her and you.

Please forgive the briefness of this note, things have happened so quickly and so startlingly that I am not yet thinking intelligently. But if you will let me talk to you I hope to explain myself clearly.

Sincerely,
Ogden Nash

August 27, 1929

Frances darling,

I've been reading your letter over all day, it's so dear, even the part that worried me. I imagine that tomorrow morning's mail will tell me what has happened and whether I really upset things. My mind has been constantly on the Cape — I can see you, but I don't know what you are doing and saying, and I want so dreadfully to know. Tell me that everything is all right, and tell me again. I've wanted to telephone, but I know you don't like the telephone, and besides I remember that yours is right out in the middle of everything and conversation is impossible. Damn the distance between us! You won't get this until thirty six hours after I write it. But remember that when I tell you now that I love you I shall be loving you even more by the time you read the words. Last Sunday I couldn't have believed that my love could ever be bigger and stronger than it was then — but it's growing every hour. Can't you feel it?

Yesterday I couldn't do a stroke of work. I was exhausted — burned out — stunned. The terrific suspense and emotional strain and then the unbelievable happiness left me without much body or mind. But today I was myself again, only better than ever before; you were the motive for everything. I've never had so much energy. You have done that; don't stop.

Haven't you a photograph or even a snapshot of yourself? I want to look at and touch, as I read and touch your letters; it helps bring you a little closer.

Frances dear, don't be afraid; it's for me to be afraid; afraid that you are too beautiful, too sweet, too adorable, actually to be mine; afraid that I am not good enough to make you happy when I have you. Yet I'm not really afraid I can't make you happy; I worship you, and I *know* that such a love can create only happiness.

Tonight I have to read two manuscripts. I try to believe that it is your hand that turns the pages; that you are sitting and reading with me. It's lovely here; real country; with crickets that are doing their best to sing your name.

Good night, and I love you, and again, remember when you read it that my love will be thirty-six hours bigger. Have you room for it? I love you.

Ogden

August 29, 1929

Dearest, dearest,

I've been living all day on your letter. The heart delighted me, even if it is a stone one. It was particularly darling of you to see it, and to pick it up and to send it.

Lord yes, the tenth is too far off even to be imaginable. Can't you leave ahead of your family and come down for the week-end of the sixth? That's four days better, anyhow. Mother and Father are here; they are so anxious to see you, and I do want you to know them. They are entirely in love with you just from Eleanor's description of you. I was told today that Sarah, Eleanor's maid, exclaimed after you left "Oh Mrs. McWilliam, that's the loveliest young lady I ever saw. If we could only have her in the family!"

Do try for the weekend of the sixth, but if you can't, you will come down for a few days around the tenth, won't you? I have two weeks of vacation coming and I'd take some of it then and save the rest for a trip to Baltimore. Gwen and Douglas will be back then. I can hardly wait to see Gwen. For six months every time I have seen her she has talked of nothing but you. She thought I wasn't properly impressed with you; the only bad guess I've ever known her to make, but her good taste excuses it, don't you think so? The spell you cast over this family is extraordinary, but understandable.

The address you want is Mrs. John Stilwell, Ardenwold, Yonkers, N.Y. A note to her would be pleasant. I wrote to her, but I couldn't tell her the whole story of what a visit it was. Some day I shall, and by hook or crook I'm going to get that apple tree. What an awful time I had getting that ring off my chain. Do you wear it just once in a while, or is it tucked away somewhere? I have so many questions. Why are you so adorable? How could you come to care even the tiniest hoot for me? Who is this man Shaw that you are dressing to go and see?

It's late now — for a working young man, that is — half an hour past midnight. Having moved to the country to escape commuting for a while, I had to go to town yesterday and the day before, and again this evening. I dined with a nice red and gray old gentleman named Walsh who wants to get a book on Ireland published. His speech was all of O'Briens and O'Rourkes and Kellys and Cohalans and his food was droopy, but he took me to the library and showed me an old 17th century map and pointed out the spot some branch of the Nash family had swashed in from Wales in 1500 to rob the Walshes, so I forgave him, and almost told him about you.

Have I ever told you that I love you? Because I do. I even loved you yesterday when I didn't get any letter and thought you hated me for trying to rush things. It ought to worry me to think that no matter what you ever do to me that is dreadful I will still have to keep on loving you; but it doesn't, and I will.

Shall I be able to see your mother in New York and thank her for having you?

> *Once more and always —*
> *I love you.*
> Ogden

Friday night
August 30, 1929

Frances darling,

I've never heard anything so gloriously silly as your suggestion that I write about something other than you. Don't you realize what would happen if I were shut off from the one thing that fills my life? Perhaps I'd better teach you a lesson. I'm enclosing a letter — just a little one, so it really doesn't count — of the kind that you would get every day if I couldn't write what I've got to write to you. Read it carefully and take warning.

Your letter arrived at half past four this afternoon, just as I had resigned myself to facing Saturday and Sunday and Monday without any.

Dear Miss Leonard —

You see, I forgot to tell you that the office will be closed tomorrow and of course Sunday and Monday are holidays, so I can't possibly get anything till Tuesday. That's too long. I remember that you get a Sunday mail delivery and I suppose this will reach you on it. I think I shall probably have to call you up on Sunday night — I don't want to go three days without a word, and I do want to know your plans. I'm so anxious for you to come here for a few days.

Your mother's letter came this morning. I didn't know anyone but you could be so nice. It makes me understand you better, and I shall answer it at once.

The day has not been exciting. A professor at Northwestern University wanted to know if we should like to publish a 500-page book on General Howe's campaign in Pennsylvania in 1777. I told him no. Right? A man in Brooklyn wanted to know if we should like to publish a book entitled "Why We Welcome Premier Ramsay MacDonald to America's Shores." I told him no. Proper? A letter came in from a woman in Indiana who says her husband is the latest and only authentic revelation of God on earth, and will we publish his book and make him rich and famous? I took it around to the head of the religious department, who is a red-headed atheist from Texas. He smiled in a resigned sort of way and told me he got a dozen like it every week. He said he got a letter from one latest and only authentic revelation of God on earth, who claimed also to be the power behind the veil, and had been the champion negro bicycle racer of the world from eighteen ninety-eight to eighteen ninety-nine; two illustrations were enclosed: one, a photograph of the author's legs taken from the back; two, a photograph of the author's legs taken from the front. I thought that was very interesting and told him so, but he said that was nothing compared to some of the things that happen in Texas, so I left.

Charlie Duell came in today with a disgustingly roguish gleam in his eye. He said that he had just had a letter from his mother, and he bet I couldn't guess what she said in the post script. I stopped him for a minute by also betting that I couldn't. He was disappointed, but said that if that was so he would read it to me. He did. This was it: "I just got a bread and butter letter from Ogden, so he *was* here!" I threw the desk and the stenographer at him, but he seemed to think it was worth it. Apparently my devotion is suspected; why not; blind Homer could look at me and see it written all over me. Besides, if they insisted on hanging around what else could they reasonably expect but for me to kidnap you? Ignorant louts, all of them, say I; but very nice.

Right here I am attacked by an empty feeling. I recognize the symptoms. It means that hours have passed since I told you that I love you. Frances, come soon, won't you? I'm so happy thinking about you, but so miserable not seeing you.

I love you.
Ogden

[ENCLOSURE]

August 30, 1929

Dear Frances,

I got up this morning. I ate breakfast. I went to work. I worked. I ate luncheon. In the afternoon I worked some more. Then I came home. I ate dinner. I read. Now I am writing a letter. Today there was no sun, there never has been any sun and there never will be any sun. Tonight there is no moon; there never has been and never will be a moon. No more are there, or have there been, or will there be birds or crickets or grass or flowers. The earth is a brown ball of dried mud that has dropped through a gray hole in the sky, and there is nothing good in or on it.

Very truly yours,
Ogden Nash

Saturday night
August 31, 1929

Frances darling,

No office today, and consequently no letter. But I don't mind so much now that I have your other three that I can take out and reassure myself with. It was just at first when I was so horribly uncertain that my bones crumbled and my flesh collapsed and my heart turned into a marshmallow when I heard nothing from you. Hereafter you may take an occasional day off — I shan't like it, but I'll be able to bear it, because I don't want you to have the feeling that you've got to do things. Meanwhile, I've started what I hope will be the finest collection of autographed Frances Leonard letters in existence, which I have no intention of bequeathing to the Metropolitan or the Morgan Library. They are to stay right with me where I can read them over while I'm waiting for the Judgment Day; and when that comes I'll only have to show them and prove that it was really I they were written to, and the grimmest jury of angels will say "There must have been *something* good about this fellow," and I'll meet you inside in two minutes. You're a darling. This last remark doesn't belong in the same paragraph with the rest, but I couldn't help it, it just bubbled out.

Exactly a week ago tonight, at about this time, we were playing blind man's buff; you were standing on the lawn, tall and white in the darkness; I couldn't see your face, but I knew every curve of your cheek and your mouth and your chin; and I loved you; and I couldn't do anything about it. I was so afraid you were tired and bored and wanted to go up. I cheated quite a good deal to keep from being caught; I thought that if I ever got the handkerchief over my eyes and lost sight of you even for a moment you might disappear. But you didn't. Thank you, Frances, for not disappearing. Do you remember how we stumbled along through the grape arbor and tried to find one little shadow on the hill side, and got all mixed up in the long grass? And how we finally remembered the steps but forgot the garden and had to climb the wall and step on the flowers to reach them? And how I had so much to say and couldn't say any of it, but just sat and looked at you, which was nice for me but must have been dull for you?

It's different tonight — I am saying so much and you are not here. Somehow I prefer the other arrangement. When shall I know how soon I am to see you again? Do you know that it's so long since I've seen you that my nose has healed? That worries me a bit, as, not being able to discover any other reason for your caring for me, I've suspected that you may have an overwhelming weakness for gentlemen with blistered noses. Tell me at once if this is so, and I'll get properly scorched before you come down.

As a matter of fact I planned today with that in mind. All morning I sat reading a manuscript on the lawn, full in the sun — very hard on the eyes, and there were three jolly fly musketeers hard at work on my ankles. I was reading a manuscript about degenerates in the artistic colony of Paris, so the flies were a welcome and comparatively healthy diversion. I played golf this afternoon; very badly in most spots and rather better in a few, and I give you my word I was thinking of you the whole time and my partner thought I was an idiot. And so I was; at least, my mind was two hundred miles away from me. This evening I read a detective ms. and decided that those people don't know what excitement is. They should try sitting in the back seat of an automobile lost between Garden

City and Cedarhurst, with a chauffeur who knows more about or at least pays more attention to what's behind him than what's in front of him — and trying to find courage enough to ask one short question that's loaded with enough heaven and hell to blow up a hundred solar systems.

Once more, dearest, before I say goodnight — I love you.

Ogden

September 1, 1929

Dear Mrs. Leonard —

It was good of you to write me so soon, and such a letter. It meant so much that I was almost afraid to open it — but I did, and found in it all I needed to complete a happiness that I'm still trying to understand. I know what Frances is to you and her father; your trusting her to me is so great a thing that it makes all my thanks look insignificant; but I do thank you, and I shall always thank you. And please don't think me impertinent when I say that as I re-read your letter I am as fortunate in finding Frances' mother as I am in finding her.

I am altogether content to say nothing to anyone for a while — I don't even think that any of my friends who have seen Frances would believe me. Of course Mother and Father do, but they haven't met her yet. They love her already from the impression my incoherent descriptions have given them, but I am impatient for the time when they can see for themselves what she really is. — I love her so completely that I know I can make her happy as long as she loves me; and I will shape my life so that she will never have reason to stop. I feel very humble when I think of her — but very proud, too: humble toward her and proud toward the world; and I am going to try to justify your faith in me.

I don't know whether my gratefulness shows in this letter; but I mean to show it not only now but as long as I live.

Sincerely,
Ogden Nash

E.W.N.
Roslyn, Long Island, New York
September 4, 1929

Dear Mr. Leonard —

Please forgive my delay in thanking you for your letter. My only excuse is that every time I get a pen and paper I find myself writing to the Cape.

I hope to tell you when I see you exactly how much that letter meant and means to me. I have always admired you and Mrs. Leonard; and now your friendliness and kind answer to my tremendous request have completely won my gratitude and affection.

Sincerely,
Ogden Nash

Tuesday night
September 10, 1929

Frances,

I couldn't go to bed without telling you how particularly marvelous you were today. You don't seem to have any idea of your own loveliness and sweetness; that can't go on, and I shall see that it doesn't. Just looking at you and talking to you was the greatest happiness that Mother and Father have had in years; thank you for that.

Any and all of the Nash family are yours, to do with what you will; however, I know which one I hope you will choose. Can you understand this letter at all? It's only another way of saying that I love you.

Ogden

Friday night
September 13, 1929

Frances darling —

I bless Chicago, if it brings you to New York. Don't you think it would be a good idea to break your trip by coming up on the 17th and having dinner with me and doing something amusing in the evening? Also I should like to see that you get a proper luncheon with the right kind of coffee before you start, and see you safely on the train. Even if I'm not very good about trains I could at least see that if you got on the wrong one it would be a Long Island one and not Dubuque or Montreal.

Your account of the goldfish's manners convinces me that I should come down and give them a wigging. The cricket tells me that he is known as a strict disciplinarian, some malcontents and hot heads going so far as to call him a martinet; so you might threaten them with a visit from him the next time they take their thumbs out of their pockets.

Don't speak slightingly of the purple ink. It was the most welcome sight in two days. A dirty little boy dropped it casually on my desk at half past four this afternoon when I had just about stopped hoping and was preparing to curl up like a sprayed caterpillar. Once I was dependent only on myself for my own happiness; now I have nothing to do with it. There are drawbacks about loving completely and absolutely; but they are like the drawback on a catapult; when the catch is released the forward rush and the exhilaration of the flight are an almost intolerable joy. I'm rather glad you didn't go on the observation platform; I want to show you that myself. Will you save it for me? The reflections of the signal lights flow along the rails after you; like red and green rivers; and whenever the train stops the country that has been slipping out from under you trembles and hesitates and then comes rushing back at you like your past life.

Frances darling, tell me you're fond of me, even slightly; remember my vacuum; I'm insatiable, and still afraid to believe in my luck. I love you.

Ogden

Saturday night
September 14, 1929

Frances darling,

This is being written five minutes after the discovery that you aren't coming to New York. My heart gave such a pleased and excited leap when I heard your voice again; it's a divine voice; why did it have to say what it did and remove all the reasons for the existence of next week? I'm telling myself that I'm getting what I deserve, or rather, missing what I don't deserve; I knew from the first that Chicago can be reached directly from Baltimore; but I was so clever and so selfish and so scheming that I didn't say anything about it. It was such a nice little plot, and such a harmless one; even if I was going to bring you out of your way by withholding the facts (I know the name of my offense: suppressio veri et suggestio falsi). I fully intended to give you a pleasant hour or two. Well, I'm dust and ashes now, and the lion and the lizard are moping over my grave; I'm buried at the cross roads with a stake through my breast; I'm drawn and quartered and my head is on a pole as a warning to all young men who may be planning to be too bright.

But Frances, the injustice of it! Think of all the kindly things I said about Chicago last night! I feel very differently now; indignant, resentful, vindictive. I enclose a curse which I shall put into effect as soon as you are safely on your way home. By the way, hadn't you better come back through New York? It's twenty-two days till the second week in October, which is five hundred and twenty-eight hours, which is thirty-one thousand six hundred and eighty minutes which is more seconds than I dare contemplate. I don't think I can stand it. After all you are responsible for the condition I'm in; doesn't your conscience tell you that you should do something about it?

I brought Dan Longwell back to dinner last night; he talked a great deal about you, mostly in superlatives, so I enjoyed the evening. Afterwards I drove him back to Garden City — my first experience of night driving. There was a heavy fog and I gave him some bad moments. The stone walls looked just like the road; I don't know what the road looked like, as I never saw it.

This morning I went to the New York office. My first caller had written a biography of Saint Martin of Tours. Would you like to know his name and address? Do say yes. He was Mr. Foley of Kalamazoo. Isn't that a grand first line for a song: Mr. Foley of Kalamazoo. In conjunction with St. Martin of Tours I find it irresistable. Anyhow, he was quite delightful; he had a very low, almost non-existent forehead and tortoise shell spectacles, and is professor of English in Western State Teacher's College and has been spending his sabbatical year following St. Martin around.

Next came Prosper Buranelli and Dr. Jack and Chas. Hedlund all in a bunch. Dr. Jack is an osteopath from Trenton. One day Chas. Hedlund went to him with a sore shoulder, and while it was being osteopathically mauled he remarked, "I must have hurt it the second time I was ship-wrecked." The doctor asked him about his second shipwreck and his first shipwreck and the rest of his shipwrecks and at once wrote to us that he had discovered another Trader Horn and how much was there in it for him? He is now Chas. Hedlund's business manager. Chas. is a broad-shouldered, double-chinned Swede of sixty, who looks at you over the top of very thick-lensed spectacles, and filters his accent through a mon-strous bandanna of a moustache. Having run away from home, sailed be-fore the mast, deserted the ship, hidden under a pile of fish to escape the police, worked in the diamond mines, served in Cecil Rhodes' body guard, fought against the British in the Boer war, hidden in the jungle from the British after the Boer war, been captured by savages in Mada-gascar, scooped snakes out of gold mines by the bucket full, etc., he is now a quiet family man and the best carpenter in town. Buranelli is the delightful little Texas wop who writes all the books that the people who have had the experiences that are to go in the books can't write them-selves. He's a most improper person; he has three households that I know of, and sings Verdi and recites d'Annunzio so well that he never has to pay for his drinks in the Italian speakeasies. He asked me to lunch with him the other day, but I was too wise; besides, I had an engagement at the Barclay. So I sent the sales manager in my place. The next day he turned a reproachful red eye on me and mumbled that the luncheon had lasted till four in the morning, perhaps later, he wasn't sure. In spite of all this, Buranelli is a splendid ghost writer and is to haunt Hedlund's book. He kept asking Hedlund if he'd ever had any native wives — Hed-lund would blush and say, "I have vife and chooldren now, I yoost von't say." Then Dr. Jack would interrupt. "Pardon me, Mr. Nash, but I'll get my share, won't I?" and Buranelli would start in again: "We've got to have something about native wives, that's what the public wants," and fi-nally Hedlund looked at me with the same roguish twinkle as the woman at the St. Regis and said, "Vell, I tell you, but don't put it in the book, sure, I vas yoost like all young men." I don't know why he looked at me; I promise you I've never had a native wife. So I flapped my apron at them and sent them home and sat down and wrote a letter. The same New Yorker that had the articles I sent you had a story about a woman who entered her dog in a dog show not because she expected him to win a blue ribbon but because she thought he'd meet some awfully nice dogs.

Now — all that stuff back there was written to amuse you. Haven't I earned the right to say that it's not what I most want to say? Frances, at the risk of wearying you I must tell you again that I love you and that you are all the beauty there is, and that I am horribly lonely and that I love you, and that I love you.

Ogden

Sunday night
September 15, 1929

Frances darling —

It's been a gorgeous fall day — blue sky, green country, bright sun and nippy wind; I looked at so many things and wanted to show them to you.

Last night, I slept as soundly as a night nurse. I think hearing your voice helped me tremendously; even though you did say you couldn't come I thought you sounded sorry, and that was something. This morning I played eighteen holes of golf with Aubrey, who beat me decisively, but I enjoyed climbing the hills and running down them and hoping to do better next time. There was a girl playing in front of us; I tried to pretend she was you, but it wouldn't work and I ended up by hating her.

I was waked up this morning by a telephone call from Mrs. F. N. Doubleday, wife of the biggest of the big bosses, asking me to tea. A command performance; incidentally my first. So at four o'clock I climbed myself into the Chrysler and set off to find the house, not having any very definite idea of where to look for it, beyond knowing that it was past a railroad bridge and to the right of a duck pond. Long Island is darned with railroad bridges and patched with duck ponds, so that didn't take me much further. I asked a policeman where it was and he didn't know; then I asked a nursemaid, and she did. What does that prove? Possibly that the Doubleday chauffeur is more fascinating than the Doubleday cook. Anyhow, I arrived; and the old lady at once took me out and demolished me at deck tennis. She's about sixty, her face is lined like the bottom of a newly raked bunker; but she's spry as a spider, and really very amusing and pleasant. I admired the dog, one of those woolly sheep ones without a tail. She said they were fond of him, but not so fond as they had been of their St. Bernard that had died. "Oh," I said brightly, "I suppose the second never is the same as the first." Just the remark that was needed, considering that she is Mr. Doubleday's second wife. But the air soon cleared and I lost a dollar at bridge and we all felt better and parted friends, and if you *will* go to Egypt this winter I'm going to wangle an invitation to Nassau out of her, so there.

This is my last night here; the children arrive tomorrow and I go to Eleanor's. I don't know whether I'll stay alone there or go to town — every day brings a million new complications. If you happen to feel like writing, the office is still the best place. But Eleanor's address is Hewlett and her telephone number is Cedarhurst 4576 in case you need some one in a hurry to help you out of Chicago.

Tomorrow morning I hope to get the special delivery letter which the United States government has been keeping from me today. The Roslyn post office closes up all day Sunday; special delivery means nothing to them. But I'm glad to know it's waiting for me. Is it kindly in tone?

Do you know how much I love you? I don't. It's some quantity that my brain can't define, or even realize. Anyhow, it's enough to fill infinite space and stick out over the edges.

Your hands are nice, too. Frances, you have no idea of how highly I approve of you. Darling, darling, are you always going to be at the other end of a train trip or a long distance telephone?

> *I love you.*
> Ogden

Hewlett, Long Island, New York
Monday night
September 16, 1929

Frances Darling —

I finally got your special delivery at noon today; it was sweet of you to do it; I made a few faces when I read the part which said you were coming to New York, but I'm pretty much resigned to missing you, and just hoping the tiniest, most innocent hopes you ever saw that you will stop off for an hour or so on the way back.

Frances, I'm not impatient. God knows the last thing I want is to have you in any way uncertain; I'll wait just as quietly as I can until you are sure of yourself; but you must allow me to love you while I wait; that's something that can't be stopped. And you mustn't make slighting remarks about yourself which reflect on my ability to recognize perfection when I see it. Of course you're not Sainte Thérèse; I don't want you to be a saint; I want you to be you; nothing else matters because there isn't anything else.

I got another royal command today. What fun. Old Mr. Doubleday hardly ever comes to the office now, as he's quite an invalid; I think he had sleeping sickness. Anyhow, his mind is as keen as ever, but if he sits long at his desk he gets shaky all over. So whenever he wants to know how things are going he sends for people to come driving in his car. The system is amusing. He lives at Oyster Bay; the meeting place is a road house called Rothman's at East Norwich, quite near Ted's house; it's the wettest spot on Long Island. I drove over with Harry Maule, my immediate boss, and the old gentleman picked us up in his yellow Packard which is some thirty feet long, and away we went, answering a dozen questions a minute. He crouched back in his corner like an old eagle and talked in a voice you could hardly hear and yet couldn't say "what" to. He's just got back from England; while he was there he took Colonel Lawrence (Lawrence of Arabia) down with him to visit Kipling. Imagine the tales when those two got together — but he said they talked mostly in Hindu and Arabic.

The drive ended in about an hour, and we got dropped at the speakeasy — somehow that seemed awfully funny to me. Maule drove me back to Garden City and on the way we had the most complete complete blowout. We were doing about forty five; the tire went with a terrific roar and we went right across the road. Great excitement but no injuries except to my gray suit in lifting the spare off the rack.

This evening I'm at Eleanor's. Gwen came up today to see Father, and she is staying here too, so we have quite an assembly. Ted's children arrived with their little mouths all full of hells and damns after spending the summer with cowboys on a ranch.

Father continues to improve and I think we'll be able to move him to town as soon as we get a place to move to.

This house has no crickets in it, so I have no one to talk to about you. I must make friends with the cat. Until I do, may I talk to you? I love you, Frances,

Ogden.

Hewlett, Long Island, New York
Thursday evening
September 19, 1929

Frances darling —

Eleanor is a sweet sister, but in some ways an odd one. There is no ink in the house, and I seem to have used the last of the writing paper. I only hope I find a respectable envelope and a moist fountain pen to address it with. If not, I shall write very badly in pencil, with a name or two spelled wrong, and when the letter arrives everyone will think it is from your old nurse. Apparently no McWilliam ever writes letters — I don't know how they communicate when parted; perhaps by sending knotted strings as the Incas did, or perhaps just by shouting very loudly.

Dearest, you've disappeared so completely that I'm in a dreadful condition, and no fit companion for anyone. No letter for three days. I know it's because of the trip and the distance, but at the same time I'm scared and twitchy and nervous and my stenographer looks at me as if I were a man-eating shark, which is the beast whose temper I have at the moment. Separation is bad enough, but isolation is just unbearable. Frances, I could write it a million times and still give you no idea of how much, how completely I love you, and how lost and lonely I am without you.

Last night I had such a delightful dream — that my pocket book got so full of letters that it burst open, and I couldn't shut it. Not that I wanted to. Did the proofs of the photographs come, and were they good or at least good enough? And when are you getting to New York, and oh Frances don't change your mind and go straight to Baltimore. Calendar makers are such fools, saying there are seven days in a week — it's been a week since I saw you and there were a thousand days in it. The telephones helped a little, but they don't really count. I know how you hate them, too — it's dear of you to talk to me — I do get the feeling from it that you are there, which is something I haven't got now.

I'm swamped with work, which ought to take my mind off you, according to all the books on how to be successful — but it doesn't. Yesterday I was in town and I wandered around the Grand Central Station because you had been there — and you looked very lovely there too, and I didn't at all like saying goodbye — and I'm writing this in the room you had when you were here, and soon I shall go downstairs and look at the sofa where we sat for a fairly important twenty minutes. But all these things are illusions, shells with the life gone out of them.

Don't think you can frighten me with talk about child-wives — but when you say "if I ever get married" you send the chills over me in regiments — goose-stepping goose-flesh. It's awful — but I love you just the same, and shall always, and always more, Darling.

Ogden

Hewlett, Long Island, New York
Friday night
September 20, 1929

Frances darling,

I found enough work on my desk today to take some five pounds of badly needed flesh off me — but no letter. This isn't a complaint — it's just to explain why this isn't the highest-spirited of letters.

I have spent the last hour going through the F. L. section of my correspondence, in an attempt to get cheered up. I find sixteen letters between November 26th, 1928, and August 12th, 1929 — that being the first of the two parts into which I have divided that particular correspondence. They are all kind, and witty, and amusing, but still they lack something.

The second part, starting with the telegram dated August 22nd and reading AM COMING MEET ME ROOSEVELT LOBBY ABOUT FOUR ON FRIDAY, FRANCES is much better. Very much. Only it stops on September 16th, which is four days back. Thirteen letters in all, dear letters, and the only thing that could carry me through this night. In one of them you say, "I don't mind leaving places, it's being left that's so disturbing." That is devastatingly true. Never have I felt so left, and if I don't get some word tomorrow — well, I don't dare even think of that. I think I have already explained, Frances, that I love you. Apparently young men visited with even mild love are apt to get nervous when they can't find out what has become of their ladies. I don't believe that there is any precedent for my degree of feeling, but it multiplies the distress of the average young man's love by infinity and the answer is, to use a weak word, discomfort. Yet it's so marvellous even to be allowed to love you and I have no right to make discontented noises at you. For I do love you, Frances, horribly and wonderfully and altogether. Whatever I do, whichever way I turn, I see only, I am reminded only, that I love you, and I love you, and I love you. It's not just simple idolatry. Of course it's instinctive, but also

I've reasoned it all out, in so far as I can be at all reasonable about you. I've compared your hair and your eyes and your nose and your mouth and your figure, and your mind and your spirit and your whole self with girls who are supposed to be something oh very extra special — and always, Frances, there's only you, all that's darling and adorable, all that I've lived and hoped for. Dearest, dearest, I'm not really living when I'm away from you — only hoping, and hope is so closely bound to fear!

But you've heard all this before, and I seem to be falling into my bad habit of saying what I want to say rather than what you want to hear. Not much excitement at the office today, mostly routine. Except that Mr. Doran told me he is going to arrange for me to spend more time in New York, which means my taking on more prominence and prestige, which pleased me.

Yates Satterlee picked me up at six. He has a job with the Curtiss Aeroplane Company, and he had a few things to finish, so he took me over to Roosevelt Field for an hour and I watched hundreds of aviators performing against the sunset. Yates is a pilot, and threatens to take me up at anytime, but I think I'll wait till he heads for Baltimore. At dinner I found out all the gossip about my lady friend on the other side of the island. Some one saw me setting out for Bayside on the morning of August 23rd with Eleanor and a girl who was described as extremely beautiful. I recognized the description, and much as I wanted to tell all about you, I said it was one of my cousins and I hope I'll be forgiven for the wicked lie.

I've been debating for two hours whether or not to call you up. I've finally decided not to, but I shall tomorrow night unless I hear from you, if I can ever find you in Kenilworth. I love you.

Ogden.

September 27, 1929

Frances darling —

First, your letter. No, first I love you. Then your letter. Believe this, dearest; it's *not* really worse for me now than if you'd never said you'd marry me; and I won't hear of your hating yourself; and you're not a silly backsliding thing. To have you consider me seriously for even a moment is so much more than I have any right to hope for; it's like giving all the water he can drink to a man who has been dying of thirst; he'll kill himself gulping it down. Not that I'm killing myself; but I do have a good many hours in a rosy delirium, and they are heavenly. The reaction comes in the intervals of sanity, and it's then that I write so distressingly. You are to pay no attention to me, but think about things until you are absolutely sure one way or the other. At least six months, and if you like, a year. I'll always wait and always love you.

Today I've been very luxurious, staying in bed and eating things on trays. The doctor's outward disdain apparently conceals a profound knowledge of medicine, because I've had no temperature since last night, and an unpleasant cough which had set in died in infancy. I'll probably get up for dinner tonight and go to the office tomorrow. The plans for moving to town are indefinite because of Father's new attack, but we're hoping to do that Sunday at the latest.

I'm changing my mind about telephones; won't you change yours? I felt so much better after talking to you this afternoon; the two hundred miles of wire couldn't stop me from feeling that I had touched you. Unless you tell me not to I shall be doing it often from now on.

I've read two books today, and liked one thing in each. One I found in the memoirs of a St. Petersburg prima ballerina: that when Russians are expecting something too awful to happen they say "God remember King David and the meekness of his heart." That delights me, particularly as I remember that King David's heart was about as meek as Chicago. The other item was in a biography of Paul Revere. After making good on his ride, Paul was appointed messenger of the Continental Congress. Emboldened by success he turned in an expense account of five shillings a day, but they cut him down to four. Somehow I've never been able to think of Paul with the awed respect which he deserves; have you by any chance read Benchley's story of the salesman who went to Boston to sell him an acid bath?

I'm an idiot. I was so absorbed in looking at you while I was in Baltimore that I never asked to see the halo photograph.* Do show it to me when I come down. And Frances I want one of each of the two new Ira Hill poses. Can that be managed?

Above all I was an idiot, and an abominably, brutally selfish one, to expose you to my cold. If I'd had any thought in the world except my own pleasure I shouldn't have allowed myself to go near you. I'm enormously relieved to hear that you didn't catch it, but I shan't soon forgive myself.

Darling, don't worry about me; don't think of anything about me except that I love you.

*See page 21. — Ed.   Ogden

Thursday night
October 3, 1929

Dearest —

This morning I overslept, and had to dash for the station in a taxi. It's fun at 7:30 in the morning because the streets are dashable, newly washed, holding neither traffic nor dirt. The taxi driver told me that taxi drivers need rain more than the farmers do, and I told him I thought his cab was a wonder, and we parted regretfully if hurriedly. Something about taxi drivers appeals to me tremendously: they're a separate race; discreet as priests, adventurous as explorers, independent as cats; they see all, know all, and I suppose do all; and nine times out of ten they are named Herman Cohen. Except the drivers of the ITOA cabs, who are all Irish and have gray hair and good manners and hold the steering wheel like reins. People are so swell when you get to know them; I've lost some of my best enemies that way; I can only keep hating them by keeping away from them. It always turns out that we have something in common, and how can you hate anyone who has the same kind of cold you have, or agrees with you that Hoover's face just cries to have maple syrup poured on it, or has a new and ingenious theory about how Lizzie Borden hid the ax that she was acquitted of doing her father and mother in with? Impossible; which is too bad; some people need to be hated; prejudices are good for the soul; I'm all for the stiff neck, but I'm afraid I'll have to turn hermit to get it. What a misfortune if by not seeing you often enough I should come to hate you. I suppose you'd be a superb prejudice, but I don't like the idea. You don't want to be one, do you? No, even as the most cantankerous and misanthropic of column-sitters or cave-dwellers I should love you more than I hated everybody else.

Frances, I keep remembering moments with you; I remember you driving to the country, and being brave about being frightened. I hated having you frightened, but it did make you look adorable. Then I remember times such as in your library when I like to believe that you were happy. And I remember you white in the moonlight when my eyes were so blurred I could hardly see you. All these things are past, so they can't be taken from me; yet because they are past I haven't really got them; and I don't know what's ahead. Except that I am going to see you next week. Would you like to be called up Monday morning?

Love, and good night, and love.

Ogden

149 East 73rd Street
New York, New York
Tuesday night
October 15, 1929

Frances dearest —

Sorry — the ink is gone — there's not even one drop in the apartment. But I did find enough to address the envelope so that the desk clerk won't sneer at me. You can laugh if you will — I'm used to that, in fact I'll confess now that I like it. I haven't been laughed at since yesterday, and I miss it.

I wish I could say I enjoyed getting back to the office, and took off my coat and sat down whistling and grinning to demolish the work piled on my desk. But I didn't. I walked in dragging my feet like a boy on the first day of school, and spent the day finding all sorts of excuses to avoid my duty. I'm always that way after a holiday — also at most other times. I should have told you that I'm incurably lazy, or have you discovered it by yourself? Chris Morley saved the day by arriving at noon and proclaiming a picnic. We got rolls and sardines and apples and cheese from a soft-spoken, lying grocer named Lloyd B. Kleinfelder, and went to a pleasant spot on the drive of the Garden City Cathedral to eat. We were quiet as mice — cathedral mice — and not at all sacrilegious, but half way through lunch a policeman appeared and said that the verger or sacristan or bishop had telephoned to have us removed. So we removed ourselves. So I have been excommunicated today. I don't mind. Ousted by the church we went straight to the devil — drove ten miles to a roadhouse and drank beer and fed pretzels to police dogs and I didn't get back to the office till four, though I would have got there sooner if Chris hadn't been too impractical to have a gasoline gauge on his car. We ran completely out of gas, about two miles from a filling station. Charlie Duell and I got out and walked and returned with a one gallon cider jug filled with green gasoline, a strange degenerate sight.

Office gossip: Dan Longwell went to the first night of "June Moon" with Edna Ferber, wore a new opera hat, and opened it with such a pop when the play was over that she fell into Al Smith's lap. Dan says the hat has the best pop any one has ever heard, and he is going to let me listen to it some time. A friend of Charlie Duell's broke his leg saying good-night to a girl. I don't understand it but I am assured that it is so. He's Nancy Maxwell's cousin, and it sounds barely possible. Myself, I generally prefer the old-fashioned hand shake.

As I look at the first section of this letter I see that the writing is already blurred. I hope it will be readable when it reaches you. It's so well-behaved, so admirably reserved and undisturbing. At least so far, which is far enough.

If I can't tell you these things in words which may upset you I must at least write them. Then you can tear them up, or not read them, or read them and go out on the board walk and forget them.

I love you Frances, I can't stop loving you, and I am not going to give up hope yet of your caring for me. I can't. You've been sweeter, tenderer, dearer, than I dreamed even you could be. Perhaps I could forget you (no I couldn't) if you were only beautiful. But I love your thoughts so, the darling ways of your mind, and your honesty and loyalty, the things you do and say that are all so divinely your own.

There. I had to tell you that. Just remember that I love you, and I'll be good. Did you get the books? I'm a bit worried about what they are. I ordered four favorites of mine and the book store reported later that they didn't have two of them and had substituted two others. But I don't know which two. They may be awful — if so, I disown them.

Love,
Ogden

149 East 73rd Street
New York, New York
Wednesday night
October 23, 1929

Frances dearest —

Today I've been very much the young man about town, staying in New York and passing wearily but unwounded through a series of conflicts with various literary temperaments. This evening there was a bookseller's dinner with many speeches and myself one of the orators. I got home just a few minutes ago and found your letter waiting for me. Of course it disappointed me, Frances; I had hoped we were fairly well straightened out. But I am not upset and I am not impatient. In the first place my love for you has grown too deep to be disturbed by surface storms. And in the second place (don't think me conceited or cocky when I say this; it's no time to reserve thoughts or disguise words; I've got to speak) — every instinct and intuition and reason I possess tells me that you are fond of me. Two people cannot be as happy together as we have been without an understanding and an emotion that is more than liking. Don't speak to me of your not playing the game. You are — too honestly. I beg of you, if you can't trust yourself for a while, to trust me. I'm not altogether a fool; I've thought clearly and continuously about this situation and I know that if I have ever been right about anything I am right now. You are not silly and weak and cowardly; you are Frances, as fine as you are lovely, a darling all over and throughout. I can wait — as a matter of fact if you told me you'd marry me tomorrow I'd have to put it off till June at the earliest. And you have not worried me, because whether I'm up or down or tumbling between the two I feel deep within me the certainty that things will be all right — more than that, that they are all right now.

Lord what a letter! Do forgive me, and don't laugh me out of town as a self-satisfied ass. I'm fighting for the dearest thing in life and I can't pay attention to appearances. Do take some of my confidence; I have enough for two. But don't think again that I am rushing you. Your wishes are mine, and your peace of mind is mine, and your happiness is mine, and when I offend against any of them it is I who suffer with you.

Now, you must help me about one thing. Please think about this carefully and answer me truly, for it is enormously important. You say you still want to be sure. Can you reach your decision better by seeing me, or by not seeing me? Am I making it harder by writing and telephoning and visiting? Would it be easier if I eliminated myself altogether for two weeks or a month or more? When I talked to you last night I thought you wanted me to come down this weekend; that was before I got the letter; still, you had written it. I am sending this special delivery and mailing it at the station early tomorrow morning; you should have it by six o'clock. I shall call you up around dinner time. I want you to tell me then — honestly — whether or not I should come down Friday evening. And tell me not from your point of view, but from mine; tell me what is best for me to do; remember that I am terribly in love and can't afford to make any mistakes. I am putting myself in your hands.

All this has been hard to write; it's after one now and my machinery is running down. But even as it creaks and wheezes, it creaks and wheezes "I love you" and means it as truly and as beautifully as if it were singing.

I lied when I said your letter didn't disturb me; in one way it did; for I am horribly distressed to think that you may be unhappy again. I'm not proud to think that I've only been able to make you miserable. That's the thing I can't bear, Frances, and won't bear; but you must help me stop it. So speak the truth when I call up tomorrow night. Meanwhile and always, I love you.

Ogden

P.S. You say I mustn't be too nice to people. What does this mean?

Doubleday, Doran and Company, Inc.
Publishers
Garden City, New York
Monday night
October 28, 1929

Frances darling —

It's now 11.35 and I'm on the train headed for home and bed after a long evening of figuring and planning. Please don't frown at the up-hill and down dale handwriting; the Long Island Rail Road has the raggedest tracks and flattest wheels in the world, and also I am quite tired. Was it really beastly of me to drag you to the telephone tonight and hold you there? I might just as well not have — there were a lot of things I wanted to say but couldn't because the plump hungry blonde who operates the switch board at the Garden City Hotel kept cutting in to see if I had finished. You didn't know that, but as you are the soul of discretion on the telephone, it was all right.

I shouldn't be surprised to find myself engaged to a dozen girls in the next few days. You may remember (by the way, how is your memory today?) that I once told you of my absurd habit of talking to myself in moments of stress. My usual remark was "why did you do *that*, you darn fool?" Embarrassing if overheard, but nothing else. Today however I suddenly found that I was muttering at intervals "Darling I love you;" I must stop, or I shall be taken up by all the unmarried maidens of a certain age in Garden City who are in the mood to apply the statement to themselves. Then what? Do you think you could help me if I got involved?

I'm sorry to report that my arm is wide awake and seems likely to remain so for some time and my hands keep reaching for something that isn't here. Oh dreadful. Too much of that and I should moulder and fall to pieces like an untenanted house.

How our conversation is improving. Has it occurred to you that I didn't get a chance to tell you the story of Frank Henry's two dollars?

Frances, this day is ending in you as it began in you. You may not know it, or like it, but you were with me as I worked; you even gave me two or three extremely good ideas for furthering this new scheme. Darling, do it always — everything is easy, everything is fun and delightful with you beside me. I love you. The word is "darling."

Ogden

October 30, 1929

Frances darling —

Today I spent nine hours composing a ten page memorandum to Nelson Doubleday embodying the ideas Dan and I worked out the night I wrote you so illegibly on the train. I then left the office rather thoughtfully. I continued to be thoughtful all the way back to town, and on the Seventh Avenue subway from Penn Station to Times Square, and on the shuttle from Times Square to Grand Central, and on the Lexington Avenue subway from Grand Central to 68th Street. I climbed to the street still thoughtful, walking slowly and more slowly from 68th Street to 73rd. These were my thoughts: "Night before last I telephoned Frances. She said she had written, and a letter I would like to get, too. But that letter should have got here yesterday. It didn't. Why not? Did she tear it up after writing it, and do a different kind of letter? I'm sure there will be something waiting for me at home — but what?" I give you my word I was in a delicate condition. Your letter was on the table, and I retired to my room to open it.

Darling, the rain stopped, and the moon came out, and the crickets began to sing, and the wax flowers blossomed out like night blooming jessamine and the goldfish raced around their bowl like shooting stars.

You have written all I want to know in this world or any other. Frances, whom am I to thank for your adorableness? If I say anything to you, you will only disclaim it. Perhaps you will at least let me give that candle to Saint Joseph.

So "Simple Stories" is now tenantless. Can the ashman read English? I do hope so; I'd hate to have the words, sentences and paragraphs that cost me such concentrated effort die entirely unread.

My curiosity is twisted and stretched till it's ready to snap, at the news that you've found a substitute for the toe of the old slipper. Where, darling, where? Have you given my brave, forlorn little talisman to Pauline, or traded it in for a jigsaw puzzle? I left it there to watch over you like a good soldier; to ward off bronchitis and night clubs and bad dreams and unhappy thoughts and other things too numerous to mention here but that we might compile a list of some time; so do keep it where it can hear you call out in case of trouble, and remember, Frances, that your voice is not very loud. I love your voice.

You say that you are glad you are going to see me on Tuesday. That delights me, darling. But I'm coming Monday. Will you be glad to see me then? I arrive in Baltimore at 9:07 Monday evening; in fact, I bought my ticket today to make sure. Will you be out somewhere Monday night, or, if in, entertaining the entire younger set? Frances, don't be; and can't you do something about the Junior League that looms like an infuriated mother bear over Tuesday morning? But here I am being unreasonable again. Reprove me, dearest, but gently.

I *am* going to Canada this week-end; leaving Friday night and getting back Monday morning. I'm rather looking forward to it, as I've never been there; as a matter of fact I've never been out of the United States. I'm going to see Rufus King, or did I tell you that? Anyhow, another publisher is trying to steal him from us, and I must hurry to hold his hand.

This is the last letter you'll get from me before I see you, as I think I'd better let you have Saturday for your own affairs without interference from me.

Only remember this: I love you, and I will be thinking of you every moment and longing to help you. We love each other; really, Frances darling, *really*. Everything else will vanish. I *know*. Now, good bye till Monday; I am praying that you don't have too rotten a time; oh Frances, don't forget that you are all my earth and heaven. I love you.

Ogden

Dear Miss Leonard —

Doubleday, Doran and Company, Inc.
Publishers
Garden City, New York
Thursday afternoon
November 7, 1929

Frances darling —

This is another daylight letter — I hate them — written with typewriters
clacking and telephones jangling and salesmen arguing and innumerable
people wondering what I'm writing, and strolling by to have a look. But
I've got to entertain an infant prodigy (why can I spell "prodigy" yet not
pronounce it?) this evening and I don't know what time I'll get home.
His name is Bayard Schindel; he is the only beloved son of Isa Glenn; he
is just twenty-one years old; we recently published a novel of his called
"Golden Pilgrimage"; and he wears spats and carries a cane — this last
characteristic is all right in itself, but taken in conjunction with the others
it may give you some idea of the sort of evening I'm in for. His object
will be to get drunk and mine will be not to; he will probably attain his,
and I will certainly attain mine. As a matter of fact he's not a bad boy,
and would be very nice if they'd only left him in the oven five minutes
longer.

As you can see from the letterhead, I'm in town. I've just had lunch
with Eugène Reynal — you don't know him but he's a good friend of
mine, so I enjoyed myself. In a few minutes I'm to see a young woman
who writes such atrocious puns in Life that they might make a good
book. Last week I wrote to her and told her that her work appalled
me; she wrote back in high glee saying she had never been so complimented, so here we are. I suspect that she has a beard; certainly her jokes
have.

I called up Mother a few minutes ago, and she told me there is a letter
waiting for me. Frances, that means that you wrote a day earlier than
you generally do after I leave. May I get a bit excited? Is it a nice letter — it must be, or you wouldn't have written. I hadn't been planning to
go home before dinner; I'd been going to get that haircut of which we
spoke — but now I want to read it before I call you up, so I'll rush
things here and get uptown for a few minutes. Your good deed for the
day — luring me home for a moment with the family.

I suppose I shall find out tonight when I am to see you again. Darling I love you; if you hadn't forbidden me to bust I should certainly bust.
Goodbye till this evening, and I love you.

Ogden

Thursday night
November 7, 1929

Darling —

I'm home early after my evening with the prodigy.

> Tonight I attempted to kindle
> An interest in young Mr. Schindel
> But though I considered
> His mother was widdered
> My affection continued to dwindle.

> The longer I listened to Bayard
> Whom the critics have greatly admayard
> The shorter I wished
> To hark to his whisht
> So I bade him farewell, and retayard.

Dull rhymes and feeble, but at least timely. I was to meet the little man at 6:30. He arrived at 7. That was just as well, as I had only reached the trysting place five minutes sooner. I asked him if he wanted a cocktail and he said he'd had some. He had. We ate. He told me he'd been in Washington doing research work for his next book and dining with the Minister from Siam. The Minister from Siam, it appears, is a very charming man who speaks Sanskrit and owes his present post to having pressed the hand of the Queen of Siam so often and so tenderly that the King of Siam decided that America would be just the place for him. The minister also read and praised Bayard's book, and got him to autograph a copy for the king; the signed book is now on its way to Siam, and Bayard is waiting for a royal oriental gift in return. A sacred elephant would be good publicity; also I am, as you may have heard, fond of elephants.

Further scandal: Last year Blanche Knopf, wife of the publisher, and an international holy cow, went to London to negotiate with Radclyffe

Hall for the American rights on *The Well of Loneliness*. Miss Hall gave her tea, and then said she supposed they might as well talk about the contract. Mrs. Knopf glanced at a dowdy female typing a manuscript in one corner of the room and haughtily announced that she never discussed business in the presence of menials. The dowdy female arose, bobbed a curtsey, said "Very good, Mum," and withdrew. Mrs. Knopf was later distressed to find that the menial was Lady Trowbridge, Radclyffe's girl-friend. Oh dear.

It developed that I wasn't to get through the evening without a drink. I was conducted to a Spanish speak-easy and given an after-dinner cock-tail of the kind they serve in Havana and the Philippines where the sun sweats all the alcohol out of people and they don't have to work the next day anyway. I then mumbled something about having a lot of work at home and getting up at 6:30 in the morning, and sped spirally from the Spanish speak-easy, which last phrase, darling, is as fine an example of alliteration as you'll find outside of Swinburne.

Regardless of all this, Bayard is perfectly pleasant and not at all offen-sive; I've merely been trying to put him into a story that will amuse you; it's my hypocritical streak again. And I was looking at him with a jaundiced eye anyway, having just learned that you can't come up this weekend. That means, Frances, that I shan't see you till a week from to-morrow night. Eight days with eight thousand hells in each day and eight thousand devils in each hell. Think of the tall handsome powerful men with overwhelming personalities that you might meet in eight days! I can't and won't think of it, or I *would* bust, and then you'd be angry with me. Thank you, Frances, for today's letter; I almost wept to think of you at the mercy of the dentist. And I got annoyed at the music teacher's remarks till I reflected that if you became a lady Paderewski you'd be touring twelve months a year.

Darling, I love you; Frances, I love you; Frances darling, I love you.

Ogden

November 12, 1929

Frances darling —

So ends this day, and I can almost see Saturday on the horizon; I'll make it if the wind doesn't die, and if the wind dies I'll swim, though

Wednesday, Thursday and Friday are wider than the Hellespont and rougher than the Channel.

I called you up this evening, but you were out to dinner — having, I hope, one of those good but not too good times. I had nothing special to say, but I did want to hear your voice again, so I was disappointed, but I'm bearing up so well that you should be proud of me. I'll probably telephone again tomorrow around dinner time; will you be in? I'm afraid I shall speak rudely to the New York operator, the Baltimore operator and Delia if you aren't, as I've never been able to stay patient for more than twenty four hours.

I had a gratifying escape last night. Yesterday noon Reggie Townsend told me that two Canadian girls, friends of his, were to be in town and he was taking them to dinner and the theater. Would I come and help him entertain them? He fixed a shiny eye on me and I said yes without thinking. As soon as I had thought I went to Charlie Duell's desk and told him he had to substitute for me. You see, Reggie (he is editor of "Country Life") is one of these gay-dog, life-of-the-party fellows who can stay up till five in the morning, go to bed and have insomnia for two hours, and get up at seven feeling strong and cheerful and ready to face Nelson Doubleday. And I was rather tired. And I'm not keen about Canadian girls. Anyhow, though I may have told you this, I'm very much in love and I don't like parties without my favorite fiancée (isn't that a swell word — I'd never realized before just what a swell word it is) or even with her unless she will sit next to me and be ordinarily polite. I know she can do this, as she has done it, and I am duly grateful.

Well, Charlie went like a little man. I saw him this morning, pallid and with lack-lustre eye. He had got home at three thirty, and then only after waging a forty minute fight against going to Harlem. I, on the other hand, had written my letter and got to bed at half past ten.

Do you know what is the most delightful sound in the world? I'm sorry that you'll never be able to hear it. It's when I'm sitting in your library, and hear you cross the floor of your room and open the door; then your footsteps in the hall and on the stairs. In four days now —

> *Good night, darling —*
> *I love you.*
> Ogden

Dear Miss Leonard —

Thursday morning
November 28, 1929

Frances darling —

In spite of the golden paper and the purple ink this letter doesn't seem to
have the imperial look I had hoped for. Will you remember that I love
you, and forgive me?

Shall I tell you all about how I saw my first aeroplane crash this afternoon? You'll probably read a much better account in tomorrow's paper,
but I'll go ahead anyway because it was quite exciting.

It all started with my taking a good-looking female author to lunch at
Rothman's. Chaperoned. By Malcolm Johnson, who is now running the
Crime Club, and Bob Buckner, an extremely pleasant Virginian boy who
owns the automobile that we had to have to get across the island in. The
lady writes for the Crime Club, and today's gathering was for the purpose of transferring her from my hands to Malcolm's.

As we passed Roosevelt Field, which you would have seen if you
could have opened your eyes last Saturday, there was a huge plane flying
over it, quite high up. It was a silver monoplane, much the biggest I've
ever seen, with four motors. As we found out later, it was the biggest
plane ever built in this country, a Fokker, with accommodations for thirty
passengers. It was going through its final load tests and performing beautifully. We admired it and drove on to lunch.

We had nearly reached Roosevelt Field on the way back when I heard
a sort of sputter. I looked toward it. The Fokker was not fifty yards away
from us, flying over a plowed field, very low, and wobbling horribly. A
shower of sparks was sweeping out from it. It sank lower and lower, always struggling to rise, always wobbling more terrifyingly. The railroad
tracks were in front of it, and across the tracks, another field, large
enough for a landing. It looked as if the pilot could make it — but the
wheels ripped into the telegraph wires along the tracks. The plane rose
slightly, heeled over on one wing, and seemed to settle gently into a
group of houses about a quarter of a mile away. The wing brushed the
roof of one, and ripped it wide open. The nose struck another, the plane
somersaulted, and its tail fell across a third. Within two seconds flames
fifty feet high shot up from the plane and the houses.

All this without a sound. The pilot cut his motors as he passed us.
The ship descended as quietly as a falling leaf. Even when it struck we

could hear nothing. It was like watching a slow motion picture, and so entirely unreal and nightmarish that you just couldn't have emotions about it. I've been much more amazed and shocked and horrified by accidents on the stage and in the movies and books.

We started for Roosevelt to get an ambulance — no one else was around except us — but the ground crew had apparently seen the plane in trouble, for before we could get there a perfect stream of ambulances, doctors, fire engines, mechanics, wrecking cars, etc. roared by us. We didn't go any closer — there was nothing we could do, and I had no wish to investigate what was probably in the flames. The houses, soaked in gasoline of course, burned to the ground in ten minutes. Nothing was left of the plane but the metal.

Tonight's papers are very vague and confused about it, but apparently no one was killed. Only the pilot and a government inspector were in the plane. They were sitting up forward and were thrown clear when it crashed — injured, but not burned. I didn't see them at all. Latest reports say that everyone got out of the houses all right. I'll sleep better for knowing that.

Incidentally, another plane fell into a building at Westbury, only a mile or two away, an hour previously. Long Island is becoming a perilous place.

Our female author was distinctly impressed, and was still talking when we put her on the train an hour later.

I told Eleanor, and she said what can you expect of an aeroplane? I have never seen any one more thoroughly cured of air-mindedness. And I think I'll wait awhile before going up again. I see that I've taken up four pages with aeroplanes. Isn't it time I told you again that I love you? Pity my hands this evening, darling — one is holding a pen, the other is holding my chin, which by the way is rather prickly. Both of them are hot, and both remember the coolness of yours. I wish your hands were in the photograph, too.

Mother and Father talk constantly of your mother. She must have been very sweet and dear with them, as I knew she would be. As for you — I've never said to you anything half as complimentary as their remarks.

I love you, Frances, and I am going to see you day after tomorrow, which is much too far away, and last night I dreamed that you told me you love me, and I believe you do. Goodnight darling. I love you.

Ogden

P.S. Your telegram has just come. I'm terribly distressed that you are ill. Stay in bed, darling. I love you — do take care of yourself. I'll come down Saturday or Sunday if I may, I'd much rather do that than go to Providence, so please don't tell me I should go Wednesday night up there. I love you.

December 2, 1929

Darling Frances —

I hope you are giving up the German* this evening and staying at home — it's no weather for you to be walking between front doors and automobiles in thin slippers. All afternoon I've been will-powering you to decide not to go out — I'd have telegraphed or telephoned but I didn't want to seem bossy. I'm sure that dentist and German too is too much for a sleety Monday.

I love you and I am lost without you. I've just spilled an inch of cigarette ash all over myself because no one in the city of New York cares enough for me to tell me when I should reach for the ash tray. How long must that sort of thing go on? Six months more of it and I'll probably be so sloppy and ash-covered that you won't want to marry me. I need you frightfully, darling.

It developes that when Charlie wrote to Isabel he called her Isabelle, and when he got a letter from her today with her name spelled right he felt very badly. But in that same letter she spelled my name Ogdon; I pointed it out, and he felt much better. So you might tell her that my already warm affection for her will crackle even more merrily if she'll throw another log on by spelling it with an e.

Will you be pleased to hear that I had a delightful trip in on the train from Garden City this evening? I sat with Henry Humphrey, whom you don't know, but who is a very good friend of mine. He is stocky and bow legged and has a little moustache and he stutters and he is going to have a baby and he is very much excited and says he hopes it will be a boy but that he doesn't much care and that his wife says that if it is what she really wants it will be a Heppelwhite side board. But that wasn't what made the trip delightful. The fun was that Henry had been away for a week and darling, just imagine, he hadn't heard my story about the aeroplane, and he listened to it open-mouthed and said Oh and Ah, and he finally made the supreme sacrifice by having me draw him a map showing just where I was and where the plane was and where the houses were, and he took the map home to his wife and I only hope the child doesn't turn out to be a 32-passenger monoplane.

Then when I had finished he told me about going to a dance at the Copley before the Harvard-Yale game, and arriving for dinner, and having the hostess take off her wrap in that student-haunted corridor, and making a mistake and taking her dress off too and standing all Peter Arno-y before the multitude much to the multitude's delight and her own and her husband's confusion. By that time we had reached New York, so I dove home for a hot bath, being very cold and wet. But you can see what a pleasant trip it must have been.

Frances, when you go abroad I wish you wouldn't do any mountain motoring. Please promise not to. My hair was standing quite on end at luncheon yesterday just at the thought of your having once done it; another time would finish me. Don't go anywhere near a cliff — not even the bottom of one, or some damned fool tourist might fall on you.

Monday's gone now, darling! Three more days are still in the way, but I've determined to live through them. I'll pass the time by wondering what dress you are going to wear, and what time we'll get home on Friday and whether you'll drink orange juice and milk with me when we get back.

I wish you could see how my adoration of you is growing — but perhaps you'll notice it when I get down there. I love you — I love you.

> *I love you —*
> Ogden

*The "Monday German," or "Bachelors Cotillon," was the ball at which the current crop of debutantes was presented to Baltimore society. — Ed.

Sunday night
December 22, 1929

Frances darling,

Who's worried about ————? Pooh! I'm not worried about anything except squeezing enough money out of Nelson Doubleday to pay for dozens of ash trays and hundreds of Chesterfields.

As for your last special delivery but one — darling, it's just about thumbed to bits. When I'm feeling too up it brings me down and when I'm feeling too down it brings me up — and then it's such a very definite letter, such a solid, compromising letter — oh darling, I love you; I love you.

I've just recalled a useful bit of my early classical education. The Romans in figuring time always tore off a day at each end. That is, they held that from Sunday to Thursday is only three days. Good old Romans, nice old Romans, clever old Romans! I think they'll just about pull me through — they and the news that you can probably stay over till Saturday.

I spent last night also in Garden City. I was in the office late yesterday afternoon and Nelson swooped down for a two hour talk — after that I had dinner with Dan and a fellow named Malcolm Johnson — have I told you about him? He's the one with the Chinese experiences. Both Dan and Malcolm are concerned with this new scheme, so we had a big pow wow which was so intense that I went to bed at ten and slept until eleven this morning — thirteen hours in a row, the first time that has happened in years. I then ate a combined breakfast and luncheon and returned to the office. Figures now conclusively prove that operation for the first six months will show a loss of $25,000, but that seems to be all right. It looks now as if we'd start in early in January. Not the least pleasant feature is that my work will be almost altogether in New York, with only a few hours a week in Garden City.

Old Mr. Doubleday gave Dan a coffee pot for Christmas and one of his ex-girls gave him a rug. We are therefore urging him to get married, as that is practically all the furniture any one needs. Dan's awfully amusing, all unconsciously, about marrying. Regularly once a year, toward the end of the winter, he decides that he ought to take the step. It has something to do with not being able to play golf, I think. Last year he was all set except he couldn't make up his mind which of two girls to ask; while he was trying to decide they both got married to other people. He was quite upset for a while, but as soon as the warm weather came he was all right. He'll very likely end up by marrying Edna Ferber.

I'd better call you up tomorrow evening — will you be home?

I love you, Frances, and haven't I been good about this weekend. I love you, if I could stop thinking about you I could do a great deal more work — but I'm glad I can't, I love you —

Ogden

Monday evening
December 23, 1929

My very darling Frances,

I'm so glad you got that new paper and couldn't resist trying it out. I
love you. Of course you're several up on me — only in quality, however.
In quantity I hold a commanding lead — about two to one in round
numbers, I should say.

I'm also glad to learn that you are not a Florence type and I am not a
John, though I had suspected as much for some time. As for getting to
market — who wants to get to market?

Do be careful about your automobiling. You say your starting is good.
How is your stopping? And have you the proper respect for railroad
crossings? I'm only afraid that my easy skill at the wheel, my ballerina
footwork on the clutch, and my trick of reaching for the gear with all the
languid grace of a drowning man reaching for a straw may have given
you a false impression of the difficulty of driving a car. I've been in town
all day — just as well, too, as a blizzard has been going off and on since
early morning. I had my first talk with DuBose (Porgy) Heyward, and
found him slim, mild, and modestly but bitterly opposed to having his
books embalmed in the immortality of a collected edition for at least
twenty years and then only if people are still reading them, which he pro-
fesses to doubt. He's just finishing a new play, but he won't say anything
about it — he's living, incidentally, in Mark Twain's old house on lower
Fifth Avenue, which I must point out to you the next time we drive to
Washington Square.

After that I saw a lady named Beth Brown, who is professionally cute.
By that I don't mean anything against her character, only her manner.
But she is just five feet tall and spends her time living down to it. She
writes books and movies and used to dance in a night club. I got on all
right with her by lying every time she asked me to tell her frankly what I
thought about her book.

Then my little pet wop Buranelli dropped in. He wants to do a book
about backstage life at the Metropolitan, and told me a story which you
may have heard but I hadn't. Caruso had played someone, let's say Martinelli, a dirty trick in a poker game. The next night they were in the
same opera. Before one of Caruso's most famous arias Martinelli had to
clasp his hand in a touching farewell. So this time he clasped and withdrew his hand, leaving an egg in Caruso's. Caruso, wearing tights with

no pockets and not caring to drop the egg, held it. I thought that was pretty good, but not good enough for a book, so I suggested his writing the life story of Moneta, who runs a gorgeous Italian restaurant down on Mulberry Street and has made millions and built a house on Long Island filled with parrots and monkeys. He then told me some good stories about Moneta, but those must wait until you come up. I refuse to expend all my ammunition by mail.

After that I saw a man named Fishman who wore a blue shirt which really defined the word blue, and a blue tie with large pink splashes as of strawberry ice cream. He's doing a burlesque of the psychology of business success books, and so far, at the age of three hours, it seems pretty funny.

This evening: gaiety, Frances, gaiety! Dinner, the theater, and a debutante dance! I'm so excited about it that I'd just as soon go to bed right now and have a good sound sleep.

I suppose it's stupid and selfish and short-sighted of me not to enjoy things without you, but I can't. Do have a jolly Christmas, and don't overdo so that you won't be able to get up on Thursday, and do stay over Friday, and please wish your mother and father Merry Christmas for me, or ask them to let me hold my greetings over to Saturday.

I adore you, darling, and I'll see you in two days. I love you.

Ogden

This poem accompanied a Christmas gift of a silver-framed mirror.

Since words of mine can never name your beauty
I send you beauty that I cannot name,
Trapped in the confines of this silver frame.
Never has lover found such joyous duty
As I in gathering for your loveliness
The loveliness that makes the earth so fair:
Here's heartsease from the golden evening air,
And silver moonlight, shy ambassadress
Of velvet summer nights, pierced with the sweet
Shrill ecstasy of tiny troubadours;
Grace of the flower that bends, the wing that soars;

These are dear, gentle beauties; these are meet.
For you I gathered them; they will not pass.
Frances, they wait you in this looking glass.

Christmas, 1929

———————

Wednesday night
January 1, 1930

Darling Frances —

Happy New Year, and I'd have called up to say it but I just didn't. Did you have a gay New Year's Eve? Gayer than I had, I hope. I was out in Garden City until half past ten, and got home just in time to hear the bells and whistles go off — twelve o'clock, I presume.

I wasn't at the office, but in Malcolm Johnson's apartment, sweating with him over an idea for a series of questionnaires that might be sold to the New Yorker and later on made into a stunt book. It's a fairly good idea, but it needs an unholy amount of working out.

Also — yesterday morning I got a check from the New Yorker — twenty-two dollars for Smoot, which is to appear in an early issue. Isn't that fun? It's been two years or more since I sold anything — perhaps chiefly because I haven't written anything except those four morbid short stories — and I like picking up the odd cash as well as breaking into print, which is extremely helpful to me in my profession.

I rather think it's your influence — the old youthful ambition and energy seem to have returned and for a while at least I'm off on an outside writing career. I've spent the afternoon doing what at the moment strikes me as an extremely amusing article on the abolition of Manhattan Transfer. Perhaps tomorrow it won't look quite so funny, but anyhow we'll see what happens. If accepted it should bring between fifty and a hundred dollars. I'll send you a copy when I get it typed — no, I'll wait and read it to you some time.

But do tell me you're glad I'm writing again — as you know, I'm an idiot, and one rejection slip is apt to discourage me unless I have you backing me up — because it is you I'm doing it for. Otherwise I'd rather go to bed early than sit up and try to be funny on paper.

Is anybody writing to Charlie about the twenty-fourth, or should I say anything to him, or what?

I love you, darling.

Ogden

Sunday afternoon
January 5, 1930

Very darling Frances —

I've not written since Wednesday — no such stretch of letterless time has been since the middle of August, and I feel rather queer. Still — I didn't get home until midnight on either Thursday, Friday or Saturday, so conditions were ideal for carrying out my instructions. So now I've been casual, and here I am spoiling all the effect by explaining it and telling you just how the wheels in my head went round. I might as well make the ruin of the scheme complete by telling you also that I hated not writing and that I love you enormously. I suppose I'm hopeless.

Thursday night was a Garden City session — the new scheme broke on a waiting world that afternoon, and there were — and still are — a million details to be settled. Long consideration has modified the original plan greatly. It now consists of the formation of something to be known as the New Books Department. Malcolm Johnson runs the administrative end; I am editor. We have complete charge of the publication of all books by new authors, obtaining new authors, etc. No salary increase till three months of operation show whether the scheme is practical or not. We're allowed to lose $12,000 in those three months — if we improve on that figure we're to be kings or something. I'm to have three hours a day added to my life by working altogether in New York; Garden City only two or three times a month. It sounds good, and I am pleased. Will you cross your fingers for those three months and wish us at least one best seller, which would just fix us completely?

Friday night I was commanded by Chris to take dinner with him in Hoboken and see his new show. It's a Civil War melodrama called The Blue and the Gray — rather tepid, and doomed, I'm afraid, to an early folding up. I was surprised to find myself getting perfectly furious with its Northern point of view — some obscure form of atavism, I suppose. The Hoboken fad is pretty well over now, and the theater was only half full;

the streets and restaurants are quiet and empty, and all in all it's much pleasanter than during the days of the boom — unfortunately, though, it's not so profitable for Chris. There's a grand new saloon in the alley behind the theater with real free lunch including hot clam broth, and what I took to be genuine trollops sitting in dark corners ogling provocatively. Chris has gone another step toward Bohemia and wears a motorman's shirt.

Last night Ted and I went to see William Gillet Gillett Gillette's positively farewell New York appearance as Sherlock Holmes. I'd never seen him or it before. He's seventy five years old now but wears a brown wig and a blue dressing gown and conducts a convincing courtship. Oh well.

I'm glad your New Year's Eve party was a good one, but you must have exhausted yourself staying up so late, and I don't like the idea of that. Did you go to the Supper Club too, and wasn't the Triangle Show Saturday night? I think you'd better go to bed again for a while; perhaps retaining just enough exhaustion to make you properly rude to any attractive men who come around.

You're not to see the article at all. I'm to read it to you when I next see you which will be — when? Don't I get some time off my New York sentence after all this good behavior?

I love you, darling,
Ogden

––––––––

Mother, still uncertain of her own feelings at the beginning of the new year, was in need of a little "space." She suggested that a good New Year's resolution would be to slow down the correspondence for a while.

By coincidence, an old flame reappeared in her life at this critical point, which made for some very rough sailing for Daddy. That the situation was weathered successfully proved a tribute to Daddy's persistence and to his growing understanding of what made Mother tick, but it also showed the basic strength of her love for him. She could have backed out entirely at this point, but she didn't.

Daddy began to take a slightly different tack in his letters now. He had learned that Mother was made uncomfortable by his constant declarations of love, and he also knew that she had a tremendous sense of humor that could be played upon successfully. By combining delicate barbs

with honeyed words he kept her interest growing. Her need for his un-
shakable devotion was real, but so was her need to be looked on as a
mortal woman — not a goddess.

———————

Thursday night
January 16, 1930

Frances darling —

This is the first time this week that I have been able to trust myself to
write. I woke up on Monday morning with the feeling that my world had
ended; a feeling that persisted until today. Really, Monday, Tuesday and
yesterday were the worst period that I have ever lived through. I don't
enjoy telling you this, but I think I had better.

I don't know why it was so awful — things have been much worse before without my going to pieces; yet somehow everything just seemed to
collapse.

Well, that's over now. I got and enjoyed your letter this morning. By
the way, you say "I can't excuse myself any more" — I don't understand
what you mean by that. Will you tell me?

I was also cheered up by our talk this evening. I'm glad, darling, that
you're feeling better and are resting a bit; also I am for the moment opti-
mistically interpreting your saying that you are more cheerful than you
were last weekend as meaning what I want it to mean. About Saturday.
As I told you tonight, I've been thinking about it for four days and I've
decided that it wouldn't be wise for me to come down. In the first place I
should probably be at my worst, nervous and annoyed and consequently
annoying. And I should not be able to see you much. Also, I believe it
would be a strain on both of us. Of course I shall not be very comfortable staying here and thinking about things, but even so it seems wisest.

Frances darling, I must ask you just one question. Is your feeling for
——— influenced in any way by the feeling that you wronged him in
originally thinking that he had turned to you as second best? This is important. So is the fact, which I have spoken of to you before, that if you
are faced with the necessity of wounding one of two people the very ten-
derness of your nature leads you to wound the one you love.

Forgive this letter. But I love you, darling, adore you; in spite of a few
things and because of thousands I *am* confident that you love me; and

just now I'm perhaps a little hysterical, having emerged only a few hours ago from a particularly unpleasant hell.

At any rate, I shall not be there on Saturday to influence or interfere with you in any way. Perhaps you will be able to get straightened out. I shall be waiting some sort of word from you. Darling, darling, don't destroy my world unless you have to. I love you.

I've now started counting the days till I see you — seven, I make it, if you will allow me to take the Senator on Friday evening. I think you should go to bed early next Wednesday and Thursday nights. And have you started yet on a tonic?

As for me — I've hired a new secretary, been photographed for the press handing a book to David Betts the Taxi Philosopher, and received two letters praising the Smoot affair, one of them from Mr. Schuster of Simon Schuster. Also I've had an idea for and put under way what should be the swellest book on censorship ever written. I meant to tell you about it last weekend but forgot. It's to be called "Banned in Boston" and consist for the most part of the passages to which Boston objected in the books that Boston banned. Also remind me to tell you about Beth Brown's delicate description of the only profession she hasn't worked at; I'll spare your blushes if you'll spare mine. It's all pretty funny.

Darling Frances, remember this — your happiness is what I want above all things. But I still believe that your happiness and mine come from each other.

I love you,
Ogden

January 27, 1930

Darling Frances, dearest Frances, dear Frances,

I adore you, I love you, I hope you are well. I'm sorry you can't see me now and that I can't talk to you, as I'm feeling thoroughly cocky and full of fighting insults which some mistaken instinct of chivalry prevents my putting on paper, while if you were here I'd take the greatest pleasure in pooh-poohing you back into your rightful lowly position in the order of things.

I've been spitting in peoples' faces and pulling beards and stepping on toes without saying excuse me all day long — I've signed the declaration of independence, my shout is To hell with petticoat government (or if not petticoats whatever garment has replaced them) and the number of women that I've elbowed off the sidewalk would, if laid end to end, look perfectly silly. I'm just about to publish a book which refers to the female figure as a collection of useful swellings, and also it has just occurred to me that I have discovered a secret that twenty million men in this country alone would pay their last pennies for, and that is how to have courtship without marriage. All in all, I'm on the top of the world, the masculine world, the only world that counts, darling, and one that you can only speculate longingly about, because you're only an effeminate creature, decorative in your way, I'll admit, but not to be compared in ultimate usefulness with a linotype machine or a Fordson tractor or even that simple and inexpensive little gadget, the pocket compass.

Of course, you can achieve a very important sort of utility if you decide to step into woman's only essential job, that of making some good man happy so that he will whistle as he goes about the work of the world, but until then — oh hide your head for shame, Frances — though perhaps you'd better hide it somewhere where I can have a peep at it once in a while when I feel a craving for sentiment creeping over me.

At seven this morning I sprang from my berth like Joris and he, as Browning so wisely didn't put it, and rushed for home where I went to bed and slept another hour, being finally waked by having one visiting nephew jump on my head and the other visiting nephew jump on my stomach, both bellowing that they guessed Uncle Og was just pretending to be asleep. So Uncle Og just pretended to paddle their impertinent little bottoms and spread his wings and soared like a lark to the office, where four weeks' accumulation of work awaited him which he had been unable to attend to at the proper time owing to an unfortunate and lopsided attachment he had conceived for a young female with a pleasant voice and symmetrical features and the modest hesitant shyness of a Jane Austen heroine without the ability of a Jane Austen heroine to carry on a voluminous and agreeable correspondence.

Aren't you a lucky girl, Frances, to have a young man who won't put his insults into writing?

I adore you, I love you,
sincerely yours,
Ogden

P.S. I could sell this letter for $50 to the New Yorker.

Tuesday night
January 28, 1930

Dearest Frances —

It's so late now that you will not get this letter tomorrow unless I send it
special delivery, and I can't decide whether or not you've earned that.
Probably not, but be on your good behavior for the next few minutes
and I'll see what can be done.

I've had a most amusing and constructive day; most of the details are
too long to go into here, so you will probably never know them. That is,
you will certainly forget to ask me for them, just as last weekend you
forgot to ask me about Beth Brown and her next book; that question
would have drawn from me an anecdote both amusing and harmlessly
risqué, together with a clever word portrait and striking thumbnail character sketch. But although warned or advised in a previous letter to ask
me, you didn't, so the story is gone forever, as I am hereafter volunteer-
ing very little information, of either an instructive or affectionate nature.
Everything must be by request. I should have adopted that policy earlier,
having already learned in the publishing business that it is the best. For
instance, it is impossible to give away free advertising pamphlets about
authors, but the minute you charge twenty-five cents apiece for them and
make people write in to get them you are swamped with orders.

However, I'll give you a brief résumé of the day's activities. 9–10
A.M., in the hands of the dentist, who filled me up with silver. 10–12,
desk work of an involved and specialized and horribly important nature
that you just couldn't understand. Then to the Dutch Treat club for
lunch. The Dutch Treat is an organization of editors, authors, artists,
newspaper men, playwrites, etc. that meets for lunch once a week and
has amusing people perform. The principal speaker today was Muriel
Draper, very arty and most attractive; full of many pointed and pithy remarks, the chief of which was that she didn't at all mind that handicap
of being a woman so long as there were plenty of men around. Very
sound.

After that I went over for a long talk with Mrs. Henry Moskowitz,
who has been Al Smith's manager since he entered politics. She is going
to do a book for us, and recounted numerous amusing tales, all of which
I should be glad to relay to you if you showed a civil interest in them.
After that a few hours of the office with many rumors of a nature which
I hesitate to commit to paper but should again be glad to inform you of

if invited so to do. Then dinner and poker, and now the thankless task of continuing a one-sided correspondence. Anyhow I love you and shall I come down Saturday afternoon?

Ogden

Thursday night
January 30, 1930

Frances darling —

Do you like the gray paper? I do — it seems to me rather cheerful and up and coming. I suppose that seeing the Harvard Club letterhead you think I am on my way home from dinner and the theater or poker or the office, but no!

I'm spending the night here, having been turned out of my own bed to make place for a friend of Ted's and Anne's who is passing through. I don't like it at all, but here I am — I've just arrived after taking Eleanor to the movies — and what movies. Rio Rita, songs, dances, spectacular presentations, the whole gamut of expensive, elaborate and infinitely dull bad taste.

Last night I got shanghaied to Hoboken where Chris was giving a dinner for H. M. Tomlinson, and didn't get home till one. I think you'd better remind me to tell you of my conversation with Mrs. Cleon Throckmorton.

Your weekly letter arrived this morning, a day ahead of time — I hope that doesn't mean you are losing your head over me; emotion is a dangerous thing; I'd hate to see you getting involved with anyone of so many and varied interests as myself. I think perhaps some placid Republican night watchman might be better for you.

I called up tonight to announce my impending arrival but you were out getting exhausted for the weekend. But I'll be down Saturday anyway, probably taking the 2:10. I'll telegraph or something if my plans change. Do you read telegrams?

I love you and think you had better marry me.

Sincerely yours,
Ogden

February 5, 1930

Frances darling —

Yes, you win your bet — I got the letter today, Wednesday — but not until I got home at dinner time, so I'll withhold payment for a while. By writing yesterday you draw ahead of me for the week, but I have no doubt that the deep silence which will surely fall over the next five or six days will more than make up for this surprising lapse into forwardness on your part.

Darling, of course I hope that you get the Florida trip. Not that I want you any thinner, or would rather have you brown than pink and white; but I imagine you'd have a good time and it would probably be awfully good for you.

That's interesting about your eyes. As I remember it, conjunctivitis itself is a comparatively simple thing to cure, but doesn't its presence denote a general run down condition? As I understand your letter, you were going to see a regular doctor today about the rest of your health. Do please let me know the verdict.

What a cheerful tone you got into your announcement that I am not to see you for five or six weeks — hardly flattering, is my private opinion. I say five or six weeks because I don't place much faith in your New York trip, and even if you do come your New York appearances are annoyingly helter skelter hotel-theater-taxi-railroad station affairs. And as I am not coming down this week-end, and you will be away the two following week-ends and leaving for Florida after that, why there we are — or rather, there you are, and here I am. Don't you think a small sigh would have been graceful?

Where are you going for those two week ends? You don't say, so it may be a dark secret — perhaps you are retiring to Switzerland like Archibald Marshall's gentleman, to get yourself a strawberry nose in a last attempt to evade my attentions. Perfectly useless, darling; I swear that even with a strawberry nose I should continue to love you, and I shall continue so to swear until I see you with the strawberry nose.

Honestly Frances, I *would* like to see you once more before you depart into the great unknown; and if you think it is a good idea, it can be done, as I have just remembered that next Wednesday, Lincoln's birthday, is a holiday here, though not in Baltimore, I believe. So if you have no other plans I could come down Tuesday evening and go back Wednesday night. As I have said, I'd rather like to do this before losing sight of you until April first or so — what is your opinion? I may telephone you about this either tomorrow evening while you are dressing for the Supper Club or Saturday, as I want to make plans for the holiday.

Last Monday night I finally got around to that huge manuscript that I meant to read over the week-end. It kept me up till 2 A.M. (hence no letter *that* night) and introduces a young man who looks to me as if he has all the makings of an important figure in American letters — what a pompous, cant phrase, but it's applicable.

Last night Dan gave a dinner and theater party for Mignon Eberhart. She wrote While the Patient Slept which has just won our Scotland Yard prize — and we have imported her at enormous expense from her home in Valentine, Nebraska. She's simply swell — fresh, young and wholesome, and thrilled by everything and every one. She's never been East before and has a heartening respect for publishers. Unfortunately she's just recovering from an operation — Dan had ordered a very elaborate dinner at the Coffee House (do you remember the Coffee House) and all she could take was milk toast.

Also she doesn't smoke; and she refuses cocktails. Today she got sick — thereby sparing me, I am happy to say, a trip to Hoboken tonight, where we were to take her to eat and theater-go with Chris. I'll be a contented boy if I never see Hoboken again. We're giving a big tea for her tomorrow if she's out of bed, and then packing her off to Valentine, tired but happy. Of such gluey gossamer is publicity woven.

The play last night, incidentally, was Journey's End, which I hadn't seen before, so that helped.

You might remind me to tell you of the conversation between Mignon and Dan, who is also a Nebraskan.

Don't wait too long before writing again, Frances — and as I close, force of habit, overcoming all my better and wiser instincts, compels me to admit that

I love you.
Ogden

March 20, 1930

Frances darling —

Both your letters arrived this morning. Thank you. I had sunk pretty low in the eyes of the elevator man, to whom I have been handing a letter to mail nearly every night and who has evidently noticed that I have been getting nothing in return. I could sense his thinking, "You have no charm, sir." But now it's all right again — his attitude today is as respectful and reverent as I could wish.

Shall I tell you what I have been doing? Say yes. I had lunch with an extremely pleasant young Southerner named Berry Fleming, who has written a book that I think I've mentioned to you — Visa to France. The book in which M. le maire paints the same picture each year and the Englishman who is off on a holiday with another Englishman's wife gets frightfully annoyed at the gross unconventionality of the lonely American who asks them to dinner without having been introduced. The whole thing is really full of charm and I shall bring it down when it comes off the press. Incidentally Fleming has the distinction of having written copiously for Punch; I don't know any other American who has succeeded in competing successfully with A.P.H. and A.A.M. and Co. on their own grounds.

Let us now skip to tea time, which finds me in Greenwich Village in the flat of Edgar Johnson, the budding Huxley I've told you about. As a matter of fact, he's not a bit Greenwich Villagy, but just happens to live there. His sister was there, a young thing, very attractive except for a rabbit-like mouth from which lathery sounds emerge. They amused me by telling me of a legend which they had created about me. It seems that Harry Maule, the old editor, from whom I took Johnson over, wrote to him saying, "Sooner or later you will have to meet Mr. Nash." To a young writer, this had a very ominous ring, conjuring up visions of unutterable ferocity, inhumanity, diabolism and stony-heartedness. So Miss Johnson would say to the shivering Mr. Johnson, you *will* write a book, will you? You *will* get Doubleday Doran to publish it, will you? *Well*, do you know what's going to happen to you? Sooner or later you will have to meet Mr. Nash! So we all had a good laugh and swore eternal friendship over a dish of water cress sandwiches and I made a mental note to write you about it, which I have now done.

However, you mustn't think that my life is all luncheon and water cress sandwiches and eternal friendship. I have a serious side, too. I spent the afternoon making up advertisements for a biography of Hetty Green which we shall shortly attempt to peddle in public at five dollars a copy. I am now a storehouse of fascinating information about that extraordinary and unlovable woman, and I shall take great pleasure, which I am sure you will share, in recounting to you the more fetching episodes in her career. She was the richest woman in America, and the stingiest. I can give you some idea of her character and the character of the stories about her when I tell you that her father gave her a thousand dollars to spend on clothes for her coming out party and she bought government bonds with it.

Aren't you eager to hear more? Well, I'm saving them till I see you.

I love you.
Ogden

Saturday night
April 5, 1930

Frances darling —

After writing you last night I started a long manuscript — 600 pages — one of those damnable ones that you have to read all of before you know whether or not it's good. It wasn't; but it was two o'clock before I could make up my mind. So I overslept this morning.

Well — I was expecting a letter. And the mail was on the breakfast table, with nothing for me. I faced the weekend 'letterless,' and thrust my fork into the egg with such frustrated fury that the dining-room windows are still yellow. "So I've been put back on the one letter a week diet, have I," said I to the egg. "Oh very well — " then the doorbell rang and the elevator man popped his head in. He was sorry but he'd overlooked one letter. Here it was. It was yours, darling, and the week end was saved.

I'm glad to know you're all right again — glad to hear you're kicking your heels up — but gladder to hear you're kicking them up discreetly. I know that absence makes my heart grow fonder than anything except presence, but I obviously don't know the formula for your heart, so it delights me to be told that you find your pleasures in the company of John and married people. Of course you may have other diversions that you don't mention, but I prefer not to admit it.

I sent three things to the New Yorker today; I confidently expect to get at least two of them back — but wish me luck, will you?

Sunday night
April 6, 1930

Darling,

Imagine my astonishment on waking this morning to find myself distinctly unwell. Internal strife of some kind — an affliction that visits me very rarely. I suspect some sausages at yesterday's luncheon. Anyhow, I've spent the day in bed, where I am now, spiritually spry as a cricket, but inwardly rather belgiumed. I hope to be all right for the office tomorrow but that remains to be seen.

I passed the time reading when I was alone, and complaining when I could get anyone to listen. I read a book called The Virtue of This Jest which was about one of those romantic poetic 18th Century London rogues, and another book called The Red Wagon which was about an English travelling circus. I read the Saturday Evening Post for April 5th, the Herald Tribune, The World, The Times, and the more inflammatory sections of the American. I read the Forum and the Saturday Review of Literature and now I am about ready to start on the Social Register and the telephone book.

Oh guess what, I'm going to Eleanor's for dinner on Tuesday night. She needed an extra man and turned to me. Always helpful, I said I'd love to come. Then after I'd committed myself she told me whom I'd have to squire. Lucy Lamar!

Today was to have been very pleasant. I was to drive down to Belmont with Eleanor to be shown the horses working out, then go to the Women's National for luncheon and perhaps golf. It was a gorgeous spring day, too. Well, what of it? I have no intention of being sick next weekend, and see that you keep the same goal in mind.

Why don't you ever play the piano for me except for half a minute once in a while before meals?

This indisposition has interfered with my work on the eclipse, but I still think I can bring it off all right.

Do you know how my mind is working? Like this: Sunday's over now, tomorrow's Monday, as good as gone, leaving Tuesday, Wednesday and Thursday — then Friday I shall see you.

Apparently I'm still devoted to you — or, as I have said so often, I love you.

Ogden

April 21, 1930

Frances darling —

I gloat, I chortle, I sing tirra-lirra by the river. Victory and triumph. This day I signed up Thorne Smith after a two months battle, and what is more, out of the very jaws of Little Brown, Cape and Smith, Brewer and Warren, Harpers, and Farrar and Rinehart, than which this life holds few greater joys. It was a death-struggle between hungry publishers, but as always truth and righteousness prevailed and Doubleday's will have the fun of publishing the story about the statues. I really am terribly pleased; and may I be just a little proud? Do let me — I'll be over it by the time I get down there.

I had lunch with Thorne and his wife today and tied up all the knots — furthermore, I got a signed copy, in very bad second-hand condition, of Topper. I've been re-reading it, for the first time in four years, and I'm relieved to find that I was quite right — it's a delightful book. I simply can't allow you to read any of it to yourself — I'll do as much of it this week-end as is possible and bring the rest home with me — thus putting myself in a position to be urged to come again soon. Dear old literature, where would I be without it?

By the way — I see that the Opera is to be in Baltimore this week. Does that affect your plans in any way? I mean, do you still want me Friday evening or will you be at The King's Henchman or Aida or something? I bought my ticket on the Senator today, so I'm all pointed for it, but if you are music hungry just let me know and I'll delay till convenient.

If I don't hear about this perhaps I'd better call up on Thursday evening. In other words, a letter reaching me Thursday morning will spare you a telephone call. Clever Ogden. I feel so good that some one is sure to deflate me. Don't let it be you.

Love,
Ogden

May 6, 1930

Frances darling,

Well, apparently the telephone is as unsatisfactory as ever. I hope you could understand me; certainly I couldn't understand you. Anyhow, the idea was that I will be down this week-end; Friday on the Congressional, to be exact, reaching your house at about eight o'clock daylight time, if that is satisfactory to you.

I was quite surprised and terribly pleased to get your letter yesterday after having had one Saturday — how nice of you.

Shall I tell you what I've been up to since I last wrote? Well — Wednesday night Aubrey and Carol and Susan came to dinner and I lost two dollars at bridge. Thursday I had a duty-date, dining with Bee Gawtry and taking her to the movies. She's extremely nice but a bit on the homey side, and the evening was pretty long.

Friday I went to Edna Ferber's for tea and thoroughly enjoyed myself. She's a great person. Remind me to tell you about Sir Roderick Kaufman. Later Dan and Malcolm came to dinner and we talked office politics far into the night.

On Saturday Eugène Reynal drove me down to Garden City. We were to play golf but we ran into Dan and Nelson Doubleday, so sat around the office until six. Then Nelson asked us back to his house for cocktails, after which Dan and Eugène and I went to Rothman's for dinner and I sat in the seat you sat in when we were listening to the Harvard-Yale game.

On Sunday we played golf — my first exercise of the year, and I burned my face crimson, scarlet and maroon. You should see my nose.

We then went to Buz Henry's for dinner and drove back to town at eleven. When I got home I weighed myself and found that I had gained four pounds. So I'm bursting with health.

Yesterday I went over to the New Yorker and had a long talk, retiring filled with compliments. And in the evening I dined with one of the editors and his wife, returning home to find your letter, for which I again thank you, and to telephone, for which I apologize, but after all it was my first telephone in two weeks, and I did want to accept right away.

> *I love you.*
> Ogden

May 13, 1930

Frances darling —

What do you think about all these letters? Are you bored? Are you annoyed? Are you embarrassed? If so, I am sorry, but I shall probably keep it up.

Do remember, darling, that the earth couldn't live without the cloak of atmosphere that some well-meaning force threw around it. I think you should be cloaked in this love of mine in the same way. Don't you? Isn't it comfortable? Don't you enjoy it? Don't you feel better for it? Certainly you do. At the same time, I know the handicap I am under from loving you so, and telling you about it. Two handicaps, as I see it. *One:* you think you can never have the feeling for me that I have for you. *Two:* you feel that such a love places too great a responsibility on you — you are afraid that you can't live up to it. — Well, I know all about that, and I've thought about it a great deal. The conclusion I have reached is: I love you; my fairly good imagination can't picture my really loving anyone else after having known you; you are fond of me, but worried because you are afraid your fondness doesn't measure up to mine (that's my fault, of course; I've given voice to every thought I've ever had about you, and every thought I've ever had about you has been something that most girls don't get thought about them — but darling, do remember, you're not most girls, you are you).

Well, that's something I wanted to get said. Otherwise — I sent some stuff to the New Yorker today which I am expecting them to accept. But wish me luck anyhow.

When shall I see you again?

Love,
Ogden

July 7, 1930

Frances darling —

Probably because of the eccentricities of the United States' mails, your July 4th letter arrived today instead of Saturday, thereby receiving a doubly warm welcome. I'm particularly pleased to hear that you are again coming — or thinking of coming — to New York. I must take the risk of seeming forward and say that I hope you really do come. It's been more than three weeks — nearly a month, in fact — since I've seen you, and I honestly don't like it. However, I leave all that in your hands. If you don't come up, though, I wish you could set aside an hour or two on Saturday and Sunday when I could pop in to see you without disturbing things. And as always, please if you are coming let me know when as soon as possible, as I don't want to be in Garden City or Rouses' Point.*

There! Now I've said at some length what I might have condensed into a few words: I love you, darling, and I want to see you soon.

The Milt Gross evening was quite funny. Malcolm and I took him out to dinner. He immediately announced that his wife and children were in the country and that he wanted to play. So I played like a little man during dinner, but when with the coffee he turned the conversation Harlemwards I deemed my duty to Doubleday Doran done and caught the first taxi home. I have not yet been able to find out what happened after I left; I only know that Malcolm didn't reach the office till noon the following day.

I spent the Fourth sleeping and writing. — nothing accomplished, but a dozen things begun. I had meant to spend the week-end working, but Saturday was so hot that I threw up the pencil and went out to Eleanor's. She has an awfully attractive place with a large garden full of what she tells me are hollyhocks. I wish you would confirm this; I hate being in doubt. Large pink blossoms springing from enormous asparagus; is that right?

I did a lot of swimming on Saturday and Sunday morning, and played golf with Eleanor on Sunday afternoon and lost eight golf balls, which amused everybody, even me. We then went out for cocktails and who should be out for cocktails too but Mrs. Lucy Lamar in baby blue, and I with no knife to cut her accent. After dinner I took Eleanor to the movies and when we got to the theater we saw it was High Society Blues, and I said I'll bet there's somebody in it called Dad, and there was, and also somebody called Pa, Dad being the High Society father of the heroine, and Pa the lowbrow father of the hero. So that cheered me up, and I went home and started a poem which goes this way:

> Well! Well!
> The day's at the morn!
> Dandy old day!
> Dandy old morn!
> Oh look!
> The hill side's dew-pearled!
> Nicely old hill side!
> Nicely dew-pearled!
> And oh look!
> The snail's on the thorn!
> Lucky old snail!
> Lucky old thorn!

Dear Miss Leonard —

Well! Well!
All's right with the world!
Hurrah for the right!
Hurrah for the world!
For oh! what a day it is today, my lads!
Oh my lads, what a day it is today!
At 11:07 A.M. I'll be 27 3/4 years old
So now as I shave I look at myself and say:

Along about then I got sleepy and went to bed, but I'll finish it eventually with something that will please and astonish you. But isn't it nice and joyful?

Then the other day I started something for you:

When with a moistened finger I
Can blot the sun from out the sky,
Tear from the moon its silver rind
And send it curling down the wind,
Blow Ocean back like drooping mist
And catch Atlantis in my fist —

the idea being that then perhaps I'd be able to describe you as I want to. But as usual when thinking of you I got tongue-tied, so I had to do this for you instead:

Here I sit, a silly lout,
Fumbling over phrases,
Never will I pick one out
Fit to sing your praises.
A word before you say good bye —
Frances, you'll discover
Truer poets far than I
But never truer lover.

And that, darling, is true. You *are* too adorable for me — I *can't* find the words I want — you outshine the beauty of any poetry, so I must content myself with whittling versicles that I hope will amuse you. For you're really responsible for this sudden energy that's carried me headlong into the New Yorker — it seems to be all I can do for you.

It's all very queer. The more I see you the more I love you, and the more I don't see you the more I love you. But I enjoy loving you when I see you more than when I don't see you. Please don't, however, suspect me of impatience. As I have said, I know what conditions down there must be, having been through a similar period with my own mother. Only remember that when you are ready to see me I want to come. I leave it to you to tell me. And that's the last of that subject.

Isn't this a juicy letter? I look forward to your gratitude.

> *Darling, I adore you.*
> Ogden

*And can you arrange your trip to leave space for a visit to the theater?

July 8, 1930

Frances darling —

I've been brooding over my inability to write the sort of verses that should be written to you, with the result that I've decided to shift the burden to your graceful shoulders thus:

> Am I dainty? asks the dove.
> Am I stately? asks the lily.
> Am I lovely? asks my love.
> Ah, darling, don't be silly!

I want you to brood over that. Do get pleasantly conceited. I won't have you going around doubting yourself. Good Lord, if you're doubtful of one of the two great realities in this life, which is your own gloriousness, the next step is to grow doubtful of the other reality, which is my love for you. Quickly now, darling, do take a quick glance into your mirror and tell me that I am right. I'll even allow you to straighten your hair and powder your nose and trifle with your lipstick before glancing, because I know how ridiculously — but how adorably — critical of yourself you are; though I've told you again and again in the face of your disbelief that weariness and dust have no power to mar your attractiveness, but only lend it poignancy. This is not a reflection on my taste; it is a tribute to, and convincing proof of, your loveliness.

Dear Miss Leonard —

I will not be contradicted. You have turned New York into a haunted city. I rode to work on the Fifth Avenue bus instead of the subway today, and the route was lined with memories of you. The Savoy-Plaza, where I met you the first evening I ever had you to myself, and I asked you to the theater and was at first afraid to ask you to dinner too, but finally found the nerve and you accepted, and walked out of the elevator in that black and white wrap and my breath quite left me and didn't return till next day. The Plaza, where I've met you so often. Bergdorf Goodmans into which you disappear mysteriously with parcels which later when you wear them un-breath me again. And turning my head to the left I could see the Roosevelt and the Barclay — all yours now, so far as I'm concerned. You are not only in my mind and in my heart, but all about me.

I have been, I think, forbidden to call you divine — I don't even want to, preferring to have you of this world. But to produce this effect on one human being, even such a one as I, somehow suggests a power that is rather more than earthly. Perhaps though not yourself divine* you are in league with divinities. Is that a good guess? I should like to know.

I had luncheon today with another of the New Yorker's young men — Wolcott Gibbs. He is supposed to be a nervous wreck and given to sudden fits of hysteria, having been that way for five years or so, no one knows just why. His first job was as a freight agent on the Long Island Railroad. One day a prize cow was shipped to his station in a special freight car. He had the car sidetracked, and promptly forgot about it. The cow starved to death, and when hot weather set in the neighbors began to complain. Investigation revealed the remnants, and Gibbs resigned. His next job was the New Yorker. His nerves were so bad that last month when he and his wife and her sister were lunching together on the 17th floor of the building that Malcolm lives in his wife left the table and jumped out the window. He is now living with a maiden aunt in Noroton Connecticut and whiling away his wifeless evening hours writing a detective story. This is all quite true and very tragic and I am a skunk to chronicle it thus lightly. My nature really is not a callous one; I only try to twist things around to divert you.

I do love you, darling.
Ogden

*No, I rebel. I won't be forbidden. You *are* divine.

July 11, 1930

Frances darling —

Are you warm? I am. Very. I'm glad to hear that you are perversely getting sun-burned and healthy. So healthy, I dare say, that when I finally see you you will sleep the sleep of a little child. This is an affectionate jest, and not sarcasm.

I have, I believe, sold three more poems to the New Yorker — two, anyhow. I'll know definitely on Monday, but meanwhile I have heard that they like them. I've also sent them two more prose bits. I refuse to be rebuffed. Perhaps you have noticed that. If you're not coming up fairly soon I'll send you all the new things that you haven't seen yet. — The first series of Random Reflections is in the current issue, and Mr. and Mrs. F. X. Pleasants is to appear next week. I've really been doing what is, for me, an enormous amount of work. Incidentally I have received two tentative offers from the New Yorker — one to join the staff in the fall, and the other to become their book reviewer. Do forgive all this "What a fine boy am I" stuff, but I like to tell you cheerful things.

I met Robert Benchley last night and had a long, interesting conversation which went this way:

"How do you do, Mr. Benchley? I've wanted to meet you for a long time."

"How do you do, Mr. Nash? I'm sorry, but I've got to be going now." And he went.

Please remember over the week end that I love you very much.

Ogden

July 14, 1930

Frances darling —

The last thing I expected today was a letter from you, but it was the first thing I found this morning. Thank you for writing at a time when it must have been so difficult.

I padded through a downpour to the office and found a kind note from the New Yorker enclosing a check for fifty-one dollars for two poems.

One of them, entitled "Hymn to the Sun and Myself," you saw the beginning of — it starts "Well, well! The day's at the morn!" and continues in that vein. The other is rather more polished, and is called "To Any Impossible She." They are trying to make up their minds whether the third one I sent can be printed without bringing in a flood of cancelled subscriptions. I showed it to you ages ago — it ends up "I prefer the purple papal people." — Anyhow, this was the biggest check I'd had from them yet, so I liked it. ～～～～～ The wiggly line represents the telephone which just rang. It was the dear old Holdens to say that they had an attractive female poetess on hand and needed help. So, remembering which side my checks are buttered on, I'll go down there. I'll report later.

Tomorrow I'm supposed to take Jake Falstaff out to Garden City and spend the night at Henry Humphrey's. So many things are going on.

Darling I love you.
Ogden

July 22, 1930

Frances darling —

This is just to tell you briefly what a joy it was to see you again, and how attractive you looked, and how sweet you were, and how much I love you, and how glad I am that the great thirty-seven-day drouth is broken.

I got on the train at quarter of two and slept like a lamb — much my best sleep in several nights. I hope you won't wake up for four or five hours, darling; you were adorable to stay up so late.

Great excitement on the way to the station. We passed a house where a girl had just been shot, and they had just put the man who shot her in the Black Maria. He looked very calm and satisfied. I expect she had refused to marry him.

Now I must breakfast but I'll try to write again this evening.

Darling, darling, I do love you.
Ogden

July 25, 1930

Frances darling —

I rather expected that you would be too busy to receive visitors this
week-end, which was one reason I was so keen to go down last Tuesday
in spite of knowing in advance that you would be a bit — well, drowsy.
But it's nice to know that you will be here again on Monday.

Will you arrive in time for luncheon and if so do you want to eat
luncheon with me? Are you busy during the afternoon and if not do you
want to be un-busy with me? And are you staying in town long enough
to do anything in the evening? I'm interested. Probably I'd better call you
up tomorrow or Sunday.

Wednesday night I came home all prepared to eat dinner and write
you a long letter and then do some work, but Eugène Reynal called me
with a hard luck story of being alone in the great city just as I was dip-
ping into my cold soup so I sighed and apologized to my angry relatives
and went out. We got seats for the Garrick Gaieties and now I'm so glad
I didn't take you. There's one splendid skit on Grover Whalen but the
rest of it looks like something put on by the Junior League of Madison,
Wis. Dreadful dreadful dreadful.

Yesterday afternoon I had to go to Garden City and I stayed down for
dinner with Dan and got involved in a jawbreaking series of arguments
about Dollar Books from which we both retired thinking the other fellow
an ass and probably a rogue as well. But no rancor.

Today a Mr. Moses Cantor of Boston buttonholed me, fixed me with
an eye like a varnished cough drop and told me that he had a little boy
nine years old who had written over five hundred poems and that as we
had published eleven-year-old William Marsh's Life of Our President he
thought etc. With a scream of rage and hate I tossed him onto the spire
of the Chrysler Building which impaled him very neatly, and though I
hear that they are going to have to demolish the entire structure in order
to get him off I have no regrets. Chrysler can afford it.

The Macfadden verse is in this week's N.Y.'er, and I have bought four
new shirts and four new neckties, one of each of which I shall flaunt on
Monday. Also I just got a note from Vanity Fair containing a polite request that I do something for them.

If you are thinking of writing a letter to reach me Monday morning
with an outline of your plans I think you had better Special Delivery it,
don't you? This is not bitterness on my part — merely foresight.

Dear Miss Leonard —

I told you about the Nash-Benchley conversation, didn't I? And about the Nash-Benchley correspondence. Well, there's a sequel. Yesterday I got a letter from Mr. Benchley's secretary saying that Mr. Benchley had just sailed for France, but would surely reply on his return. Don't you eagerly await the next instalment of this gripping story?

I don't know when the Improbable She is to make her debut, but I think very soon. So you like her even though she isn't you? Of course she's not entirely not you, but she has several characteristics that you haven't. For instance, if you have ever admitted that I am your favorite beau it must have been to your diary alone. Also, I believe I have your permission to go. And I'm not sure that you like to be wooed.

I saw a line from Chaucer today that applies to you more closely:

"In thee magnificence assembled is."

Till Monday — and after —
I love you.
Ogden

July 30, 1930

Frances darling —

You'll find no news in this letter — you'll only find me talking about you. I am so filled with thoughts and memories and hopes of you that there is room for nothing else.

I have heard and read of people who were constantly falling in love, and feeling each time that this was the real thing, and the last time was a mistake. I never really believed it, because it didn't coincide with my own experience — even in my rawest youth when I liked some girl's way of walking or doing her hair I didn't confuse it with love, but recognized it as unreal, temporary and unimportant.

But now, in a way, I'm like the people I didn't believe in. For I have a new love every day, and the love of the day before seems trivial in comparison. Yet I don't scorn that love of yesterday, for it represents all I was capable of at the time. It's nearly two years now since I met you — six hundred and twenty nine days, to be exact — and on each one of those days you have become dearer to me. Perhaps in another fifty years I shall be loving you as you should be loved. Perhaps if every man in the world loved you as I do now the total would be right — but I should hate that. I'd rather work up to it by myself. And I really have made a good start.

I saw Raymond Holden today and he said I was to send in some more verses at once, as the New Yorker is now receiving imitations at the rate of three and four a day, but insists on the original and only. Nice?

I hope for a letter tomorrow, but I am reconciled to waiting until the day after. But I'd like to know your telephone number. And I long for you more than I ever have.

> *Good night, darling, and*
> *I love you.*
> Ogden

August 5, 1930

Frances darling —

Just to show you that I too have some respectable letter paper. But, you see, I write so often that I can't afford this as a general thing. Imagine the expense of one and often two long letters a day on this handsome and costly stationery. What would become of my theater ticket fund? My new shirts and ties? My haircuts? Those fascinating books? And all my other cunning devices for making myself likable and eventually indispensable. No, it's not to be thought of. You must accustom yourself to the slummy looking yellow sheets. The heat hangs on — over 90 again today. The firm sent out word to all employees this noon that anyone who wanted could leave after two o'clock. That's only happened once before in my memory. Of course it happened that I had so much on my desk that I didn't leave till six, but my stenographer promptly lit out leaving me well up in the hot air.

Tonight I'm going down to sleep in Malcolm's flat. He stepped on a nail while bathing and developed a badly infected foot which the doctor cut open this evening. As his family live in Boston he has no one to keep an eye on him, and I imagine he needs some help, for a while at least.

The Vanity Fair woman called up again today so I am stopping by there in the morning to see what it is all about. Perhaps it is fame and fortune — who can tell?

Last night I told you that after mailing your letter I was going to try to get a bit of writing done. Well, I didn't. My hand just stuck to the paper and wouldn't budge so that all I could write was a circle that got bigger and wetter as I worked, and there's no market for big wet circles. In art, perhaps, or even music, but certainly not in literature.

Mr. Doran is not taking any of his books to his new office so I raided his shelves today and carried off half a dozen prizes.

I'm glad you liked The Selby's. I rather imagined you wouldn't like the Huxley; as you know, he sets my teeth on edge and gives me an odd and unpleasant feeling in the tummy. He seems to me to be a maggot popping up his head from the corpse of society. But, though a maggot, he *is* brilliant — so what is a poor publisher to do?

Your letter this morning clearly promises that you will write again soon. Do, Frances. Letters at least represent some small part of you and as such are very precious to me who love all of you.

Ogden

August 6, 1930

Frances darling —

Another boiler of a day following a boiler of a night — but this has ceased to be news. Obviously either the Equator has moved to 42nd Street or the earth in payment for its sins is getting closer to hell every hour.

I've been doing a lot of talking about work, but no work, or at least very little, and that unattended by cash and notoriety — by which I mean that I haven't been able to write anything to sell to anybody.

I did go around to Vanity Fair this noon. Apparently they are very hard up for new people, for while I was talking to the Associate Editor the Editor sailed in full of cordiality and ideas, and no sooner had he started than Frank Crowninshield, the suave old Holy of Holies, sent for me and it ended up by my staying for lunch. Everyone was very flattering about the New Yorker stuff and wanted something like it, as well as the Taupe Year article brought up to date. So I gave them everything the New Yorker has rejected, including the infamous Preface to a Wedding Trip, which now has travelled some fifty thousand miles — there should be only one l in travelled which evens up for your two p's in developping yesterday. I don't know whether or not they will bite — Crowninshield is a shrewd old bird, so probably not — but please cross your fingers for the next few days and if you come across a new moon or a haywagon I could do with a good wish.

Today's paper speaks of bad forest fires on Cape Cod. Are these anywhere near you? I wanted to call you up this evening to find out, but not knowing where your telephone is located I decided not to bother you. You might let me know whether you can speak in comparative privacy or whether it's a community procedure.

Malcolm's foot is much better, and he'll be back in the office tomorrow or the day after.

In spite of writing nothing, I did get five dollars from the New Yorker today — for calling their attention to that Bobby Jones thing I told you about, which they will themselves whittle into a paragraph for Talk of the Town.

And I saw an advance copy of this week's issue which will contain — indeed does contain — that second batch of short Random Reflections.

> *Do you know that I love you?*
> Ogden

August 10, 1930

Frances darling —

I'm just back from an open-air week-end which was hot but healthful. After talking to you on Friday evening I went to Garden City and sat up until two o'clock arguing publishing procedure with Dan.

Yesterday I played golf all day and today I sat around. In a few minutes I shall go to work.

I got another nice piece of news on Friday. The New Yorker has raised me from 75 cents to a dollar a line, so I'm getting into the big money class. And tomorrow morning I'm to see Simon and Schuster about doing a book. Dan wants Doubleday to publish it, but for various reasons it might be better to have it done outside. The chief thing is to get it out as quickly as possible. Everybody seems to think it will be quite a success, so I am permitting myself to hope, if not to expect. Anyhow, I'll probably have some news by the time I see you.

> *I'm awfully glad I love you.*
> Ogden

The book would become *Hard Lines.*

After the death of the family matriarch, Nannie Jackson, in July 1930, my grandmother decided my mother needed to be given a breather from Daddy so that she could make up her mind once and for all. She herself was exhausted from overseeing Nannie's last illness and had planned a trip to Europe to recuperate, so she suggested that my mother accompany her. Mother was torn between relief and doubt. She had come closer than she would admit to herself to depending on Daddy's presence in her life.

Mother broke the news of her impending trip abroad when Daddy visited her on the Cape.

August 23, 1930

Frances darling —

Here I am, once more confronted by your photograph instead of you. It is not so good-looking, but on the whole it is more civil, and cannot wink, grimace, frown, or tell me to stop talking like that. Yes, I rather think the lady in the photograph is the girl you might have been; we get on extremely well together; our friendship of some ten months has ripened into something warmer and deeper, and a lifelong attachment is in the immediate offing. All this might have been yours — but you adopted the same attitude to me as to steamed clams — you'd never tried me, but had an idea you wouldn't be able to swallow me. Some day you will realize that I am not a steamed clam, but a pop-over; take care that it isn't too late. I'm damned if I'll give you anybody's left eye.

Uppity? Certainly. Nasty? Oh boy! Look at the two nice letters I got, in addition to that voluptuous check from good old Frank Crowninshield. Some people *like* to write to me.

The crack of dawn today found me busy packing and I was right on time for Ambrose, even after having some milk and swiping a book. As I told you this morning it's a gorgeous book, one born to be read aloud, and on second thought I shall not return it. I'm going to keep it and wait for an opportunity to read it to you, and if you are half the girl I think you are you will enjoy it as much as the Water Gipsies. It lasted me all the way to Boston; my eye didn't wander once except oh yes when Ambrose stopped and took me to a hot dog stand for breakfast. I had two hours in Boston which I spent wandering around in book stores. Once on the train I immediately rushed for the diner and ordered and ate a luncheon that would have done you credit. There was no charm sitting beside me to divert my attention from my steak, and I made a handsome job of it, winning, I believe, half a dollar for my waiter who seemed to have had a bet with the waiter at the next table.

The watch chain has been much admired. In fact no sooner had I emerged from the station than a prosperous stranger stopped me, complimented me on my chain, and offered to sell me the Chrysler Building for $500.

Have you decided yet about coming down? It would be marvellous if you could make the Cedarhurst week-end — you wouldn't have to go out any where — but I suppose that's too much to hope for. But do if you can. Anyway, I'll see you soon. And I love you, darling — I love you.

Ogden

August 28, 1930

Frances darling —

Coo, you *are* a clever girl, and no mistake. Your letter arrived just in time to prevent me from putting you firmly out of my mind and taking up with Jeannette McDonald, who is about to open here in a new picture and has often said, I have heard, that she would like to settle down with some slightly broken-hearted but nevertheless amusing young man with a sunburned face and legs. As a matter of fact I thought it was quite a nice letter and anyhow I'd much rather go to Baltimore than have you come to Cedarhurst. Don't forget to let me know as soon as possible when you are coming up so that I can make arrangements about entertainment.

I wrote two new pieces last night, or rather, I wrote one new piece and polished up the Marc Connelly one that you didn't like. Today I took them around to the New Yorker — also the ribald rhymes about the turtle and the fish — and the New Yorker seemed to like them, but I'm never convinced till I get a check. If they take everything I'll have earned just a little more than the price of a black taffeta dress.

I heard a marvellous true story about Louis Bromfield and the movie magnates — much too good to tell now. Remind me of it — also of Stephen Benet's Hollywood adventures, particularly the monogramed underwear one.

It now looks as if you would be in this country when the book is published after all. That is to say, complications have set in about the November date. The New Yorker has eight unpublished bits still on hand and can't possibly print them all in time — and they can't be used for the book till the magazine is through with them. So we're planning now to wait until January, which incidentally will give me time to add a lot more material. I'm feeling more optimistic all the time — flattery yesterday from Edna Ferber and today from Oliver LaFarge, and both of them have promised to say it in print when the book comes out. The gentle and highly important art of logrolling. But I won't kiss anybody's baby.

Dan and I were looking out my window at the Chrysler Building today and had a sudden impulse to go up it. So we put on our hats and went out and went up it — 71 stories. Very impressive and I'll probably take you up when you come.

I see Pauline *is* engaged. Noble institution, matrimony, and just the thing for Baltimore girls. Broadening. Perhaps not so broadening as a trip to Europe, but still very broadening. I approve.

Nancy Maxwell has just got engaged, too. I heard it yesterday from Susan. Nancy went to Santa Barbara, gained twenty-four pounds, and got engaged. I'm glad. She's a nice girl, she needed the twenty-four pounds, and I approve of engagements. They're broadening. Now you know what I think of engagements and marriages, and I'll go to work. You'd better write me soon or I'll call you up or something. Darling idiot — adorable shell — highly desirable flibbertigibbet — distracting angel — consider me seriously. I love you.

Ogden

September 8, 1930

Darling —

This makes two letters today, and if precedent is precedent you haven't written even one, but you were so very adorable over the week-end that I feel impelled to relax discipline for the nonce. Besides, it has been a whirlwind day, and I want to tell you about it.

First, a colossal annoyance, which began as an achievement. At ten o'clock this morning I signed up Captain Dieudonné Coste, through his representative, for a book. At two o'clock this afternoon I found a good man who would write the book, and write it in six days — a vitally important point, as Coste starts his good-will tour next week. And at three o'clock the firm rejected the book, leaving me nothing but my pride and my fury.

It was just then that Harold Ross, the editor of the New Yorker, called up and asked me to come over and see him. I needed air, so I went out for a walk, ending up in his office. And he definitely offered me a job at a thousand dollars a year more than I'm getting. It would be to take charge of all the departments in the magazine — theater, movies, books, sports, music, shopping, automobiles, travel, etc. — see that the right people did the right kind of work on them, re-write when needed, contribute stuff of my own, and generally go to work. I've been thinking and talking it over ever since. I don't know. It would be an important and serious move, and I must weigh the consequences. I don't want to decide while I'm mad. But I'll go to Garden City tomorrow and see what Nelson has to say.

Ross is an odd man — very much of a genius in his line just as you are in yours. He said he had had another man in mind at first, but he had found out that he was an optimist, so it was all off — that they couldn't afford to have an optimist in the office. Then he told me I wrote nice verses and said he had showed one to Marc Connelly and said isn't that funny, and Connelly had said No I don't think so, so Ross looked at it again and the second time it didn't look funny to him, but now he has one that he is sure is funny and he is sending it to Connelly who had better like it or I'll boycott him and all his ilk.

There. That's the news of the day. Now for you, Frances. Breath-taker, face-maker, mosquito-gazer that you are — impudent, sleepy and talk-less — subject-changer, turner-around and laugher-at-me — I love you for the reasons that I should unlove you. I adore you for the traits that would lead a sensible man to throttle you and get acquitted. But then, you are not all hateful. You have many charming characteristics which I have not time to describe — probably you can call them to mind.

Darling Frances — I do love you, and you know it. Otherwise I am all right.

Ogden

Mother's stay in New York before sailing was everything Daddy could have hoped for. She confessed that her original purpose for making the trip was now lost, for she really had made up her mind that she loved him. But her mother had spent so much time and money in planning the trip that she couldn't back out now.

She left a note with him at dockside promising to come home to him and to their marriage. Though he was losing her for six months, my father knew now that he had ultimately won her and that by facing the separation with patience and humor, he could in one fell swoop both give her her freedom and bind her to him.

The European correspondence details his life during her absence. A job change and a best-selling book were part of that life.

October 3, 1930

Darling — darling, darling —

How am I to crowd three weeks of my love for you into one letter? But even when I have only stumbling words, or no words at all, to tell you with, I think you know. Better, I *know* you know. And darling, I do know now that you love me, and we are to be happy always. With that extra five minutes at the end of always.

Now — of course I hate to have you go away and I shall miss you horribly. At the same time I think that in many ways it is a good idea. You know what an important period in my career this winter will be. Well, I'm going to work so that I'll have a lot to show you when you get back.

As for you — darling, take care of yourself. I know this trip will be a wonderful thing for you — do take advantage of it. All our worries *are* over now — let your mind be at rest, and don't think any more of complications that are past. I intend to have only happy thoughts from now on, and I'll be really annoyed if you don't do the same. I want you to be strong and cheerful and very lovely when you get back, because we've got a lot to do. But it *is* all right for you to be shy while you're gone; in fact I strongly prefer that you should be.

Remember that I'm giving up all the loveliness in the world for six months. Not giving it up, but rather lending it to Europe. For you *are* all loveliness, Frances, and I have always adored you, even in the moments when I wanted to beat you. You are romance, and daydreams made tangible, and the misty charm of far-off things made real.

I spoke to you of the strength of my love. It *is* strong, darling; lean on it when you need to; never think that I am forgetting you for a moment; you are too deep in my heart.

Write me whenever you can; and take good care of my heart, which I herewith confidently deliver into your lovely hands.

You are beauty and enchantment and all the dear virtues; and you are going to marry me when you get back.

Be happy, darling, and I love you.

I love you.
Ogden

October 5, 1930

Darling, darling Frances —

I was quite numb yesterday. The whole process of your going away was utterly unreal — it acted rather like novocaine on me. The first pang of realization came when I found that Isabel and Dan had arrived after I left you, and that I *needn't* have left you for another half hour. Since then I have felt pretty awful. There's a sense of loneliness that I've not yet been able to cast off.

I got back from Brooklyn about midnight and found Mother and Father still awake, and very happy after their evening with you, which was perfect. I then went to bed, but I did not go to sleep without taking ten minutes to say goodnight to you. Did you remember to do the same for me?

I slept like a drugged man, which I suppose I was — who has ever been so full at one time of happiness and desolation? — and woke to think of you again. Oh darling, you are so unutterably precious to me — do take care of yourself!

I took your father to lunch at the Harvard Club, and got him a good seat for Once in a Lifetime. He delighted me by telling me he thought your trip wouldn't last the full six — or six and a half, rather — months. You see, I still think three months would be wonderful for you, but anything over that would put us both under a bad strain. I've waited a long time, darling; so have you. Let's not keep it up too long.

Well, that's that. I shall be much more cheerful in future letters, but it takes a little time for that gaping hole in my breast to heal.

Dan got the pleasant idea of cheering me on my way and took me to a vaudeville show yesterday afternoon which oddly and fortunately turned out to be extremely amusing. I then had dinner with him, and not contented with his afternoon's work he took me to see an animal movie called Africa Speaks in which two men are killed by lions right in front of the camera. I know exactly what they felt like. I hope my wireless expressed my emotions without being indiscreet, but I had to say something of what I felt. If I can think of some more words I shall send another this evening.

I enclose two newspaper clippings, but make no comment on either of them.

Now I've got two manuscripts to read and I hope a bit of writing to do. And oh yes, do you remember the poem about So-and-so, who wouldn't say yes and wouldn't say no? Several people have told me it's the best yet.

I love you, darling, now and always; and I have no fears for you. I know you are coming back to me. But I can't help missing you horribly.

Darling — darling!
Ogden

October 7, 1930

Darling —

I'm ashamed to report that I've gained four pounds in the last week. I think it all started the day we drove to Salisbury and I ate all the chicken and all the sandwiches. At this rate I shall be a monster long before the six months are gone, and if I choke on a hambone they will have to lower me out the window like a piano.

Well, Dan and I did see Kaufman last night, and did make our final plea, but it was a failure. The other people bid $250 more than we honestly thought the thing was worth, so there was nothing left for us to do but retire ungracefully. I consoled myself by winning $3 from Dan at pool, and stopped at a cafeteria on my way home and had a bowl of thick soup and a ham and egg sandwich, followed by a quart of milk before climbing into bed.

Thorne Smith blew in like a dead leaf this afternoon with the final three chapters of his book — very good, with a moving last paragraph. I'm quite apt to judge the entire quality of a book by its last paragraph. Listen, darling — from June on I think we'd better have a bit of reading aloud every evening. I've got two gorgeous books to begin with in Thorne Smith and The Shiny Night. The Shiny Night, by the way, should last until our second or third anniversary. But Lord what a story: You'll like Seth and Elizabeth who loved each other for sixty years — the only book love I've ever come across that reminds me even remotely of my own.

This letter goes to Dresden. Are you receiving mail at all regularly? And are you writing regularly like a good girl? Of course it will be another two weeks before I know about that. The periods of time involved in this excursion of yours are appalling — I just try not to think about them.

Darling, I'm so glad you came here to the apartment. It is filled with the memory of you, and I can sit on the sofa and close my eyes and imagine you beside me, and the joy of it is worth the misery of coming back to empty reality. And do you remember that silk handkerchief that somehow got covered with lipstick? I'm not letting it go to the laundry; it is safely tucked away with your letters, there to remain until you come back and redden it again. Come back! What important words! Well, you *are* coming back — even if you hadn't promised I'd know that. All's clear now, Frances, all's well — and I love you. I love you.

Ogden

October 13, 1930

Darling, darling Frances —

I hope I'm not spoiling you with all these letters. This is the second today, but the first one really doesn't count, as it was just an explanatory note about the cross-word puzzles. But if you do feel your head turning from so much attention remember that I probably have my own pleasure at heart as much as yours. Every time I bring pen and paper together it gives me a splendid sense of power, for I feel that I am reaching across 3000 miles and catching you to me — perhaps an unsatisfactory form of embrace, but a pretty good one under the circumstances.

I consider myself much too important to you to take the slightest chance of being forgotten, even for twenty-four hours. You've *got* to have the constant sense and knowledge of my love — and although now I believe that even if I broke both arms and couldn't write a word till you got back you'd still feel it and still, bless you, darling, return it, what's the use of taking chances? Not for Ogden, where you are concerned. Nice girl, good girl, lovely girl, adorable girl — oh adjective adjective adjective Frances, what in the hell did you have to go away for? I know that before putting up a big building they always rip a huge hole in the ground for the foundations — but I don't need to have one ripped in me to make the structure of my love secure — it's rooted deep in me already; it won't even die with me, but will outlive me by always and, if you aren't too sleepy, five minutes.

I spent most of yesterday going over manuscripts. In the evening Malcolm called up from the office, so I went down and fooled around until midnight, after which I had some scrambled eggs and bacon and a glass of milk at Child's, and came home and had another glass of milk, and thought about you for a while, and then went to sleep still thinking about you.

Today being Columbus Day is another holiday — the tail-end of a two-and-a-half-day one — and it makes me angry not to have been able to use it as I'd have liked to — in a trip to Baltimore. I don't know what the Pennsylvania Railroad and Vernon 1212* will think has become of me, but it's very likely that they soon will begin dragging the neighboring rivers and ponds in the belief that I have met with foul play.

> *Darling, you are always,*
> *always in my heart.*
> Ogden

*The telephone number of the Yellow Cab Company in Baltimore. — Ed.

October 19, 1930

Frances darling, lovely, precious —

Your two steamer letters came yesterday. Adorable girl, dear love — aren't you clever? I had figured out that yesterday morning was the first possible moment I could hear from you; I slipped out to the front door in my dressing gown before breakfast and opened it slowly, determined not to be disappointed if they weren't there — but they were, they were! Dear letters, too, Frances, that I have read and re-read till at the end of thirty-six hours they are beginning to fall apart. My heart is so full of you, darling, and it is such happiness to know that you love me — and to be told.

Do hurry and come back; it's wicked for us to be apart for so long; so needless. The great happiness is *here*. Not that I want to get married before June (well that's not really true, because I'd like to this afternoon, but June for many reasons is the best time) but I do want to see you again, to touch you, to hear you, to know the joy of being with you. Darling, I'm frightfully in love. And though I've proved that I can live without you I'm damned if I want to keep on doing it. It's one endurance test that I'm quite ready to terminate.

A manuscript I was reading yesterday contained a Chinese poem. About a father whose baby girl has died. He has forgotten his grief in his important work, he says; he has forgotten her baby ways and soft kisses. "But today, he met her old nurse in the road, and for an hour his sorrow overtook him again."

I was struck with it, it so closely expressed my own situation. I try so hard to absorb myself in my work and occasional diversions; sometimes I almost think I have driven the desolation from my heart; and then suddenly some little thing will remind me of you, and all's to do again. I don't know who it was that said "To part is to die a little," but it's an understatement. Emily Dickinson's "Parting is all we need of hell" is nearer the truth.

In other words, I miss you. — Wouldn't it be awful if I used up all my patience before I got married and had none left for afterwards? Better be careful, darling.

I'm just self-centered enough to be pleased to hear that you were upset when Isabel and Dan arrived after I had gone. Because that was the one thing that shattered my stoic calm. Somewhere, some time we have that hour to make up; and I won't rest till we've done it.

Last night I went to the Reynal's for dinner — just Eugène and his mother and a giantess from Philadelphia named S —— S —— . We went to the theater — a play called "The Greeks Had a Word for It" — quite rough and very clever; a bit like "Strictly Dishonorable," but better, I think. We were joined there by a boy named Ben Kittredge, who had just got back from ushering at John Brown's wedding. He said it was a great success and all the Kinsolvings, including the various bishops, did beautifully with the champagne. A photographer hid in the church and snapped pictures during the ceremony and the ushers pounced on him and threw him out and broke his camera. But apparently he had hidden the films in his pocket because the pictures were printed in the Philadelphia papers four hours later.

Now I must go to work and edit Thorne Smith's manuscript, removing the vulgarest of the vulgarities.

Frances darling, I love you and your letters are heavenly. I don't need long ones; you know what I want. One line is enough. — Sixteen days have gone now — 365 years in a day, 24 days in an hour and 60 minutes in a second. I know you are coming back in April, but will April ever come? I adore you.

Ogden

November 3, 1930.

Darling Frances —

I suppose I'd better take up the week-end chronologically, or as chronologically as I can. Not having a very orderly mind I'll probably do a bit of jumping around.

Or shall I talk about the people first? People are more interesting than schedules. — Well, I'll just write it as it comes.

As I think I told you, I went down to Cold Spring Harbor to stay with the Gawtrys for the West Hills races, a sort of minor Maryland Hunt Cup. I do like the Gawtrys, who are thoroughly nice. There is Mr. Gawtry, who is a hard little ball of a man with a wind-beaten face and gray hair and a very British accent and a pipe three feet long. And Mrs. Gawtry, a comfortable schooner-like woman, very placid; she was a Van Rensselaer and has the pleasant, kindly dullness of the tribe. And Bee and Olive, the girls; good sports and rather attractive, if a bit on the large side. The whole family mad about horses. One other girl and one other man were staying in the house. She was Sylvia Hillhouse, whom I've known off and on for years, as she's a great friend of my ex-sister-in-law's sister and I've seen her around Newport a good deal. She's taller than I am and has a rather sharp tongue, perhaps the result of approaching spinsterhood, as she's close to thirty and no sail yet in sight. But she's very smart looking, and I like her too. The man was named B —— S —— , an architect with a shiny red face and a Peter Arno moustache and a six-year-old son and a wife in the insane asylum.

I got down to Cold Spring about noon and was immediately whisked off to the West Hills club for lunch, which turned out to be of the same sort as that at the Maryland Hunt Cup. Little tables all around with not enough chairs, and long tables with food on them and hundreds of males clustering round them balancing plates, egged on by their women-folk.

I saw old Mrs. Doubleday and made a tremendous hit by getting her a table and five chairs when her own escorts failed. I'm in training to be a good husband, you see. — Bee Gawtry is very public spirited and conscientious; so she had charge of selling programs, so I carried around great armfuls of them for most of the afternoon.

It's beautiful rolling country down there, quite thickly wooded, and of course all the woods were red and yellow and orange. It was quite raw and cold, but the sun kept breaking through and the light was gorgeous. By climbing to the top of a rise you could see most of the course and also stand within a yard of the horses as they took one of the brush fences — then when they had passed you ran like sin down the hill and arrived just in time to see them finish. There were five races, and three riders were carried away in ambulances, and I lost seven dollars. Two of my horses were leading when they fell. Alligator, whom you may remember, won the big race, the West Hills Cup, by about six inches.

That was over about five, and we drove several thousand Arctic miles to the Gawtrys' house which is right on Huntington Harbor — a grand rambling white Long Island house, surrounded by enormous trees, and full of dogs. B —— S —— and I were blue and chattering in the teeth and goose-fleshy all over, as the Gawtrys are very healthy and scorn closed cars, so Mr. Gawtry made us each down a noggin of very old Irish whiskey, and then we had one of those splendid teas which consist mostly of sandwiches and muffins.

We drove twenty miles to the Bob DeGraffs' for dinner. Bob is a nephew of Mr. Doubleday's and very important in the office — pink cheeks, yellow hair, blue eyes, and six feet two of Dutch obstinacy, I'm very fond of him, and his wife also. They have an attractive done-over farm house full of antiques; very small, but they managed to get thirty-five for dinner into it by using small tables. I sat between a girl who didn't make much impression on me and one of Charlie's old lady friends, now married, named Roberta Thomas, who is another of those horse-women, and whose husband is an M.F.H. or something and organized the races.

Many of the horsey people are attractive, but Lord, they're difficult to talk to. It's another world. After listening silently for half an hour to my three table-mates exchanging remarks about spavins and fetlocks I sat up and told my little story about Adolph Menjou. It fell flat, because none of them had ever heard of him. Their whole life seems to consist of breaking a couple of ribs in the Greenspring Valley, getting well in time to break a hip in Essex County, rushing to Meadowbrook to fracture a collar bone, and getting very angry if it doesn't knit in time for them to get up to Millbrook and fracture their skulls. I met an awfully pretty girl named Louise Bedford who had at different times broken her hip, her leg, her ribs, and her collar bone. Her baby was three weeks old on Saturday, but she had been beagling all the first part of the week, and then sent the baby back to the hospital for the week-end to make room for the guests.

Anyhow it was a good dinner and there was lots of champagne which resulted in everybody's singing John Peel. Everybody except me. I didn't know the words. After dinner we drove another twenty miles to the ball, which was held in a huge house belonging to a man named Robbins whose wife was a Russian dancer. Being very polite, shortly after arriving I asked her to dance with me. And hostess or no hostess, I was stuck with her for fifteen minutes. I unlimbered all my most effective conversational openings. I told her of some of my friends who had married Russians. I talked about Russian literature and the Russian theater. She answered nothing but yes and no. Finally I said I thought that the Russians were charming even when they were silent. Then she remembered that she should go and greet some guests who had just arrived. I understand that last year her hair was orange, but now she has dyed it silver. I saw loads of people I like whom I haven't seen in years, and we didn't get home until quarter to five.

Sunday we spent in quiet recuperation until tea time when we drove another twenty miles — everything down there is twenty miles away from everything else — to the Reggie Townsends. Reggie is editor of Country Life, and one of those born jokers who is always the life of every party, but I like him. His wife is handsome but odd and moody; studies choral singing. That afternoon she talked to me about singing and about an attack of indigestion from which she was recuperating. Her mother has a harp and plays it.

I got back to town late Sunday night full of horses, choral singing and Madeleine Townsend's indigestion. Mrs. Gawtry asked me if the New Yorker was the same as Town Topics and I was so tired that I said yes.

Darling, I wish you were here to go week-ending with. The more nice people I see the more I realize how particularly nice you are. I love you, Frances darling — I love you.

Ogden

November 16, 1930

Darling Frances —

I've just finished writing a note to enclose the verses etc., and I now begin my news letter separately, believing as I do that two envelopes are twice as much fun to get as one. I'm sure you join me in this belief and gobble them like popovers and spinach soup, and why don't you come on back some day and have some popovers and spinach soup, and do some cross word puzzles with me and get or pretend to get annoyed when I laugh because you make your G's like 9's, and go to Girl Crazy with me and hear Gershwin's music, and take a drive through the Park up past the Hudson River Bridge, and I won't take you up the Chrysler Building again or even through the museum, though you will probably want to go through the Museum after I have read Thorne Smith's The Night Life of the Gods to you. There! that's what's waiting for you. I offer you the city, and the full heart and empty purse of the loneliest young man in it. Do come and get it.

Yesterday being Saturday, I left my office at noon and went down to Simon and Schuster's, where I spent two hours having lunch and going over the preliminary advertising plans for the book. My head swims from their confidence in it and their regard for it. They are treating it as a sure best-seller and making the most elaborate and costly preparations. The danger is, of course, that if nobody wants to buy it the thud will be all the louder and more humiliating. However I refuse to be humiliated until that happens; and meanwhile all the signs are good; so that when you get back I may be in Hollywood getting first-hand information about Garbo, or in Honolulu on the first leg of a leisurely trip around the world. Do you believe that, or do you believe that I will be pacing the dock? Guess which, darling.

I've now had two luncheons and a dinner at the expense of my publishers, and after my years of paying and paying for other people's fun, I thoroughly relish every minute and every mouthful. I love being an author, and I've almost decided to take it up permanently though I'd consult you first, as that would mean you'd have to have me around the house all day — or no it wouldn't, I'd have to have an outside office to write in as if I were in the same house as you I'd never have the inclination to work but would fritter away the precious moments sitting on sofas with you and inspecting your very comely face and getting my fingers all tangled in your hair.

I've got to have my photograph taken for publicity purposes next week and if it doesn't turn out too oddly I'll send you one. I've already been invited to speak before a little group of women next January, and if you heard a dull, growly, thundery noise rolling across the Atlantic the other day it was me saying no. Not for Ogden unless there's quite a lot of money in it. I'm getting horrid mercenary now that I'm looking forward to assuming an obligation in June. Darling, don't you think it will be rather nice to be married?

Yesterday afternoon I went to Ted's and Anne's and listened to the Yale-Princeton game on the radio. Yale was supposed to win by 50–0, but only won 10–7 and was lucky at that, as Princeton carried the ball 80 yards in the last two minutes and lost it on Yale's one yard line just as the game ended. Young Lang Lea played most of the game and sounded very good.

I'm going to the Harvard-Yale game at New Haven next Saturday, but I'm afraid the Harvard lads are in for a sound beating. I've refused an invitation to fly up. Right?

Last night I played bridge with Ted and Anne and Eugène Reynal, and lost five dollars because I bid a little slam at a time when I should have kept my silly mouth shut.

Today I've been sitting around the apartment, working off and on, writing letters to a girl I'm in love with, and thinking about you a great deal. — Dick Simon tells me that he read the verse about New York to his sister and she said, "Oh I want Ogden Nash for Christmas." But I don't think you're ready to sign a release just yet, are you? Frances darling, I love you.

Ogden

November 19, 1930

Darling Frances —

Your very darling letter, written in Merano but not dated, came in this morning and as a result I've been horrid uppity all day, annoying everybody with my wreathed smiles and intolerable air of knowing a simply wonderful secret.

In the first place, I'm really glad you're not going to Egypt. Not for selfish reasons, but somehow Egypt seems to me like the end of the world, and I had been slightly miserable at the prospect of your being so far removed. Spain sounds much, much better. And of course I am still cherishing the infinitesimal hope that perhaps you will come home a little sooner than the schedule calls for. You've been gone exactly six and a half weeks now, and I don't like realizing that six and a half months is exactly four times as long. — Don't think for a moment, however, that I am in any way worried or upset. I'm not. You have even convinced *me* now that you love me, so at heart I am very peaceful. But I do miss you, darling. Is that all right?

The second thing I liked in your letter was your upbraiding me like a wife of ten years standing for not having done any verses or novels. Frances, will you really stick pins into me from time to time? You *will* be a wife of ten years standing one of these days, you know — and I can assure you that for me at least those ten years will be a great deal shorter than the coming winter. I do love you. Incidentally, you should have received by now the new verses that I have done. But do write more letters like that. Darling, it means everything to have you say that you are proud of me — it makes things fun, and makes me want to do a lot more. As for the novel, it may be along fairly soon after we are married — not before, as till then I shall follow my custom of devoting most of my prose to you. Even though I know, as I have said, that you do love me, and would doubtless keep right on loving me and knowing that I love you even if I stopped writing every day, I place great faith in letters as a reminder.

One bit of news about prose though — the New Yorker has bought my theater-pulpit piece — the first non-verse of mine they've ever taken. So I'm delighted with them and me. And you. I enclose the piece, and hope that you will like it as much as I do. Remember that it's not anti-church; but it *is* directed against clergymen who turn churches into circuses.

The poker game last night was down on Long Island, so I didn't get home till 2:30, after losing five dollars.

Today I had lunch with another English publisher, George Blake, of the house of Faber & Faber. He wants to do my book over there, which would be nice for me, but, I should imagine, rather bewildering to the English.

The afternoon I spent with Thorne Smith, going vigorously and ruthlessly over his manuscript and frightening him to death with my fierceness.

The question of this New Yorker job is coming to a head, and it looks so good that I'm not sure I can turn it down. I expect to decide one way or the other within the next ten days. I shall of course let you know at once what my decision is. But I've got a great deal on my mind at the moment.

I notice that this is letter number 47. I got number 12 from you this morning. Are you ashamed of yourself? Don't be. Just keep on with the sort of letters you have been writing; darling, they make me completely happy. Oh Frances, dear, dear love, I adore you.

Ogden

November 26, 1930

Frances darling —

Now I'm all up to date on my correspondence and can begin to tell you what has been happening.

I spent all Thursday evening with Raymond Holden of the New Yorker talking about the job they want me to take. Friday I was out in Garden City, spending the morning in a book meeting and the afternoon in talking to Nelson Doubleday. In the evening I went to a party given by Wolcott Gibbs, also of the New Yorker.

Saturday I went to New Haven to see the Harvard-Yale game with a party consisting of Charlie, Dan, and Allen Lane, the young English publisher I spoke to you about. Harvard amazed everyone by winning 13–0, so it was a pleasant afternoon. I had a date to meet Kenneth and Louise Safe after the game and go back to Providence with them, but I missed them in the crowd and came back to New York. Yesterday I read manuscripts till I couldn't think, much less write an intelligent line. This afternoon I had an hour's talk with Harold Ross, the commander-in-chief of the New Yorker, so now I have a pretty clear idea of what they have to offer. I have a week before I need to give them an answer, and I shall spend it in talking to Garden City and thinking very hard. I'm highly interested and quite excited about what is going to happen, but fortunately not worried, as I shall win either way. I seem to have everybody where I want them right now.

As for my homework — I just got a check for sixty dollars from the New Yorker for that stage-pulpit piece — very satisfactory, as it only took an hour to write. — And it now looks as if at least one English publisher wants my book — did I tell you this? — if I will go over it and write foot notes explaining such Americanisms as Senator Smoot and Ovingtons to the insular British public.

I just got your fifteenth letter this evening — from Bologna. How you are jumping about! You must be exhausted. Of course you got no mail during all that time between Vienna and Florence; I'm sorry I didn't know the schedule. But I've just looked up my own mailing schedule, and a slight calculation tells me that you must have found sixteen letters and one cable waiting for you in Florence, which I hope helped a bit. — I am now anxiously awaiting your revised schedule.

I hear from Baltimore that Richard's engagement has been announced and that he is to be married on January 17th. I'm naturally wondering whether you will come back for it; but I do no hoping.

Darling, I adore you and you have been away for fifty-one days. Please don't ever do it again. I love you, Frances.

Ogden

November 28, 1930

Darling Frances —

Your first Florence letter got here today. No, I haven't read "Queen Lucia," but how did you know? Had you looked at me (in those far-off days when we could look at each other) and sized me up as the sort of man who hadn't read "Queen Lucia"? And what are the symptoms? A redness of the eyelids — a tendency to sniffle and make puns — an aversion to polo? I'd like to know.

Darling, as soon as my first successful play is produced I shall buy you (1) some sheep that will have young ones on demand — (2) some similarly obliging goats — (3) some grape-vines slung between fruit-trees — and (4) a pink house with a few angels painted on it. Till then will you put up with (1) an apartment, quite small but in a respectable neighborhood — (2) one combination cook-waitress-chambermaid, probably Scandinavian but surely friendly — (3) all the food I can buy you — (4) all the clothes I can buy you — (5) dinner out and the theater once a week — and (6) me. Do say yes.

I wish the book *could* be out for Christmas, but it can't. I meant that it would be manufactured by Christmas. Publication is January 15th if all goes well. As for the title, I don't know yet. No one but me likes Rancor to Windward, so that's out. S. & S. want to call it the Golden Trasherie of Ogden Nasherie, but that makes me feel like an X-ray photograph of my own tummy, so *it's* out — definitely out. Then Dan and I wanted to call it Love Among the Republicans, but all the salesmen said it would be taken for a book on politics. Queer beasts, salesmen. So it will probably be called Hard Lines, which was suggested by George Blake, one of the visiting English publishers.

I hear that Dorothy Parker got back from Europe this week, so I am hoping to see her — but not alone. Incidentally, when the book comes out, the Herald Tribune wants to print her letter as a review. Darling, it is such fun working for you — and I do feel that I am getting somewhere. I've put in six years of hard work learning my profession, and I think that now I am beginning to do a bit of harvesting.

I shan't be able to write you over the week-end, as Dan and I have been invited to go to the country with Edna Ferber. It sounds nice, and I'll tell you all about it on Sunday or Monday.

> *Darling, Frances darling,*
> *I love you, I love you.*
> Ogden

December 3, 1930

Frances darling —

At last we reach the letter with the important news — and I'm so damn tired that I can't even write intelligently. But I'll continue the story tomorrow and reveal any details that I don't get around to now. So —

The last offer made to me by the New Yorker was too good to miss, so after two weeks of thought and prayer backed up by a very thorough and careful investigation of both the New Yorker and Garden City, I signed up with them this afternoon.

I start out at a salary of fifty dollars a week more than I'm getting now. That will give me a regular income of about $9100 a year. In addition to that I get paid for everything I write, which will run to another $2,000 or so. Darling, we can do so nicely on that! That pink house with angels on it is getting closer.

I shall probably be given two days a week to do nothing but write in. If things work out well I get a large raise and a bonus of New Yorker stock at the end of the year.

This is not a hasty move on my part. I've been considering it ever since they first approached me, back in July. It's an awful wrench to leave Doubleday's, where I've been very happy for six years, but this is a big opportunity — and I *must have* opportunity.

They want me right away, but it will take me at least a week to clean up. Then I'm very anxious to take a week's vacation. I only took five days last summer and I've been working pretty hard — I think a short trip would be a good investment. I'm thinking about Nassau or Bermuda, but I may just go to Baltimore. I expect to join the New Yorker about Christmas.

Well, that's that. I hope it makes you as happy as it has made me. Darling, darling, I adore you.

Ogden

December 4, 1930

Darling Frances —

Life continues its intolerable pace. Last night I went to a party given by Dorothy Parker and didn't get home until after four — a bit too late to write. And tomorrow night Nelson Doubleday is giving me a farewell dinner. And the book is about ready to go to press. And I'm rushing around cleaning up things in the office. And I'm trying to arrange a trip for myself. What with one thing and another I'm rather on the jump.

Darling, I do wish you were here now. It's all such fun, and I'm sorry you're not with me to share it. But I'm riding right on the crest and am somewhat astonished and embarrassed to find myself the bright boy of the moment. I don't know how long it will last, but I'm cashing in while I can.

The Parker party was grand, and I became very chummy with all the cream of New York's wit and humor — Donald Ogden Stewart, Kaufman, Connelly, Benchley, Woollcott, Brown, F.P.A., Edna Ferber again, and all the rest of the luminous boys and girls. Mrs. Parker was swell. Small, dark, not pretty but very attractive, and not hard, but wistful. She told me that I was her hero, and then said that the story in

Dear Miss Leonard —

Vanity Fair was the best thing she had read in years and that she had
sent it to Ernest Hemingway. So I said thank you Mrs. Parker.

I enclose another advertisement.

The trip looks as if it were really going to happen. Probably Bermuda,
and I think Charlie will come with me.

Doubledays want me to sign a three book contract and will pay $500
or $1000 just as a retainer, but I'm considering things before agreeing.

Darling, darling, it's all for you. Do be pleased.

I adore you.
Ogden

December 8, 1930

Frances darling —

In case you'd look to know the kind of man who wants to marry you —
who insists on marrying you — and who by gosh is *going* to marry
you — I enclose a note from Chris Morley to Dick Simon. I can't say that
I'm pleased to find that I have a Roquefort flavor, and I don't know what
cauchemar is, but I *should* like to think of myself as descended from the
Elizabethan Nashe, who, though accounted a sorry fellow and a tale-
bearing cad by Ben Jonson, wrote what is probably my favorite poem
about Spring and Cuckoo, pu-wee, tu-wit-wit, jug-jug.

My heart almost broke at the dinner Nelson Doubleday gave me; it
was such a spontaneous and sincere tribute. Twelve of my best friends
from the office, caviar, terrapin and champagne. Nelson made a long and
overwhelmingly friendly and complimentary speech, and then presented
me with a green gold cigarette case which will hold twenty cigarettes and
which several people have since told me is worth between four and five
hundred dollars. He also said that he wants me back within five years.
All in all it was pretty pleasant, particularly as Nelson, who is rather
rough and cold-blooded, has never done anything like it for any one
before.

Yesterday I became an uncle for the twelfth time, Anne and Ted having themselves a handsome red-headed son, so we are all delighted.

I'm still trying to decide whether to go to Bermuda or Baltimore. And
I wish I knew where you are and are going to be.

Darling, I love you. Don't you know it? And how much nicer March
is than April! Now I can give you a birthday present. Also, in July you

shall have a black taffeta gown at my expense. Lord, I can hardly wait to be submitted to your extravagance.

> *All my love, Frances darling.*
> *I adore you.*
> Ogden

December 11, 1930

Very darling Frances —

The piece about the stage and the pulpit appeared in last Friday's New Yorker, and yesterday I received my first anonymous letter, which I enclose. Do enjoy it. It's fun to have my courage questioned by some one without enough to sign his name.

On Tuesday I had a final conference with Simon & Schuster, designing the jacket and sending the book to press. Advance sales are good, and it looks as if we'd get a running start. As I think I've told you, January 15th is the publication date, so if you'll cross your fingers and do a bit of wishing — (damn, why did I mention your fingers? They're lovely, and I miss them, and now I'll be thinking about them all evening) — between now and then, darling, you'll earn my gratitude as well as my affection, and perhaps a fetching gown or two besides.

That evening Joe Auslander took me to dinner at the very large house of a very large gentleman who has written a three-volume work called "Napoleon, Poet of Action." — the trouble is that Joe himself is a parlor poet, though a good one, and as he lilts from parlor to parlor his worshippers approach him crying, "Master, we too have manuscripts. Won't you get them published by Doubleday Doran?" So Joe says "Why certainly, I'll get hold of Mr. Nash at once," and does, and I spend the next six weeks ducking, dodging and explaining. Ugh. However in this instance I'm doing an injustice to the gentleman whose very good dinner I ate. He is not a worshipper, but a hard-headed psychiatrist named Dr. Pierce Clark, who has spent his life among homicidal maniacs, having been for a time in charge of all the New York State lunatic asylums. He feels that after this preparation he is peculiarly qualified to write the final word on Napoleon. — Anyhow, I'll not have to read it, as my book days are over for the time at least.

Wednesday (yesterday) at 4:30 I signed my last letter and my last memorandum, and finished my Doubleday Doran career. It was, and is, a

Dear Miss Leonard —

very queer feeling. I think you know that my work there was a good deal more than just a job to me. For six years it was my life, holding all my interest and nearly all my friendships. The wrench at parting was pretty stiff. But I *know* I did the right thing, and that I have speeded up my progress by about five years. So do be pleased about that too, darling. That $200 a month extra will be awfully useful. And as I told you in my first letter about the change, there'll be a lot more at the end of the year if things work out as they should. Frances, I love you.

Gwen is staying with us for a few days, and last night I sat up till all hours talking to her. She saw both Isabel and your father recently, both looking very well, but I'm sorry she has no Baltimore gossip. By the way, I was probably wrong in my dreadful prophesies about Pauline, as I have seen her and her husband, together and apparently very happy, several times since I started the scandal.

Great excitement last night; I went to put the $400 Nelson Doubleday cigarette case away in my most private place, where I keep the ring — and when I got there the ring was gone. Well, it's not much of a ring, but it's the only one I've got, and I have a definite use for it in three months or so, so I was a bit upset. I hunted for an hour, and finally found it — slipped down in a crack between two drawers of the bureau. I was relieved, darling, and you'd better be, too, unless you'd have liked a brass one with an imitation stone. Of course I don't know how you feel about those things. — Anyhow, it convinced me that you should have taken it when it was offered. By the time you are ready for it the jackdaw of Rheims is quite likely to have hopped off with it.

I have definitely decided that I'd rather spend money in the late spring than now, so I'm going to Baltimore instead of Bermuda for my rest. That isn't unselfishness — it's simply anticipation. Now it's up to you to join me in June, so that I shan't have hoarded all that wealth for nothing. You can spend it on spinach soup, concerts, radios, victrolas, taxi rides, clothes or anything you like — so long as you spend it. Extravagant and luxury-loving Frances, I'm tired of spending money on you. I want to give it to you and have you spend it on yourself. Please put me in a position to do so. Darling, make some demands.

I suppose this is my Christmas letter, isn't it? A merry one and a happy one, beloved, to you and your mother. — As long as you *are* happy there I'm glad for you to be away, but, as who said? if you begin to get a little bored, that's all right, too. Is Christmas in Italy fun? Tell me all about it. Also please send me your corrected itinerary. I'll only be in

Baltimore about a week, so keep on writing here. And a cable to 106 E 85 only costs about fifty cents more than one to Doubledor and I'd enjoy one.

> *Merry Christmas again, Frances*
> *darling, and I adore you.*
> Ogden

December 22, 1930

Darling Frances —

Such a day! As I write, the clock is striking midnight, and this is the first moment I've had to myself and you.

To begin with, this morning I started work for the New Yorker. That in itself is a bit bewildering, and I shall be a babe in the woods for two or three months, but I think I'm going to enjoy it. I like the feel of the place, and I like the people. I like having only one boss instead of a board of directors to deal with. I like the atmosphere which I believe is going to be a stimulant and lead to more and better work on my part. I like the prospects. In a word, I like the job, though I don't know yet what it is; and at the end of my first day I'm convinced that making the change was the wisest thing I ever did. — I find that nobody gets to the office before ten, which is nice, and nobody leaves before six or seven, which I'm used to. Furthermore, when you leave the office, you're through — no more of this home-work with manuscripts and dummy descriptions. That in itself means that I'll be able to do a lot more writing, and more writing means more money, and more money means more pink houses with angels on them and bigger bills from Bergdorf Goodman and oh lots of things. Darling, I love you.

I had luncheon with Max Schuster who says things are going beautifully. Publication date is three weeks from day after tomorrow. The first edition comes off press a week from today. I'll send your copy to Paris.

A huge box of roses arrived for mother today, and the apartment is filled and fragrant with them. They came from Salisbury and a written card on them said they were from Mrs. Thomas Leonard, but I guessed at once that that was a clerical error and that they were really from your mother. I know that Mother herself will write, but I just wanted to tell you myself how much delight they gave her. So did your Christmas card with its message, darling. I can easily understand why I grow increasingly fond of you.

I had just sat down to dinner when Walter Phelps, an old friend and good friend of mine from Providence, called up to say that he was in town for the evening. So it was up to me. I got seats for Three's a Crowd. That's the new revue with Clifton Webb and Libby Holman and Fred Allen from last year's Little Show. I enjoyed it tremendously. Rather rough, very funny, good music and dancing. Libby Holman sings better than she did last year, but hollers worse, so I don't think you'd like her so much. But there are two dances that are even more hair-raising and gruesome than Moanin' Low. — Gosh there are a lot of things I want to take you to. I think you'd better spend quite a lot of time in New York — particularly as it looks as if I'm not going to have the elastic week-ends that have been so convenient in the past.

I'm really feeling right on the crest these days. Everything is breaking right; I had never hoped to jump ahead so fast. My job now is to keep moving, and I'm just in the mood to do it. I thrive on success; it seems to breed more success. So wish me luck, Frances. I'm really getting to look rather commanding, and losing much of my reserve and hesitancy. So with that, and the fifteen pounds I've put on, you may find me a different person from the one you said such pleasant things to before you sailed. Perhaps you won't like me at all. If you don't I won't do a thing except strangle you. Darling, do let's be awfully in love with each other, and get married (to each other) and live (together) happily ever after. I will if you will.

I sent Edna Ferber some caviar after that week end in the country, and received this note from her today:

> For gents who send me flowers and gin I have but pleasant looks.
> I feel no girlish tremors over lads who give me books.
> But when caviar is sent me by Frederic Ogden Nash
> I'm swept by warm emotion which is nothing short of pash.

Frances darling, good night,
and I adore you.
Ogden

December 26, 1930

Frances darling —

Christmas has come and gone, I've sent two cables and got one, mailed 82 letters and got 23, I'm still solvent, still have my health and ambition and an imposing new job and, so far as I know, the same old girl. So the year closes more pleasantly than it opened, and I'm filled with shiny plans for 1931. But I'm looking for a partner, as it will take two to work them out. Preferably a partner between five feet eight and five feet nine who doesn't know how many l's there are in marvellous or how many p's there are in depressing — though I rather think that if I get the right person we'll never use the word depressing. Why Ogden, is that a proposal? Idiot, of course it is. Aren't you pleased?

Having had strict orders from Simon and Schuster, I spent an hour in the photographer's chair this afternoon, and found it more wearing than the dentist's. He's one of those modernistic photographers, named Sherrill Schell, who does pictures of eggs and triangles and skyscrapers for Vanity Fair, and he practically ruined my eyes with his lights. He took about two dozen poses — Nash looking up, down, sideways, frowning, whimsical, thoughtful etc. So my private life seems to have vanished forever. — Do you want one, or have you enough now?

I did another verse today which I can't remember now but which begins

> I know that a little verse is a versicle, but I don't know if a little
>   phrase is a phrasicle
> But I do know that at the moment I am feeling too too alas and
>   alackadaisicle

and continues rather sillily. I also did two short anecdotes. All are in the hands of my co-editors to be tested for funniness.

Darling, I'm still giggling over your cable, and I hadn't giggled since you left. I guess I must be in love with you.

Ogden

P.S. I've just reached a decision — I adore you.

"Nash looking thoughtful."
(*Photo by Sherrill Schell*)

December 30, 1930

Frances darling —

For one reason and another I missed writing you during the last three days, and now I'm going to do a rather nice thing. You know, the sort of nice thing that the hostess does in upsetting the coffee pot immediately after a guest has upset the tea pot. I mean that I'm just not going to make up those missing letters, so that when you get back I won't be able to look smugly at you and say "Well *I* wrote every day." But anyhow I'll have written damn near every day.

And speaking of letters, I got just the kind of letter from you this evening that lights up the whole week — an adorable letter, with you in every word, so that whenever I read it I feel terribly close to you, and can almost hear you being amusing, and disrespectful, and idiotic and wise and lovable. Yes, it seems that you are lovable and everybody knows it but I know it better than anybody else. Darling, it occurs to me that I should like very much to kiss you. As I shouldn't dream of such a thing if you were here, you can see that absence *is* making my heart grow fonder. Go on, darn you, stay away ten years and I'll probably even propose to you.

Oh and also, speaking of dreams, I dreamed the other night that you were back, and you said; "Did you miss me?" and I said "Yes, frightfully," and you said "Oh you shouldn't have," and I said "Well as a matter of fact I didn't," and then you got mad. So like you that I could hardly believe it was a dream.

I enclose a proof of a rude verse I wrote about Sinclair Lewis, who won the Nobel Prize, which was all right, and then made an ass out of himself and his country, which wasn't. I think all noisy boors should be socked in the eye, and I am trying to do my humble part. This thing will be in next week's New Yorker. — The job is going beautifully though I still don't know what it's all about. But I'm writing three articles at once, one of which may be good, and re-writing several others of other people's, and being kept very busy, and feeling awfully on top of the world.

Did I tell you that the office doesn't open until 10:30 in the morning? If a husband with a job like that isn't an inducement to matrimony for a girl of your tendencies I don't know what would be. Breakfast at 9:30 instead of 8, darling. Think of it!

Now may I interrupt this interesting conversation to say that the first edition of the book came off press today and that your copy was mailed to Paris this afternoon so that it should be waiting for you when you get there. It's awfully good looking — Simon & Schuster have done the swellest job of their career. Do like it, darling — after all, it's yours. It will be published two weeks from tomorrow, just about when you are reading this. Dick says the advance sale will run between 2000 and 2500 copies, which is an excellent start. After that, it's up to the public, which is of course unpredictable. But if it dies it will have been buried decently by the time you get back, and if it goes it will be just at the top then, so that's all right.

I heard André Maurois speak at a luncheon today. Very French, very shy, and very amusing. He is lecturing at Princeton this year, and seems to like it. I wonder if I should have gone there?

Darling, *what* a lot of talk, and all the time I've been aching to tell you that I love you. My mind is full of you, Frances, and my heart is full of you, and it is all loveliness, and I wish you were here — but of course I don't wish it hard enough to make you think I couldn't get on without you.

> Frances, Frances darling,
> *I adore you.*
> Ogden

December 31, 1930

Darling Frances —

It's quite late — just five minutes this side of next year — and already the bells and horns and fire-crackers have begun. I'm sorry, in a way, to see the old year go, so many nice things started during it. But I'm happy to see the new one come in, as I'm expecting it to bring great pleasantnesses rather more completely than 1930 did.

There strikes the clock now. Happy New Year, darling, and I love you now and always.

Today I finished two things, a prose piece and a verse. I think the New Yorker is going to take them both, but I can't be sure for a day or so. If they do, I'll send the silly things to you, but if not I won't. I refuse to appear before you now except when I'm robed in success. — I'm glad to find that what I thought would happen when I took this job seems to be happening — I'm getting a lot more work done. Ideas are in the air, and it's easier to write them down than it is not to.

Just think, darling, you'll be sailing for home in $\quad$ 31
$$28$$
$$\underline{27}$$
86 days

and you've been gone $\quad$ 27
$$30$$
$$\underline{31}$$
88 days. So the half-way mark has been passed, and in addition to that you'll be in Paris in three weeks. And as I think I've told you, after your wanderings of the last three months, I feel that Paris is practically around the corner. Do buy a lot of nice clothes there, darling, so that you'll just knock my eye out when I see you. But leave room in your wardrobe for one dress. I do want to buy you a dress.

Here's today's advertisement and today's puzzle.

I love you darling, and I am praying that God will help me make this your happiest year as it will be mine.

Ogden

January 1, 1931

Darling Frances —

Today being New Year's, I am enjoying myself, sitting around the house and trying, without much success, to think. It's a curious thing, but I've never been able to do any work on a holiday — only after having spent eight or nine hours at the office. So you see how unusual I am.

Tell me, darling, is "le Harvard" a short, skinny young man, with red hair, pale eyes, sandy lashes, and pink eye-lids? And does he wear a blue suit and white sneakers? Because last night I dreamed about you again. I met you as you were getting off the train from Paris, and I wanted to kiss you, but there were a lot of people around, so I said please come for a walk, and you did, and we walked along a country road, but an awful young man, the one I have just described, kept following us, about five yards behind. When I walked faster he walked faster, and when I slowed down he slowed down, and he never said anything, but just kept looking at the back of my head. I asked you if he was "le Harvard" but you wouldn't answer, so I decided that he was. Then, as he was quite small and looked as if he had been ill, I wanted to turn on him and beat him up, but you said not to. And I said angrily Oh very well! and that was that, and I woke up and looked at my watch and it was five o'clock. So I went back to sleep, and apparently you were sorry for your outrageous conduct, because you let yourself be dreamed about again, and came back with a lot of lipstick awfully well put on and wrote something on a piece of paper and gave it to me and I read it and it said Will you please marry me? And if you don't know my answer you'd better stay in Spain.

So you've been dreamed about twice in one night, darling. I do like dreaming about you while it's going on, but it's rather dismal waking up afterwards to nothing more real than a photograph, which while a very nice photograph, doesn't know the meaning of lipstick and couldn't say Well well well or laugh at me to save its life. I miss being laughed at.

The reason that my mind is running so on lipstick is that I've just been straightening out the box in which I keep your letters, and I keep in with them the handkerchief I carried the evening you sailed, and the red has almost faded off it and I don't know whether it's going to last till you get back, and that annoys me and darkens my otherwise cheerful outlook. I wish you'd send me a dab from Paris. And once more, my love, how about that photograph? You *know* you promised you'd have one taken. Here I've sent you two handsome snapshots already, and I've also had a real photograph taken which I shall send you shortly, but what have I had from you?

Oh, I must tell you about my photograph. I did tell you that the photographer was pretty modern and arty. For two of the shots he made me pose without my coat, though I protested that even if they came out well I was not an actor and would not allow them to be used, but he pacified me and assured me that it was purely for his own satisfaction. And now I have the proofs and the two shirt-sleeves ones are much the best, and I don't know what to do. By the way, I said above that I'd send you one shortly, but perhaps it would be inconvenient to carry around and you'd rather wait till you got home. Or perhaps you'd rather have an oil painting or a bronze bust? I don't know, so please tell me.

I am glad you are beginning to have some misgivings about your culture. Perhaps you are getting an inkling of the responsibilities of the position you are to occupy. Never mind, darling, your pretty face and gentle nature will carry you far. Now, aren't you sorry you aren't here to slap me?

Pay no attention to me, Frances. Except when I tell you, as I do now, that I adore you.

Ogden

January 3, 1931

Darling Frances —

Today opened with a merry flurry. Do you remember the advertisement I clipped and sent you a few days ago — the last one? I didn't tell you at the time, but it scared me to death, because, through some oversight on the part of Mr. Simon or Schuster, Edna Ferber was publicly listed among the admirers of the book — whereas she had never spoken or written a word of admiration to me or to them, though I have heard indirectly, through Dan, that she does like it. From past experience in other matters I know her to be very touchy, and a hell-cat when roused, so my heart was in my boots and my boots in the cellar. I wrote her at once telling her that it was a mistake; would not occur again, please forgive, respectful admiration etc., a very nice letter. I haven't heard from her yet, but this morning Dick Simon got a boiling hot letter calling him a publishing racketeer and threatening to put the matter in the hands of her lawyer — which last would have been interesting, as her lawyer is also Dick's lawyer.

What's legal etiquette under the circumstances? At any rate Dick was worried and annoyed and called me up about it, and we talked it over and decided that he'd better get in touch with her. So he called *her* up and her first word was a sweet melting apology and she went on to say that she had been in a bad mood when she wrote the letter and hadn't meant a word of it and though she had at first resented the unauthorized use of her name she presently understood that it had been used by mistake and not with intent to defraud, and she wished she hadn't written the letter, and having written it wished she hadn't mailed it. Then she said she thought the book was a swell book and that she would be delighted to lend her name in any way.

For my own information I looked into the matter to see how it happened in the first place, and I found that Max Schuster had written the advertisement up in the country and had filled in the names of the endorsers from memory and had unfortunately remembered two that just weren't so. Yes, heaven help me, *two*! Not only Ferber, but also Samuel

Hoffenstein. What is worse, Hoffenstein's name, you will note, is spelled
Hoffen*skin*. Dear oh dear oh dear. We haven't heard from that one
yet. — That's the prickly side, but it's all fun.

Now for the other side. Advance sales continue gorgeous. The big
wholesale house, Baker & Taylor, today placed an initial order for 500
copies. The president took his copy home last night and reported today
that he thinks it the funniest book in years, which is nice, as he has the
power to make a book almost by himself. Brentano's took 100. Two
Doubleday shops took 100 each because they liked the book; a third said
they didn't like the book but would take 100 because they liked me. A
few days ago I sent a copy to Oliver (Pulitzer Prize) LaFarge. I saw him
today and he said he spent all last evening reading it to an enthusiastic
audience which included his mother-in-law, who stole it when she went
home.

I also got two nice letters which I shall quote with explanatory notes.

Do you remember the verse I wrote up at the cape that you didn't
like? It contained the names of Benchley, Marc Connelly and Frank Sullivan. So I sent them each a copy with an inscription saying I hoped they
didn't mind having their names mishandled. Frank Sullivan writes back:
"I am proud to have a copy of your book, which I predict will do more
to improve the condition of the slaves than any book since Uncle Harriet
Beecher Stowe's Tom. I am prouder still to be mentioned in it. I will settle
for two per cent of the gross for the use of my name, and those of Connelly and Benchley. I control the American rights to both."

Then I sent a copy to Milt Gross with a modest inscription saying that
after re-reading the verses I was more than ever of the opinion that one
picture is worth twenty thousand words. And he writes: "Just a line to
tell you how delighted I am to have your book and how much more delightful than the possession of same is the reading of it. Some of the
verses and couplets just pack dynamite in them. As for one picture and
20,000 words etc., let me see the guy that can draw a Bopodist."

Also nice letters from Newman Levy, and Amy Loveman of the Saturday Review of Literature. That's about all of today's news of the book.

Last night I finished the funny prose piece and this morning I turned it
in. The boys have two prose pieces of mine now, and I await with
interest.

Still a good deal of talk about me, isn't there? I'm sorry. But things *are*
happening to me, and it *is* fun, and oh darling, I do wish you were here
to share it. And it *is* all for you and all yours.

Last night I deciphered the post marks on all the letters you've written since sailing, and made up a month by month schedule. I find that you wrote 10 letters in October, 11 in November, but, so far, only 4 in December. I'll get one or two more December letters tomorrow off the Mauretania, I think, but even so the month will compare unfavorably with October and November. What was the matter, darling? Not too much Harvard? I love you anyhow.

Ogden

January 5, 1931

Darling Frances —

Last night after writing you everything that was then on my mind I felt much better, went to bed, slept like a baby — in fact, better than any baby I've ever come in contact with — and awoke this morning gay as a lark. So I'm the glad boy again.

The New Yorker cold-bloodedly gave me back my two prose pieces today and *still* I'm cheerful. (Oddly enough I don't miss you so much when things go wrong; I'm not a sympathy-craver; it's when things are going very, very right that I want to have you here to crow to.) One of them I myself didn't think was much good, so I tore it up; the other I did and do think is excellent, so I immediately sent it over to Vanity Fair, though it isn't exactly in their line. And I enclose herewith proof of a poem which describes rather well my mood of yesterday.

I got some more letters this morning which I shall quote to you.

Stephen Vincent Benét writes: "It's a swell book, and I'm glad to have my name on the wrapper of a swell book. Incidentally, I like 'Old Men' very much — and the whole family is learning 'No, *You* Be a Lone Eagle' by heart. Also, we once had a turtle."

Nelson Doubleday writes a thank you letter and signs himself "affectionately." That's the miracle of the century, and I'm still palpitating.

And Edna Ferber — after the storm, peace. Here's what she says: "I want first to tell you that I think the book is gay, and amusing, and refreshingly mad, and I am as pleased as can be at your sending me a copy with the flattering inscription. I am very showy about leaving it out where people can — must, in fact — notice. My fury at the use of my name, without my permission, took on fishwife proportions. I wrote Simon & Schuster a letter which was, perhaps, inexcusable except for the fact that I happen to be a little cuckoo on the subject. It has happened to me before, and I hate it worse than practically anything in the world. I threatened, I am afraid, suit, mayhem, and death by slow torture. It was altogether a most unladylike letter (it was: Ed.) and I am a little ashamed of it. (She ought to be: Ed.) I hope the book will go very well indeed. (So do I: Ed.) How do you like being with the New Yorker? It would be nice to see you. Edna Ferber."

So I wrote back and said how much better I felt after getting her note, and that I was still up to my Adam's-apple in regret and confusion, but that I was very grateful and that if she ever needed a job done, from eavesdropping to parricide, I would do it for her. And now that episode is over, I wonder what the next will be?

The day at the office was quiet enough, if you except Ross's usual blow-up. Ross, who made the New Yorker what it is, and who really is a genius, is probably the strangest man in the world. He comes from San Francisco where he was known as the worst ship-news reporter and the best card-shark on the West Coast. His hair sticks straight up, his teeth stick straight out, his eyes slant, and his expression is always that of a man who has just swallowed a bug. His collars flap, and he wears high shoes. Once a day at least he calls you into his office and says "This magazine is going to hell." He never varies the phrase. Then he says "We haven't got any organization. I'm licked. We've got too many geniuses around and nobody to take any responsibility." He has smoked five cigarettes while saying that. Then he takes a drink of water, prowls up and down, cries "My God" loudly and rapidly, and you go out and try to do some work.

I got another letter from you this morning. That brings your December total up to five — written on the 4th, 5th, 15th, 16th, and 22nd. Tomorrow's boat will have to bring quite a batch to bring you anywhere near October's ten or November's eleven. And what, darling, were you doing between the 5th and the 15th? That's a dark gap that I should like explained. Or perhaps I shouldn't. We'll let it go this time, but see that you do better in January, February, and March.

Frances Leonard writes from Rome, "Gosh what an admired young man! I should think you'd be glad I wasn't at home." What does she mean by that? She's all wrong. Then she says, "You must be uppity." That's better, nearer the truth. Then she goes on about night clubs and churches and somebody named ———— who I hope gets a cactus in his throat and a squirt of grape fruit in his eye, and somebody named ———— who I hope gets boils and hiccups. Then she tells me not to be *too* much admired when she knows very well whose is the only admiration I care that — snap! — for. That's the girl I've taken a fancy to. I guess we writers are too impractical. I ought to get married. I'm not safe alone.

Darling, I don't care how long you stay away, but I do miss you I mean I don't miss you but I do wish you were here. I mean I love you. Frances, will you marry me? (There now — you've been proposed to in Paris.) I adore you, darling.

Ogden

January 7, 1931

Frances darling —

The fan mail continues to pour in from everywhere except Europe, the European correspondence being more in the nature of a trickle — splendid when it does come, but you can't count on it. Today's kind words are from Mrs. H. L. Mencken, who writes from Baltimore (Baltimore? Baltimore? Who was it I used to know that used to live in Baltimore?) to say: "Certainly it is the most enlivening stuff I have read since the fall of Atlanta. Henry, I might add, enjoyed it as much as I did and is giving it the noble review it deserves in the Mercury."

In addition to that, I enclose a clipping from Vanity Fair and one from today's Daily News. The Vanity Fair one is a bit behindhand, as you can see. The Daily News one amused and astonished me because a little while before I left Doubleday's I went to Hellinger and asked him to do a book for us. He presented an outline and I turned it down and he wasn't a bit pleased, so I was hardly expecting anything kinder than silence from him.

Do you know what I'd like? I'd like a cable from you saying that you've arrived in Paris. I sort of feel better when I know that you've got to places all right. That's why I cabled you at Barcelona last night. And if you don't behave nicely when you get to Paris I shall call you up. In fact, if the advance sale keeps on the way it has been going I may do it anyway. Wouldn't that make you feel important and embarrassed at the same time? And annoyed? I can imagine the conversation.

Me: Hello
You: Hello
Me: What?
You: I said Hello.

Dear Miss Leonard —

```
Me:    Oh.
You:   (Silence)
Me:    Frances, how are you?
You:   All right.
Me:    What are you doing?
You:   Nothing much.
Me:    Darling, I love you.
You:   Oh.
Me:    (desperately) I love you.
You:   Oh.
Me:    I said I love you!
You:   What?
Me:    It doesn't matter.
You:   (silence)
Me:    Well. . . .
You:   Well?
Me:    Well, good bye.
You:   Good bye. — Click.
Me:    What did I do that for?
```

A nice talk like that would put me right on my feet. I think, darling, that you and I are not born telephoners.

I got your Christmas letter from Rome this morning. (That brings your December total up to six; I may still get one more December letter, which will make a total of seven. Seven letters in a month of 31 days as against eleven in November which only had 30 days. There's something very odd about that. What do you suppose was happening?)

Frances dearest, I'm so sorry to hear that you were sick and had a horrid Christmas, though I gather from your post script that you were better the next day and probably got off to Naples on schedule. Darling, I don't *want* you to be sick over there. But I suppose you're quite pleased because you probably lost some weight. I don't like that idea, either; if you don't bring me back as much Frances as you took away I shall probably act badly and make you conspicuous on the dock.

Frances, you say again that you are proud of me. That's twice now. Are you really, darling? I'm trying so hard to make you able to be, and it makes me so happy to believe that you are. It's you, you, you that I'm working for and want to work for always. Oh darling, I do adore you! Also I'm quite absurdly pleased at your saying that you'd like to see me.

That's twice you've said *that* now; once when it was raining and you wanted to be read to, and once when you were sick and again probably wanted to be read to. Anyhow, *I'd* like to see you, too, so there. And I'm glad my letters and cable cheered you up a bit.

I had luncheon today with Charlie, who went down for the Supper Club with Isabel and spent the week-end; and seems to have had a grand time. Richard and Mary were of course the center of activities. You say your father reports John as being most subdued, but he was healthy and sprightly when I saw him, and capable of entertaining both Millers at once all by himself; and Charlie also says he was in good shape. John told me he hadn't written to you, and looked very shame-faced about it. — Did you hear that the Baltimore Country Club burned down two or three days ago? Completely destroyed, I believe, and one fireman killed.

The Gormans have taken Mrs. MacMillan's house in Guilford, just around the corner from where you live when you are at home if you are ever at home, for January, February, March and probably April. How useless.

So you want to know your most striking faults? Wait till I see you. But I'll tell you one now. You say three times in your letter that you are stupid. Stop running down the girl who, if only my unofficial fiancée, is certainly my official beloved. Darling, you are completely adorable and I love you.

Ogden

January 8, 1931

Frances darling —

Well, here is today's advertisement — the last before publication. And will you for the heaven's sake look at the enclosed quotation from a review that will appear in the February issue of the Atlantic Monthly? Did you know you were loved by a foolish, nimble and entertaining versifier? Did you know that he would do your heart good? And did you know that he was a young Gilbert risen in our midst, and badly needed by the present world? Gosh, darling, I hadn't realized the éclat that went with my hand when I offered it to you. Conditions have changed. Still, I'm a man of my word; a bargain's a bargain, and I'll stick to it even if it costs me money.

I'll tell you something. For the last three days I've been thinking about you all day long. Steadily, with just a little time off to work in. Not that I don't generally think of you pretty often anyway; but for some reason you've figured far too prominently in my head and heart lately. I wonder why? Am I telepathic, and is something happening; or am I just getting more deeply in love? I don't know. I enjoy it, but it's all very disturbing. You're so real when I think about you — and so far away when I pinch myself. It's a weary world for the waiting one who sits at home and spins while the loved one ploughs the deep and goes adventuring in strange lands. I'll probably end up in a cottage on the sand dunes waving a handkerchief at passing ships by day, and at night setting a lantern in the window to guide my sweetheart home. Just a legend, that's what I'll be, and when I die sentimental tourists will weep over my grave and many hot dogs will be sold around it. Ah welladay. Don't you like the way I mingle humor and pathos?

The photographs of myself came today — very handsome. I hadn't realized my charm. Perhaps *you* haven't. Have you cabled yet? I've thought of something awfully nice to say to you. Perhaps I'll do it tomorrow. Darling, I love you.

Ogden

January 9, 1931

Frances darling —

Your cable — or rather, radiogram — from Pollensa arrived just after dinner this evening. I had been expecting it to come from Barcelona, and hadn't the vaguest idea where Pollensa was. But it had such a Slavonic sound that for a few awful moments I thought you might have changed your plans once more and gone to Poland or Russia — particularly as I consider you quite capable of doing it. Then I spent ten minutes with an Atlas and found you right where you should be, on Majorca.

So you arrived without sailor complications, did you? It seems to me that your cables are getting pretty cheeky, beginning with Business Man's Christmas Greeting Number Nine and carrying on with this important message. Have you no respect for my thinning hairs, my newly added fifteen pounds, and my rapidly increasing reputation? Hasn't the courtliness of foreign culture taught you the deference due to one who is older and taller and heavier and far, far wiser than you? Have you learned nothing from the Latins about the inferior position of women in the scheme of things? Or perhaps you just think you are safe because you are where I can't get at you; you are taking advantage of the Atlantic Ocean to ridicule my finer feelings. Is that sporting? Is it amiable? Do I love you for it? Yes.

No enclosures today except the inevitable puzzle. Which reminds me: do you really use all the puzzles I send or am I mutilating the papers to no end? And *what*, darling, are you doing with the barrel of letters you have received from me by this time? I'm consumed with curiosity.

An amusing true story came in today about a woman who was going to take her little boy to the movies and asked him what he wanted to see. "War Nurse," said the boy promptly. She remembered having read in the reviews that War Nurse was pretty lurid, even torrid, and said, "Oh no dear, wouldn't you rather see Africa Speaks? It's a lovely animal picture with lots of lions and tigers." The boy insisted that he wanted to see War Nurse. "But there are *animals* in Africa Speaks, dear," said the woman frantically. "There are animals in War Nurse too," said the boy, showing her the advertisement. It read "Come to War Nurse and see men and women turn into beasts."

Also a perfectly reputable man, one of our regular contributors, arrived with a true story about Coolidge's bootlegger in Northampton, Mass.; all about what he buys and how he haggles over prices. Ross wouldn't use it; said everybody had a right to their private lives, even Coolidge.

Well, darling, I've now crossed Harvardites, architects and sailors off my list of worries. What's next? Do let me know.

Frances, I think that every man has once in his life a hint, a swift vision of unattainable beauty. I have had mine. The difference is that mine is real. Darling, you are all beauty and all loveliness, and I wish you would become real again, and I adore you.

Ogden

January 15, 1931

Darling Frances —

I didn't write last night, and I shan't apologize for it. I was so nervous I couldn't hold a pencil, and simply spent the evening pacing the floor. I had a horrid feeling that the reviewers were going to take my skin off in the morning, and I wished very heartily that I had never written a book.

Well, it's out now, and everything looks wonderful. The first reviews, which I am enclosing in a separate envelope, are incredibly, ridiculously good. Book stores around town report good sales. A second edition went to press this morning, the first, of 4000 copies, being nearly exhausted. The pre-publication sales were 3200, about 1000 above expectations. All the signs point to success, though we can't be certain for about a week. But whether it soars or flops, it's all fun now. Gosh, I do like hearing pleasant things.

Darling, your cable came this evening. That *was* sweet of you. It perfected the day. It's very warming to think of you thinking of me way over in Palma de Mallorca.

Now I'm too tired to write any more — too tired for anything except to love you, and love you, and love you. Good night, darling.

Ogden

January 15, 1931

Frances darling —

Here's the first batch of reviews — perfectly astonishing. I don't know when I've seen such unrestrained enthusiasm. I really had been scared to death, and it's all a great relief. Will you save them?

I was amused at the line in Harry Hansen's review: "the girl who won't say yes and who won't say no, and who is said to be a real person." I don't know who started *that* rumor. Certainly not I. *Is* she real?

Darling, I love you.
Ogden

January 16, 1931

Frances darling —

The only review I got today is slightly equivocal, not to say barbed, but being an honest old thing I am sending it to you anyhow. It is my firm conviction that there are two sides to every question — except one, on which I brook no argument.

Reviews are pleasant, or, at least, pleasant reviews are pleasant — but of course what I'm really interested in is sales. Today's reports are good.

As I told you yesterday, the first edition of 4000 is about gone. A second edition of 3500 has now gone to press. I stopped in the Grand Central Book Shop on my way home this evening and they told me that they have sold nearly a hundred books in two days, and that two out of three people coming into the shop ask for it. Dick tells me that Macy's are also doing extremely well with it. So at the moment the prospects are golden, but we can't really be sure for another ten days or so. I still don't believe any of it — I keep re-reading the reviews to convince myself, but I have a feeling that it's all an elaborate hoax arranged at great expense to make a public idiot of me. This attitude is obviously wrong, and I shall try to correct it — develope a swelled head and take everything as my due. Do you think you'd like that?

This morning, at the command of my publishers, I submitted to being interviewed by a fat oil gusher named Mrs. Alice Dixon Bond, who lectures to women's clubs about books and authors. She told me that she thinks my youth and sincerity are wonderful. Have you ever noticed them?

I got a terribly nice letter from your father, to whom I had naturally sent a copy of the book. But still no word from Isabel. Perhaps she has broken her arm.

I had luncheon today with a man named Cathcart, who is business manager of the Saturday Review, and in their office I ran into Bill and Steve Benét and Chris Morley, all of whom were so kind that I was embarrassed. Bill was the one who wrote that swell review saying I was right about everything. Gosh, people have been nice to me. It will take me years to work off my gratitude. And it *is* nice to be liked — to have people really wishing you well. And everybody, from Dick and Max to the booksellers, has just turned somersaults for me. And you sent a cable. That was best of all, darling. Never forget that I love you.

Ogden

January 17, 1931

Darling Frances —

The cheerful surprise of the week — along with your cable — was a letter from you which arrived this morning. I hadn't expected anything to be

mailed between Naples and Barcelona, and had reconciled myself to an
arid ten days or so. The Genoa letter, therefore, came as so much velvet.
I'm sorry about the food on the freighter. It doesn't sound like a pleasant
trip, and I disliked the idea from the moment I heard of it. However, I
know from your cables that it turned out all right, and it's all over now,
so I'll try to think of nicer things, such as your getting to Paris on
Wednesday.

Gwen called up from Baltimore tonight to say that there was a big review of the book in the Evening Sun stating that Mr. Nash is the Abraham Lincoln who has emancipated poetry. (Mother immediately said,
"Well, I'm no Nancy Hanks!")

Richard's wedding was today; I'm sorry I couldn't get down for it. I
enclose a notice of it from the Herald Tribune. Gwen also said she saw
your father yesterday, and he is dining with them next week — that is, if
the stove is fixed. She was giving a good-sized dinner before the Assembly, and right in the middle of it the gas stove exploded and blew the
cook into Union Memorial; not seriously injured, but thoroughly startled.

Then here's a review from this week's Time, with a striking likeness of
the nimble Abraham Lincoln of poetry decorating its abdomen. — And a
monster advertisement from today's World, in which, I am sorry to say,
my publishers seem to have played up the more vulgar elements of the
work. Harmlessly vulgar, to be sure, but nevertheless vulgar. This is mis-
leading; I am really a very refined person.

You write me that you and your mother are vexed because you won't
see the book till after it's been published. May I politely remind you that
I extended a cordial invitation to you to be present at that interesting
event — even going so far as to postpone it from December to the middle
of January to make it more convenient for you? Or — shall I just shut
up? Whichever you like.

Today is Saturday. At four this afternoon I had just tucked next week's
issue comfortably to bed when Ross arrived with two stories that had to
get in — so the whole thing had to be done over again and I was there
till seven. The week-end problem in the Spring looks serious, but I'll find
a way.

Darling, your letters *do* make good reading. Furthermore — oh very
much furthermore — I love you.

Ogden

January 19, 1931

Frances darling —

No enclosures today, except the crossword puzzle. One or two things happened, though. Macy's called up Simon & Schuster to say that Hard Lines was the best-selling book, fiction or non-fiction, in the store. And the Evening Post called me up to know if I would pose for a drawing by one of their artists, and I said yes, so I am to do that tomorrow. And on Wednesday somebody is to make an etching of me. By Thursday I expect to be very tired of sitting still, and even more tired of my face, which at best has never excited me very much. At least not since I was two or three years old — for I *was* a beautiful child. Much better-looking than you were, I insist — and now look at us! Just another of Fate's tricks. If we had only grown up as we began, I probably shouldn't care *when* you came back.

I had luncheon today with Joe Alger. Joe is the one who wrote The Cricket of Carador with me. I don't think you've ever seen that unlucky book, have you? It was a children's story, published in 1925 by Double-day Page. Neither Joe nor I ever got a penny out of it, and fewer copies were sold than you could count on the thumbs of one hand. D. P. had a lot of copies left over that they didn't know what do with. I believe that when all else failed they tried to trade them to the Figi Islanders for co-coanuts, but the Figis balked and held out for beads. Anyhow it was all very sad, and I'm pleased that the recent event is so different.

The cigarette box arrived from Dresden today. Frances, it's a beauty. I like it better than the tortoise-shell watch chain, but I don't know yet whether I like it as well as the horse. I'll tell you in a week or so. — Darling, isn't it calculating of you to plan your arrival just in time for a birthday present? Clever, but a bit obvious. What would you like? I have a very nice ring — I think you've seen it before. It's been worn once or twice, but it's practically as good as new, and it's yours for the asking —if you ask politely. Darling, I love you.

Ogden

January 24, 1931

Frances darling —

The Telegram and the Post honor me today with what the boys call "personality stories" which I bravely pass on to you. By the way, I have *not* got cross-eyed since you left — neither do I carry a plug of tobacco in my lower left jaw. I can't help it if that's the way I impressed the lady who drew me. Also the fact that all the time she was working she was talking to an unexplained gentleman in a bathrobe who lay on a sofa between her and the light may have something to do with it. Wasn't it very fair-minded of the interviewer, under the circumstances, to use the phrase "nice-looking"?

I had hoped for a cable from Paris by this time — I don't know whether you are just silent, or whether you have stopped off somewhere and haven't reached there yet. So I just tell myself to be calm, and by gosh I *am* calm!

I got your nice, long Balearic letter — you really are doing pretty well, darling; please disregard my occasional tantrums.

> *And remember — I love you.*
> Ogden

January 28, 1931

Darling —

I am going to the Oliver LaFarges' for dinner tonight and afterwards to somebody's house-warming, so I imagine I'll get home too late to write. Hence this voice from the office. Have I ever written to you on the type-writer before? I think not. Unsentimental, unromantic things, typewriters. Byt din't you th9nk I t8pewr"te beaytxfullly? Showlnk off axain, you see.

I got your second Balearic letter this morning, and for some reason it seemed to me to be almost the nicest letter I have ever got. Perhaps because you used my favorite phrase twice; perhaps because the whole tone of it seemed to bring April nearer. Anyhow I went to work like a lion.

Aren't you clever to have done a tapestry? Poems are made by fools like me, but you can make a tapestree. And you've stopped working on it in public because you keep your mouth open while working? Darling, if you'll only come back you can keep your mouth open — you can grow adenoids and goiters — you can muss your hair and dirty your hands and walk bowlegged and wear blue goggles — and *still* you'll be the loveliest sight in the world. Come on, Frances, try it — see if I'm sincere.

And here it is in cold type: I love you and I love you and I love you.

Ogden

January 31, 1931

Darling Frances —

Imagine my pleasure on seeing the authority quoted by Doubleday Doran in the enclosed ad. The extract is from a review which will appear in to-morrow's Herald Tribune — I'll send it to you. But what fun to be a sign-post! Is there any more fame left?

You ask — and very prettily, too, darling — if I know yet what I am doing on the New Yorker. No, I don't, though I'm beginning to get a glimmer. Mostly I listen to Ross's woes. Also I try to get Dorothy Parker to write a piece for us every week. Also I try to see that all the depart-ment writers — fashion, sports, theater, racing, etc. — get their de-partments in on time. Also I handle the profiles. Also I read manuscripts. Also I talk to people who come in with bright ideas. Also, every Saturday afternoon I stay in the office till six or seven arranging the Talk of the Town (those anecdotes, gossipy pieces, etc., up in the front) for the printer. My big job I think will be in the process of time to harness some of the waste power around the office. My impression at the moment is that there are far too many people, doing far too little work. The specta-cle galls me, as at Doubleday's everybody does about two men's jobs. I don't know what the solution is. I may get so darned efficient in cutting down duplication of effort, etc., that I'll end up by eliminating my own job.*

S. & S. called up this morning to report a sale of over 4000 books this week! It's appalling — I reel with amazement. We look like a real best seller. The total to date is somewhere between 10,000 and 12,000.

Darling, thank you a million times for your cable. I'm so glad to have you in Paris, and I had lost you for ten days. I thought you were prob-ably stopping off somewhere, but I didn't know for sure.

The snapshots were in letter number 76, mailed on December 19th to Naples. Probably you have them by now. Also, I had a regular photograph mailed to you today. Not a shirt-sleever; rather a stern one. The shirt-sleeve is too arty — I don't dare show it till I can laugh at it with you.

> *Darling, I adore you.*
> Ogden

*He would — in three months. — Ed.

February 4, 1931

Darling, darling Frances —

In reply to your letter which came this morning: Yes, the Paris proposal holds good for Palma, and as you said yes to it, you had better consider yourself affianced. And here is a Palma proposal for Paris: Frances will you marry me? — And just to round it off, here's a Paris proposal for Paris: Frances darling, will you marry me? — Please answer these questions promptly and correctly. — Also you are kind enough to inquire whether I will marry you. I had thought that that was the idea from the beginning — at least, from November, 1928. Perhaps, though, I've never made myself clear about it. Yes darling, I will marry you at any place you want (except Atlantic City) at any time you want (not later than next June) and be quite cheerful about the whole thing. Oh Frances, beloved, you fill my heart so; I'm simply one great longing. Sixty days more! Such a lot of days. Use them well, darling.

The office was very fluttery today, with Ross darting and booming around like an infuriated bee. No casualties, however. In fact, I managed to write another verse. It's name is:

> "My Child Is Phlegmatic . . ."
> — Anxious Parent

I like it very much, and if, or I may even say, when, the New Yorker accepts it I shall send it to you. — Also I re-wrote the grim short story and it has almost been accepted, but I don't know definitely yet. Life is so suspenseful.

Darling, I loved your letter. Darling, I love you, and I want to be with you always — except once in a while when it would probably be better for you to go off somewhere. Darling, if you weren't going to marry me I'd be so appalled and sickened by the thought that there is not, and never has been, and never will be anyone so adorable in every way — but you *are* going to, and — well, Frances, I'm pleased.

> *Good night, darling.*
> *I love you. I love you.*
> Ogden

February 6, 1931

Darling Frances —

Something happened today that amused me quite a lot. — The super-sacred cow of the New Yorker office is E. B. White — the one who wrote Is Sex Necessary. He has the only quiet office in the place, and the messenger boys are commanded to stop whistling when they pass his door. If anybody says Good Morning to him he is apt to send a memorandum to Ross complaining that people are bothering him. — He does no editorial work — simply writes all day long. He is the one who writes all the Talk of the Town stuff. Also, of course, he writes other things. And he is the apple of both Ross's wildly rolling eyes. As a matter of fact he is a very nice shy young man, and the hocus-pocus that surrounds him is mostly Ross's doing. — Well, anyhow, I ventured into his little chapel today to ask him about something, and he looked at me and said, "I wrote a poem about you yesterday."

"Did you?" said I, slightly startled.

"Yes," said he. "Would you like to hear it?"

"Certainly," said I,

"If I were Ogden Nash I would marry a girl in black taffeta / And sit around the house all day and laffeta," said he.

Really, Frances. That really happened. I'm not inventing a word of it. I promise. Isn't it extraordinary? Because that's exactly what I'm going to do. What in the dickens do you suppose put black taffeta into his head? I've never mentioned it to a soul except you.

Oh, and I got an offer today — very odd. Hannan Shoes called on me and wanted me to write and sign for them a series of six verses to be used in advertisements. Asked me to name a price and said they'd consider it seriously, no matter how exorbitant. — But I'm afraid there's no price exorbitant enough to compensate me for the cheapness of such a proceeding, so I'll probably pass it up. Now if it were Bergdorf Good-man, and they would pay in clothes — what would you advise me to do then?

No reports on sales so far this week. I rather expect they'll be small, though, as the shops stocked up so heavily last week.

The New Yorker bought that grim short story today, so I'll have a proof of it soon to send to you. It won't run until May; I think you'll be home then, won't you?

Darling, you say two things in your letter that make the whole world seem marvellous. First, that you love me. Second that you are proud of me. — I want to tell you two things. First, I love you. Second, I am terri-bly proud of you. Darling, you will never know how I glory in your love-liness. I feel such pity for all the rich, forceful handsome men you don't love. I'm growing a frightful superiority complex. My pride in your beauty and your grace and your sweetness is really terrific. Pride? Dar-ling, it's turning into unbearable arrogance.

Frances, I adore you.
Ogden

P.S. What are you buying in Paris? I love you.

February 10, 1931

Darling Frances —

I got home this evening to find your first letter from Paris waiting for me. I love you.

So you like the book. Well, darling, it's all yours, so I'm glad. And thank you for defending its purity against Mlle. Motteau's Gallic insinua-tions. Perhaps you had better tell her that the artist is a *sale Boche* who was raised in perfidious Albion, and that the drawings were put into the book over my vehemently protesting body. You may also assure her that I am frightfully sérieux and very much comme il faut. *Am I sérieux!* She should have seen my face for the last four months. Sérieux is an under-statement. That explains my appearance in the snapshots; show her those, and also the photograph which you should have by now, and ask her if that is a frivolous face. A male Penelope, that's what I am, sitting at home spinning and unspinning words while my true love gads about in the Metro. A pretty undignified position for a prominent author — *Sérieux*! Faugh.

You ask me if I have puffed up a little. I'm not sure, but I think I have. It still makes me writhe to have people flatter me to my face and quote my verses to me, but all the same I thrive on it; and I do enjoy reading nice things about myself. As a result I've slightly revised upwards my idea of my own importance, but I keep it all strictly to myself, and show no outward arrogance. I think you'll find me tolerable; probably harder to browbeat and lead by the nose than when you left, but still much the best — in fact the only — man for you to marry. Yes, darling, my mind is definitely made up, and you might just as well begin to reconcile yourself to the idea of a life time of my company, starting this spring. Reconcile yourself to it? Hell, look forward to it! I'm really delightful now; I hear it on all sides. "My dear, he's as witty as his books; and so handsome!" You'd better come on home.

Just for the information of the little Czech girl, I am not only not related to the Nash cars, but I am also not related to Golden Rule Nash, the Minneapolis manufacturer who gave his business to his employees, or to Mrs. Jean Nash, the best-dressed woman in Europe.

So you've turned down le Harvard? Very good. But why do you describe him to me as red-headed and pink-eyed and dressed in a blue suit and white sneakers, and then tell Isabel that he's an attractive young man on the Riviera? You know — not jealousy, just curiosity. Not jealousy at all. At all. He's the one I wrote the verse about people who go abroad about. I hope an octopus gets him in the Mediterranean.

And you think an engagement ring is all right in its proper place but not as a birthday present, do you? Hoity-toity, miss! And who's to be the judge of what's the proper place? The proper place is your finger, and the proper time was last September; once having let that pass you are a lucky girl to be offered it again on April 12th. You don't consider an engagement ring a suitable birthday present for you just returning from six months in Europe! My stars! Did *I* send you away for six months? Did *I* say I wouldn't give you the ring unless you went off and gave me a chance to think things over? Did I — well, I'm speechless. And I suppose I'd better start thinking about what to give you for your birthday. But I warn you that the ring comes first. Not even one little useless silver woman do you get until the ring is properly on your left hand. If I'm to give you a present it's got to be a real present — one that no girl could accept from a casual admirer. A ten or fifteen dollar present — a jewel or something equally resplendent — the sort of thing that can only follow an official betrothal. So think that over. Darling, when will you be ready for the ring? It's so lonely-looking. And gosh, I want to be announced. I want to be married more than I want to be announced, but can't both be managed? I've been in such an odd, uncomfortable position for a year and a half now. Lord, it's been a long time. Do hurry up and give me some standing in the world.

Dick Simon called up to say that last week, when we expected to sell only 500 books, we sold 1800; and 5000 more have gone to press. What a time we're having! I shall celebrate by beginning work on a poignant short story — one that I weep even to contemplate.

Darling Frances, darling Frances, beloved and beautiful and absent Frances, I adore you.

Ogden

February 13, 1931

Darling Frances —

Here is the new verse for you. Do you like it? It's very true. That's the great thing about Nash's verse. It's so true — so sane. Beneath his mad laughter, his careless nonsense, there lies a vein of wisdom. The work of this new figure in American letters — The Deserted Poet, as he calls himself — marks a turning point in our civilization. It is devoutly to be hoped that Mr. Nash will marry and settle down.

This particular verse was really written in reply to a letter from Henry Humphrey thanking me for a copy of the book and saying that he and his wife had enjoyed it but that unfortunately his child was too phlegmatic to pay any attention to it.

Also I'm sending you an advertisement from Publisher's Weekly showing the enthusiasm of Pittsburgh, Houston, Chicago, Hollywood, Northampton, Minneapolis, Cincinnati, Los Angeles and Buffalo — such nice cities, all of them.

I didn't get away from the office till 8 o'clock this evening. I had to wait for Dorothy Parker's stuff to come in, and waiting for Dorothy Parker's stuff to come in is a full-time job. And the trouble is that when it finally does arrive it's so good that you forget how mad you were while you were waiting. It's too bad she's so absolutely irresponsible; she'll never do anything until the last minute — until after the last minute, in fact. She's worn out about eight people at the New Yorker so far, and bets are now being made on how long *my* nerves will stand up under the strain. Little do they know the training I've had.

An agent came to see me this afternoon who seems to think she can get me a movie contract. I told her to go ahead; no one can anger me by offering me money. I also got a letter from College Humour asking me to do a monthly page. I'm to talk to them about it next week. — Both these things are of course very nebulous, and I have no idea of whether or not they will work out. Still, it's all good fun.

The next ten days will be busy ones for me, as Raymond Holden, who has been breaking me in, is leaving on a vacation and I am left to my own devices and his job as well as mine. Well, the experience will either kill or cure me. There's a possibility I may be able to get to Baltimore again for Washington's Birthday. You remember Washington don't you? He was the American Jeanne d'Arc. Darling, can you still speak English?

I adore you, Frances.
Ogden

February 16, 1931

Darling Frances —

Not a very exciting day; mostly routine, with a large part of it spent on the telephone trying to find Dorothy Parker, who hides in queer places hoping that no one who wants to make her work can reach her. It's a man-killing job to force her into the theater, and another to make her read a book — and as she is reviewing books and the theater it's fairly important to see that she does one or the other — perhaps both.

I had an amusing interview with a man from the advertising agency which is promoting the Empire State Building. He said how nice it would be if I would write a long poem about the building, one that they would use in their advertising. I said I'd already rejected one advertising offer. He said this was different — very dignified, very high class. I said I thought I didn't want to do it, but if I changed my mind, how much would I get? "Oh," said he in astonishment, "would you want to be paid?" — That concluded the interview.

Today was my first of struggling single-handed with my half of the magazine. All right so far, but who knows what the morrow will bring? I'm not one to count on anything in the future — except you. — Can I count on you sufficiently to buy that elaborate birthday present before you get back, or must it wait further decisions? You'd better answer that question quickly, and as it should be answered; the longer I have to look around in, the fancier I'll do.

Well — forty more days will see you on shipboard. I don't know yet what ship, but bless the anonymous old thing anyhow. I still miss you darling, no matter how many times you may tell me not to.

Furthermore, I adore you.
Ogden

February 17, 1931

Darling Frances —

In spite of not having heard from you for a week I am sending you herewith a juicy lot of enclosures. As for my not having heard from you, that is not your fault, but the steamship companies'. There hasn't been a boat in for seven days. The France arrives tonight, however — and if *she* hasn't something for me, you shall see a tantrum that *is* a tantrum. Incidentally no boats coming means no boats going, so I expect my letters to you have been held up. But you take those things so calmly; it's very annoying. I suppose because you can be so sure of me. Well, I'm sure of you, too, and how do you like that?

About the enclosures. First there's a little batch of extracts from reviews, in which you will find that you are engaged — oh, very unofficially and distantly — my fiancée once removed, sort of — , but still engaged, to a supreme wagster who is — faint praise — funnier than Will Rogers, if not so rich.

Then there's the copy of a dispatch in the London Evening Standard. My favorite paragraph in it is the one saying "The New Yorker Magazine, which serves the same purpose in New York that a college magazine does among the undergraduates . . ." — Wait till Ross sees that.

Finally, there are the proofs of the rather gruesome story I told you I had written. It's based on fact to this extent — many of the racketeers are taking houses in the suburbs where they live quietly and respectably between operations.

So if I haven't much news, at least I've sent you something to read.

Darling, I love you.
Ogden

February 18, 1931

Darling, darling Frances —

I think we're even. No, you're far, far ahead. You say you can't find words to tell me how much you like the book. Well, I say that I can't find words to tell you how I adore you. And at the moment I'm the champion word-finder of America, too. So there we are. I feel much worse than you do.

Darling, what a marvellous morning you gave me! Three letters — glorious letters. I'm really excited about your clothes. How many weeks will it take you to show them all to me? Do start slowly, and with awfully simple things; let me get used to seeing you again before you knock my eye out altogether. Oh Frances, Frances. Frances, I'm wickedly impatient. How impatient? Ask our friend the dove.

Thinking about your clothes finally goaded me into getting some new ones for myself. Not exactly getting; just ordering. I picked material today for three suits — they're to be made in England, and I won't have them for six weeks, but they'll get here just before you do, and I hope to look very swell indeed. I've been going in rags and tatters for years, and I'm sick of it. From now on dapper is the word. Having written a book, I refuse to look sloppy and literary any longer. I'd throw my glasses away if I thought I could live two minutes in the street without them. Never mind, darling, I won't wear them around the house if you'll lead me to things.

To-day's Parker episode. Her book page was due at twelve. I called her up at eleven to ask her how it was coming. "Oh," she said very sweetly, "I've got a big surprise for you. I've decided not to do it." So, what fun I had in getting a substitute page. A cooing serpent, that's what she is.

I've done quite a lot of work last night and tonight. I think I told you that College Humor wants me to do a page every month. I've finished about half a sample page, and it looks all right so far. If it works out it will mean a bit extra that will come in handy if I'm to be tied to an extravagant girl. — Darling, do keep on being lavish about clothes — I'd much rather look at you than eat. I also did a short piece for the New Yorker; *I* think it's very funny — well, *pretty* funny — but what the New Yorker thinks remains to be seen. And tonight I did some verses. —*That's* the mood I'm in these days, and you've done it, darling. I do love you, I do love you, I do love you.

Dan came to dinner tonight. He's getting fat. Everybody's getting fat. — Nelson Doubleday's wife is going to Reno; as soon as she gets the divorce she is going to marry again, a man whose wife has also just gone to Reno. It's a dreadful shame, and Nelson is badly broken up. I am deeply sorry for him.

My own happiness today was completed by a letter from your mother, which I shall answer tomorrow, as it's nearly one o'clock now. But the letter goes under my pillow tonight.

Darling, darling, I adore you.
Ogden

February 19, 1931

Darling Frances —

It's been a day of hustle bustle, helter skelter, pell mell, dither and ado, full of all sorts of slurrying and scurrying. Millions of things going wrong, including Dorothy Parker — though I imagine it's some years since she first did. No irremediable catastrophes; just a lot of things getting balled up and having to be fixed. Lots of bother but, when it's all safely over, lots of fun.

Oh also, my most embarrassing telephone conversation occurred this afternoon. A feminine voice — well here's the actual dialog, word for word.

Me: Hello.
Feminine Voice: Is this Mr. Nash?
Me: Yes
F.V.: This is Louise on 56th Street.
Me: Who?
F.V.: Louise; Louise on 56th Street.
Me (*completely bewildered*): What?
F.V.: I've got a new brassiere I think you ought to see.
Me (*weakly*): What did you say?
F.V.: I say I've got a new brassiere and I think you ought to come around and see it.
Me: I'm afraid I don't understand.
F.V.: Isn't this Mr. Nash, the editor of the New Yorker?
Me: One of the editors, yes.
F.V.: Well, this is Louise, the Corsetiere on 56th Street, and I'm selling a lovely new kind of brassiere and I wish somebody from the New Yorker would

come and see it, because I think it deserves a write-up in your shopping columns.

Me (*with a whoop of relief*): I see, I see, I see! Thank you for the invitation. I'll tell Miss Long of our Feminine Fashions Department and she'll stop in. Good-bye.

Everybody seems to like the verses I wrote last night, so I think they'll be bought. Also, I get very encouraging reports on the prose piece, which is in the form of a 3-minute play, so I think *that* will be bought, too. What a splendid world we live in. — The College Humour situation hasn't jelled yet, but is on the way.

Darling, of the three letters I got yesterday the one I liked best — almost — was the one with no news at all in it; because you'd written it just for the sake of writing it. Do that often, and become even more beloved. — So you are translating some of the verses for Mlle. Motteau? Which ones? I wish you'd write them out and send them to me if you get time; there might be a New Yorker piece in them. We recently printed Jabberwock in French, with huge success.

I'm sorry to find you back at your old trick. What do you mean by being ashamed of yourself for not being enthusiastic about the book? Silly and adorable darling, you're much more responsible for the whole thing than I am; if I had't had you to write it for and read it to, there would have been nothing.

Also I'm bothered to hear that you think I'm never going to have to have my hand held or be comforted. If you aren't prepared to see me through rejections, Parker-trouble, Ross-itis, self-recrimination and delusions of misery, all of which I am occasionally subject to — all I can say is Huh!

One more complaint and I'm through. You're not having a photograph taken because, you say, I'll see enough of your face. Oh I will, will I? Do you think that even by seeing it through all Time (plus the blessed five minutes) I'll ever catch up on this six months? Think again, darling. Don't bother with the photograph, but just reflect on the absurdity of your own remark about your own face.

Darling darling <u>darling</u> Frances,
I adore you.
Ogden

February 24, 1931

Darling, darling, darling:

This time I *am* speechless, but I'm determined to babble on anyway,
whether I make sense or not. Your cable, knocking two weeks off my
sentence, arrived this morning. Lord, Frances, how marvellous! You'll be
sailing in eighteen days, and home in less than four weeks! That's the
part that gets me. Even when the term had shrunk to seven weeks and
then to six I couldn't actually realize that it was ending; your coming remained somewhere outside of time and space, where it has been since
October; something to be very dimly dreamed of, but too nebulous for
the mind to grasp. But now — it's the twenty-fourth, and the next
twenty-fourth will find you here. No more twenty-fourths without you!
And after tomorrow, no more twenty-fifths, and so on. Only three more
issues of the magazine to be made up before you land. Only — darling,
do forgive my ranting; you're seeing a genuine exhibition of ecstasy. I've
just sent you a rather incoherent cable, but I think that it conveys my
feelings. Darling Frances, I do love you.

Also, I got a letter from you this evening, the kind I like, without any
news but with a nice sentiment in it, and I'm expecting some more to-
morrow morning, so what with one thing and another I'm ultra-uppity.
Good old Minnetonka! Good old Atlantic Ocean! Good old Ambrose
Lightship! Good old Sandy Hook! Good old Quarantine! Good old
Frances!

So you adore Paris, do you? Even that fails to disturb me tonight, and
I don't know whether I'll do a verse about it or not.

A quiet day at the office, as it always is at the beginning of the
week. — I dropped in on Dick and Max for a while. Very satisfactory
news of the book. Sales three weeks ago, 1800; two weeks ago, 1100;
last week 1600; total to date, 15,300. Another edition of 5000 went to
press today. The book is on every list of six best-sellers, all over the
country, its position varying from second to sixth.

I got a frantic telegram from College Humor demanding a page of fun
immediately, so I hastily smoothed out a rough idea and sent it on. I
bought a copy of their darned magazine the other day, and got so de-
pressed while reading it through that I had quite given up the idea of
writing for it. Horrible stuff, cheap and collegiate in the worst sense. All
gin and petting. And I found myself trying to write down to them. However, a dollar is a dollar, and here I am, Ogden on the make, so the scru-
ples went overboard.

That about finishes what I've got to say. — Darling, when, where and why did you make this glorious decision? Tell me all. I love you, Frances, and I love you, Frances, and I love you Frances — oh darling, I adore you!

Ogden

February 25, 1931

Darling Frances —

Last night I was much too happy to sleep thoroughly, and, instead, tossed about in a delightful sort of delirium, counting days, hours and minutes. This morning I upped early, and found two more letters waiting for me. Such letters, darling! Bless you for the lipstick one, and do it again. You're so clever, so amiable, so everything! I think I should love you more; I wonder if it could be done? But I know for certain that if it can, I'm the one to do it. All right?

And how adorable of you to say yes, yes, yes you will marry me. There's a firmness in that phraseology that makes a strong appeal to me.

I'm glad you like the photograph in spite of the genre artistique but wait till you see the shirt-sleeve one. — By the way, your new sailing date means that you will get here before my new clothes do. Can you bear me in tatters for a week or so? I'm sure The London creations will be well worth waiting for. — After all, I'll have waited six months to see your Paris ones. — I am shocked and humiliated to find that I have been mis-spelling the name of la famille Mottheau, but I place the responsibility on the shoulders of your father, from whom I obtained the offending ver-sion. My profound apologies to Madame et Mlle. Mottheau.

Darling, things *are* perfect, aren't they? Don't *you* be superstitious, be-cause *I* am; I spend hours each day knocking on wood. Leave all that to me; I'm used to it. All *you* have to do is come on home and marry me; it's easy.

Yes, certainly I answered the Saranac letter, and very nicely, too. I've answered all my letters except the green one from the lady who wanted me to bring her new glamor and new romance, and the anonymous ones. I've had a few of those, some of them altogether unprintable. There are strange people in the world.

Dear Miss Leonard —

You liked "To Be Hanged," did you? Good for you. It's a Crime Club book over here. Malcolm wanted to reject it and I had a big fight over it. That time I was right, as it's done very well.

But have I told you about my most notorious rejection? Last Fall I turned down the memoirs of Grand Duchess Marie against the advice of George Doran. Viking published it in January, and it's outselling Hard Lines. Pretty funny.

The New Yorker today bought the verses I wrote two or three nights ago; Ross says they're particularly good and is howling for more. As a matter of fact they're not very wonderful; all right, but nothing special. But I didn't argue with him. — And that brings my report up to date.

Seventeen days till you sail. Now you're just two hair-cuts away — only one, if I time it right.

Darling, darling, darling,
I love you
Ogden

February 27, 1931

Darling Frances —

Today being again rather slack in the office, I amused myself by doing another verse or two. Here's one of them, based partly on the inability of the oyster to make up it's mind whether it's a lady or a gentleman:

> The oyster's a confusing suitor,
> It's masc., and fem., and sometimes neuter;
> But whether husband, pal or wife
> It leads a peaceful sort of life.
> I'd like to be an oyster, say
> In August, June, July or May.

Then I did one called The Anti-Saloon Leaguer:

> The Anti's tone is pugilistic;
> He floors you with a quick statistic;
> He juggles graphs and charts and jiggers;

Ignores the facts and quotes and figgers.
I do not envy your position
If you oppose his holy mission.

And then, believing as I do that all propagandists and crusaders are equally reprehensible, regardless of which side they are on, I wrote exactly the same thing over again and called it The Anti-Prohibitionist. — The idea being to run one right under the other. I'm quite pleased with it, but I don't know how Ross will like it. — It's nice to think that by the time this last batch appears in the magazine you'll be here to read it, and your cries of joy, amazement and mirth will travel direct from your lips (thank you *again* for the brief illustrated letter, darling) to my ear, instead of through the medium of pen, paper and the Cunard Line.

There! That's about all for this evening. I'm now going to return to a short story I'm struggling on — the one with so much irony and pathos in it. I don't expect ever to finish it, but I enjoy suffering — over stories, that is.

Darling Frances, I love you.
Ogden

P.S. Darling, don't stop writing just because you're coming home. Keep it up to the last minute. — I wish you'd tell me more about your clothes. I'm really getting ridiculously excited. No, not ridiculously. Properly. I'll see you and them in a little over three weeks now — but meanwhile I'd like to hear everything. I love you, darling, I love you.

Ogden

———

A very significant piece of news that Daddy hadn't dispatched to Europe was that his job at *The New Yorker* was not working out. In an interview with Roy Newquist which appeared in Newquist's book *Conversations* (Rand McNally, 1967), he said, ". . . Harold Ross hired me under two misapprehensions: first, that he wanted a managing editor, and second, that I would be a good one. At that time the job of managing editor of that magazine was like being caught briefly in a revolving door. In my case the revolution of the door took ninety days which was, I believe, the usual period of tenure at the time."

Luckily, an earlier offer made in December 1929 by John Farrar to join Farrar & Rinehart still stood, so Daddy went to work there as an associate editor.

The letters after my mother's return were few and short, for the engaged couple were together a great deal in the ten weeks or so before their wedding. Grandfather Nash's death on April 27 changed some of the wedding plans, for at that time the old rules of mourning were quite strictly observed. For instance, in the letter Daddy wrote his cousin Frank Nash after Grandfather's death he said, "I am to be married in Baltimore on the 6th of June — Father had set his heart on it, and told me only a few days before he died that if anything happened to him we were not to delay the wedding. The last words he wrote were a list of names of his friends who were to be invited. There is a little side door to the church and a pew whose occupant cannot be seen by the congregation, so Mother is coming."

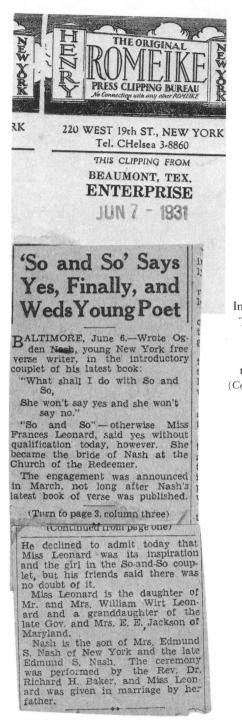

THIS CLIPPING FROM

BEAUMONT, TEX.

ENTERPRISE

JUN 7 - 1931

'So and So' Says Yes, Finally, and Weds Young Poet

BALTIMORE, June 6.—Wrote Ogden Nash, young New York free verse writer, in the introductory couplet of his latest book:

"What shall I do with So and So,

She won't say yes and she won't say no."

"So and So"—otherwise Miss Frances Leonard, said yes without qualification today, however. She became the bride of Nash at the Church of the Redeemer.

The engagement was announced in March, not long after Nash's latest book of verse was published.

(Turn to page 3, column three)

(Continued from page one)

He declined to admit today that Miss Leonard was its inspiration and the girl in the So-and-So couplet, but his friends said there was no doubt of it.

Miss Leonard is the daughter of Mr. and Mrs. William Wirt Leonard and a granddaughter of the late Gov. and Mrs. E. E. Jackson of Maryland.

Nash is the son of Mrs. Edmund S. Nash of New York and the late Edmund S. Nash. The ceremony was performed by the Rev. Dr. Richard H. Baker, and Miss Leonard was given in marriage by her father.

In June 1931, even Beaumont, Texas, took note of Daddy's East Coast—establishment marriage. *Hard Lines* had made him a national figure. (*Courtesy of* Beaumont Enterprise)

Frances Leonard Nash, June 6, 1931.

The Family Years

OVERLEAF:
"*A bit of talcum*
Is always walcum."
Father and daughter, fall 1932.

DADDY BEGAN his married life as he was to continue it — by including his new wife's parents in his happiness. The closeness between my grandparents and their son-in-law was something that I now know was unusual, but when I was a child it seemed the most natural thing in the world. The strong concept of "family" was still at work to sustain another generation of children.

My Leonard grandparents were physically a part of our household at many times during my early life. I saddled them with the remarkable titles of "Minnie" and "Boppy" — a matter of wonderment to my father, to whom the origin of words was a constant fascination. He tracked "Minnie" down to his satisfaction (apparently a Scottish diminutive for mother or grandmother) but "Boppy" forever eluded him. It simply remained a source of frustration, much like the rhyme for "orange," which he futilely pursued over the years.

Shortly after returning to New York from their honeymoon in Canada, Mother accompanied Minnie to summer quarters at Hyannis. The custom of families with adequate means taking "cottages" for the summer was widespread then. The wives and children would be spared the heat of the city for the season, while the men would join them for weekends and their usual two-week vacations. All through my childhood, life followed this pattern for the most part. It only differed from my friends' summers in that I had my father full-time instead of just on weekends, for by the time that I was two, Daddy was self-employed: a free-lance writer who worked at home.

Chateau Frontenac
Quebec, Canada
Saturday
June 20, 1931

Dear Mrs. Leonard:

Ever since I got here I have wanted to write you — I have so many things to say, so many things to thank you for. But time has slipped by. This is not the particular letter I wanted to write; it is only to say that I shall feel terribly disappointed if you don't stay with us in New York. Of course you know that Frances wants you; so do I, deeply; your room is ready for you; and your being right there will mean evenings full of talk — and there's so much to talk about — and no bother about getting back to the hotel.

You see, Mother is not coming back to the apartment at all, but going directly to Long Island with Eleanor when she leaves Gwen. And it's my apartment. And Sandra, our Finnish maid, has had nothing to do for six weeks and I'm afraid she'll be getting stale. And just at first, with the novelty of the honeymoon worn off and New York pretty hot and unattractive and lonesome I'd hate to have Frances too much by herself.

So please, please, do come.

Affectionately,
Ogden

Tuesday evening
July 7, 1931

Darling —

Five o'clock at the office, and not very cool, but a good day's work lies behind me. I played the most marvellous game of publishing I have ever played. I tackled an author so hard I fell down and hurt my knee on a contract. Gosh! I cried. Not much; just enough. Then I went back in and played the best publishing I have ever played. I beat everybody, 1–0. As a matter of fact nothing very much happened; mostly fooling with wrappers, etc. I had lunch with Wolcott Gibbs, and gave him a short verse and a longer one for the New Yorker. I enclose last night's batch. Two are new — the others are salvaged from the dreadful page in College Humor.

The Newport trip sounds amusing, don't you think so?

Darling, I adore you.
Ogden

P.S. I enclose the envelope of an announcement returned by the Dead Letter Office. I love you.

[ENCLOSURE]

Reflection on Nature's Being Sometimes Inscrutable but Always Wise

Alcohol is an intoxicant
So gin can often do what Moxie can't.

Reflection on the Depression — What's a Depression?

It's comforting to be assured by Washington that your dollar will buy
    much more
Than ever before,
But unfortunate that trying to make this year's 99 cents do the work of
    last year's dollar
Is like trying to get a 16 neck into a 15 collar.

Reflection on the Advantages of Citizenship

1/5
Works on half shift;
4/5
Live on ifs.

July 29, 1931

My adorable and beloved Frances —

Seven miles is not very far ordinarily, nor seven hours very long, but
when they lie between us they seem multiplied by infinity. My heart is
swollen with longing for you, and my mind is filled with your fragile and
iridescent image. There is a silver echo of your voice in my ears, and my
body tingles at the remembered flame of yours.

For some reason, God has seen fit to grant me the woman of all
women, the always hitherto intangible, unattainable idea of every poet's
dream and every man's desire. You are eternal youth and truth, tender-
ness and passion, and bright beauty that at once pierces and eases the
heart. You are the vision that for a million years has drawn man up from
the beast; and suddenly the vision is incarnate, and in my arms.

You are my light and air, my food and drink, my very inmost life.

I worship and adore you
through all the eternities.
Ogden

Tuesday
August 4, 1931

Darling —

I love you. And it's perfectly ridiculous how pleased I was to hear from your mother last night that you had grippe. I'd been so worried about you, it was a relief finally to know something definite. I'm glad you're in bed, and I'm glad you're being read to, and I hope that the grippe will explain everything, and it's much, much cooler today, and all in all I feel a great deal better.

I arrived at Eleanor's house last night and was immediately jumped on from behind a bush by Alec; he had no clothes on except a pair of drawers, his face was blackened, and he was brandishing a spear. I took a chance and guessed that he was a cannibal; he was quite disgusted with me, however, for not knowing at once that he was a head-hunter. One of little Eleanor's beaux has gone away, but the other keeps things going by sending her notes via Alec. She ran head-on into a tree the other day and as a result looks a trifle frayed, but she still has enough spirit to interrupt or contradict an uncle or so. The cat has recovered from pneumonia and the dog from paternity.

Dick and Max seem to be more confident than I am that the book will be finished on time.* They're beginning to advertise it already — I enclose their page from the last Publishers Weekly. Last evening I did no work at all — just talked to Mother till bed time. Oh well. Procrastination is an old habit of mine; it's fun; and, so far at least, I've always managed to get things done on time. I hope I haven't forgotten how.

I'm now just about to dip into a soda, procured for me from a neighboring Schraffts by my incomparable secretary — really the only thing she does well. John and Stanley get them too and we all sit around and sip and talk about the wonderful things we're going to do. And it's cool, cool, *cool* today; and I know, because I have lived, have lived, have lived, in the heat, heat, heat.

Darling, darling, I adore you and you are in my heart always and it seems much too long till Friday. I love you.

Ogden

*The book was *Free Wheeling,* which would be published in October. — Ed.

Monday
August 10, 1931

Darling, adorable darling,

Monday's half gone — I've already got my teeth into Tuesday, Wednesday and Thursday — then Friday I see you again — and have you for ten days. *Darling,* I like to think of that. Perhaps I'm a pig to ask you to submit to New York for those five days — I don't know. What do you think? We might go out to the country or something. — I had a fine trip down — no ladies in my berth — and slept solidly all the way. Margaret Sanger occupied the office for an hour this morning; I could only look at her and think "Why couldn't you have come in June?" But she's very nice, and quite attractive — not at all the crusading type. I bought myself two more pairs of white flannels at lunch time; also a dark brown gabardine coat which I hope you will like. My train, the Knickerbocker, gets to Providence at 4:57 daylight on Friday. Bathing suit, please.

Darling, I shall call you up tonight. I do hope you have good news. I hate to have you worried this way. But whatever happens, I adore you — oh, much more than ever.

Ogden

The "grippe" turned out to be me. The year 1932 was a year of changes for the young Nashes: a new baby, a new apartment, and a growing worry over money. Despite the success of Daddy's two books, supporting a wife and child in New York City at the height of the Depression was not easy. The salary he earned at Farrar & Rinehart was being cut again and again as the firm struggled to keep its head above water.

I was born on March 26, and in June when the summer heat moved in Mother took me to Baltimore and the comfortable existence at 4300 Rugby Road. Minnie and Boppy delighted in housing their first grandchild for the summer and Mother felt sure that I would be in the best of hands. My grandparents' household was well-staffed and ran like clockwork, for my grandmother was a truly gifted housewife. Although aided by "help," she had been well schooled in all the arts of homemaking, as were most girls of her generation. She could cook and "put up" as well as the cook, garden as well as the gardener, sew and knit as well as a seamstress, and launder and press fine linens as well as the laundress. Though a baby nurse was supplied for me, I am sure that Minnie oversaw my every waking hour when Mother was in New York, and that she was far more intuitive than the nurse could have been about my needs and care. Life at Rugby Road had a magical quality about it that remains in my heart a half century later. While I surely cannot recollect that first summer of my life, the fact of it must explain why I always think of the great stone house in Guilford when I hear the word "home."

Tuesday morning
August 9, 1932

Adorable darling —

I gave you most of the news over the telephone last night, but I want to talk to you this morning because I love you and I miss you and my heart and my mind are very full of you and I have to do something about it.

Isn't that pleasant about the royalties? Think of Hard Lines earning $200 in the last six months — a year and a half after publication. That doesn't happen often. And $425 from Free Wheeling is pleasant, too. I'm almost persuaded to write another book.

By the way, don't say anything to anyone about Eleanor's rent going down $400 — apparently its secret and confidential etc. and I'm not supposed to know about it. But I'm glad I do. Which reminds me to call Mr. Port.

Ann is going to be with David in Blue Ridge till Sunday, so I've asked Ted in to stay with me — I'll set him in a corner with Mr. Clunk so I'll be able to get on with my work. Three manuscripts last night kept me going till twelve, so I wrote not. But I'm awfully hopeful. Are you tired of my being hopeful? I was amused to see that yesterday every stock in Wall Street went way up except Radio which sank gracefully.

The Gershwin book has just arrived from Dick — I'll bring it down on Friday — that's quicker, I think than trusting it to the Post Office.

Yesterday we boiled, today we simmer. The city is hazy and people are trickling around like steam-drops on the lid of a tea kettle. But we had luncheon with Macy's buyer yesterday and she said business is better there.

Built in 1927 by my grandparents,
4300 Rugby Road would be
home for the Nashes during most
of my childhood.

I saw Aubrey's baby yesterday afternoon and got very hungry for ours. And darling darling *darling* for you. I adore you.

Ogden

More changes were coming within the Nash household. Daddy's salary at Farrar & Rinehart would recede to $25.00 a week by the next spring — which is what he had been making with Barron and Collier before he went to Doubleday's. This became a truly desperate situation, for another baby was due in September.

However, on the plus side, *Happy Days,* Daddy's third book in as many years, was also due out in the fall and, as one letter mentions, he was offered a contract with the *Saturday Evening Post* (for twenty-six verses a year at $100 each). This contract was a turning point in my parents' life together. After much careful thought, they came to the conclusion that with the money Daddy was capable of earning from free-lancing and from his books that they would be better off financially if he could devote his time to his own work. So they decided to bid farewell to expensive New York and to look for a house to rent in Baltimore, where Daddy could pursue his writing with far less overhead.

Mother and I again spent the summer at Rugby Road and Daddy wound up things in New York, commuting for the first part of the summer but then coming south for good. It was fearfully hot that summer, and Mother had acquired an eye infection that, together with the heat and her pregnancy, made her completely miserable. Her greatest pleasure, reading, was denied her, so Daddy read to her. I'm sure that Daddy remembered the time so long ago when he, too, had been unable to use his eyes. He knew how it felt — and he knew how to help.

The summer drew on, Mother's eyes improved, they found the perfect house, and on September 30, my sister was born. Later years would find the Baltimore baby a confirmed New Yorker, while the New York child would be wedded to Baltimore — one of life's little ironies.

Our names are family names. I was named after my father's aunt, Linell Chenault Rogers, a choice for which I am eternally grateful since, while in one poem my father called me "my daughter Jill," which I wouldn't have minded, the name Lalage (Kipling's "When I left Rome for Lalage's sake") was also under serious consideration and might have been my fate. My sister was named for Isabel Jackson, Mother's first cousin

And then there were two — Mother with
me and Isabel.

and dearest friend, who, at twenty-four, had tragically died of meningitis the year my sister was born. Her death came as a tremendous blow to both my parents and all thoughts of the possibility of "Jennifer" for my new sister were discarded. People often assumed that because "Linell" and "Isabel" rhymed — sort of — our poet father had chosen our names specifically for this reason. I must say it almost drove us crazy and I'm sure it did him too; not to say that he didn't occasionally put the coincidence to good use in his work (e.g., "The Rainy Day").

So the end of 1933 found our family complete, settled in Baltimore in a house with a bay window on Underwood Road and with a new way of life for the breadwinner.

Nineteen thirty-four brought a consolidation of our new life but no letters, for my parents were never apart. They enjoyed the company of family and friends in Baltimore. Granny Nash who had gone to live with Aunt Gwen after Grandfather's death saw us often, as Daddy would drive us out to the country for weekend visits.

Beryl Summers, the RN who spent so much time with her, also often oversaw our care as children, and is still a dear friend. And Delia Ratigan, a wonderful Irish nurse, came to our family the day my sister was born. Delia was to remain with us long after her place as "nurse" was obsolete.

My other grandmother, Minnie, was a warm and abiding presence in our lives. She sang to us, she played games with us, she read to us, she rubbed our backs when we were sick and told us wonderful stories.

Nineteen thirty-four also brought our first summer at Little Boar's Head, the tiny enclave on the New Hampshire coast that would turn out to be the constant thread throughout our lives as a family. The Baltimoreans who summered there, as well as vacationers from other cities, became my parents' lifelong friends; their children would be the same for Isabel and me.

It's hard to describe the feeling of that summer colony before World War II. A different time — a different world — it shimmers in the mind like a mirage. Memory records special things — the Fourth of July parades led by a much-respected elderly gentleman who would be followed by all the children, each one — even the toddlers — carrying small American flags. The home-based fireworks that evening were another golden memory. They were always preceded by a picnic and then, as darkness began to fall and the fireflies began to glimmer, we children were allowed to light sparklers from the sticks of punk that had been lit earlier and lay smoldering in an enclosure of stones on the lawn. We would run,

The Nash girls in 1934.
Oh, for those bygone days of
tricycles and wicker
perambulators . . .

*"I love you, Mummy,
says Linell."*

"Love Mummy too, says Isabel."

whirling them over our heads or trailing them behind us with their trains of little shooting stars, and when their life gave out we would collapse on the grass and watch as Boppy and my father would set off rockets and catherine wheels, or hurl "torpedoes" at the sea wall.

Nineteen thirty-five was a year filled with both promise and pitfalls. Daddy's fourth book, *The Primrose Path,* was coming out, and his free-lance work saw 157 pieces sold. By now both Isabel and I were walking and talking, and Daddy began writing for us as well as about us. But rough weather was building up fast. The summer at Little Boar's Head, while filled with friends and fun, brought a source of contention into the open that had been growing below the surface of things for some time. My father was drinking too much. Whether or not he was over the edge is arguable. He was turning out reams of work; he was not shirking his responsibilities. But he was definitely pushing the term "social drinker" to the limit.

Mother had grown up with the specter of alcoholism in the form of an uncle who had caused the family much grief. She also knew the effect alcohol was having on Daddy's brothers and so was terrified by what she was seeing in him. While she may not have felt that my father had become a full-fledged alcoholic, she couldn't let the growing danger continue without taking a stand against it. So she issued an ultimatum. She would go on a six-week trip with Minnie to England and France (October 19 through December 4). She hoped he would use that time to get his drinking in hand — she wouldn't be there to nag or scold or exacerbate the situation in any way. His drinking and its control were his responsibility and had to be dealt with by him; by the time she returned she expected him to have resolved the issue, for the continuation of their life together hung in the balance.

It's interesting to note that drinking is only mentioned once in his letters to her at that time. That was in response to an angry letter from Mother, which in turn had been prompted by a letter to her from "a friend." Daddy concentrated mainly on his old formula of wooing her — recounting funny anecdotes and then overwhelming her with love. But this time he could include the children in his witchcraft.

When Mother came home, she found her strategy had worked. While Daddy had by no means turned teetotaler, her fears of alcoholism were laid to rest, and life was sunny again. Today what she did would have been termed "confrontation" or "intervention" in terms of a treatment program for a problem drinker. She faced the danger at a time when my

father could still weigh the importance of the extra drink against its consequences — a world without Frances.

The Disappearance

I

Have you seen Linell?
She was three years old;
Her eyes were gray
And her hair was gold.
She had three dolls,
They were all named Maggie;
She wore pajamas
And the knees were baggy.
She wore a dress,
It was sprinkled with flowers;
She left her blocks;
I can see the towers,
She wore a hat
With an Indian feather,
And galoshes, in case
Of nasty weather;
And when she was sick
She went to bed,
And when she was better
She got up instead.
Oh, where she is hiding,
I can't tell.
Has anybody *possibly*
Seen Linell?

II

Has anybody seen
My absent child?
She seldom fussed,
And she often smiled.
She threw a penny
To the organ grinder;
Wherever she is,

I want to find her.
I looked in the corner
I looked on the stair;
I couldn't catch a glimpse of her
Anywhere.
Is she in the cupboard?
Or a bureau drawer?
I tried and I spied,
But I never saw her.
She had a bike
With a jingly bell
Has anybody *possibly*
Seen Linell?
Did she tell the postman
She was his?
Why, who's that coming?
Here she is!

The World for Frances
June 5th, 1935

Here is the moon, my darling love,
You are silver-cold as she is,
And here the sun in a burning cloud,
For you are fire as he is.

Here are stars for your fingertips,
As the stars remote and gold,
O queenly proud and snowy chaste,
O flaming sweet to hold!

Yours the scent of the flowering night,
Mystic dark and fragrant,
Yours the touch of the little winds,
Tender and shy and vagrant.

Here is the flower upon the stalk,
Your proud and lovely head,
And here the swift and delicate things
Where grace is in your tread.

I give you music cool and soft
Of waters gliding slowly,
The murmur of a limpid voice,
As yours serene and holy.

No beauty haunts the sweeping sky,
No beauty walks the earth
But folded you and moulded you
And blossomed at your birth.

I bring you gifts already yours;
Smile on a sorry giver!
O blessed love, O blinding love,
Receive me too for ever!

Absence

Dear love, the day drags out so long, so long,
The sun seems mired in a sticky sky;
The useless minutes shamble slowly by,
The chimes compound with such reluctant tongue,
Almost I think that life is daytime only;
Then suddenly the tedious sun is quenched;
This world, our room, is with swift darkness drenched,
and I am more than ever lost and lonely.
Oh love, dear love, behold me now without you,
The house, hungry for life, untenanted,
The spirited body, and the spirit fled;
How can I not adore, and yet not doubt you?
My shoulder restless with no heat upon it,
My empty arms as futile as a — sonnet.

For Frances —
October 22, 1935

Wednesday
October 23, 1935

Dearest darling Frances —

I warned you work would be starting. Well, it has. Four poems in the last twenty-four hours, all of which I enclose. Also more preliminary work on the show — collecting and sorting of ideas from my mass of complete and incomplete ventures. It looks good, and I grow more optimistic about it daily.*

Other enclosures are "letters" to you and Mrs. Leonard from Linell, and a rather nice photograph of Gwennie from Sunday's *Times*, which I enclose for no special reason.

A great blow to Linell this afternoon. Ellie Stinson was to come over, but it rained — cooler, too, thank heaven — and Ellie had a cold, so the visit fell through. Linell said "I want to go over and steal Ellie." I explained Ellie had a cold. Linell said, "That's all right, Daddy, I'll nurse her." Then she added rather ominously, "She'll never see her mummy and daddy again."

Isabel plays a new game of her own. She stands in front of you and looks at you mischieviously. Then she says "One, two, free, seven, ten, GO!" On Go, she casts you a triumphant and roguish glance and practically perishes of her own wit.

Both children have now several times mistaken my knock on the door for yours. There are cries of "Here's Mummy coming to take care of me," and then I go in and I'm not Mummy.

Your father went to the Philadelphia Symphony tonight and John and I to the Parkway — a dreadful, amateurish picture based on the life of Stephen Foster, but accompanied by a delightful cartoon and a newsreel of Ethiopia and the Yale-Penn game.

Darling love, I adore you, and I don't like looking at your bed, which I can see from here. My precious, my glorious Frances, I am more yours every day. Sweet angel, good night.

Ogden

---

*The "show," *Family Album*, would never see the light of day. — Ed.

October 27, 1935

Darling angel —

Yesterday was the Navy–Nôtre Dame game. I've never seen such a crowd in Baltimore — every seat in the Stadium filled, including temporary stands across the open end. It was a fine game for the first quarter, and then Nôtre Dame scored two touchdowns, and there was nothing more to it. But it looked to me more like Navy weakness than Nôtre Dame strength; or is that just my prejudice against N.D.? Army beat Yale, I am sorry to say, 14–8, and Harvard lost respectably to Dartmouth, 13–6. But Princeton got mad at last, and slaughtered Cornell 52–0. So much for football.

I gave a dinner after the game — Tommy and Alice, Eleanor, Jack and Julia, two New York friends of theirs named ———, and your father and John. Clarence and Frederick did an extremely good job, and everything was a great success, except the ———s, who are as unattractive a couple as I've seen in some time. He's not so bad except that he looks like a skeleton, but she is a honey. I had her on my right at dinner. First she asked me if I ever read the New Yorker. I said yes. Then she said she read it from cover to cover every week. Then she said Julia had told her I wrote, why didn't I send something to the New Yorker. Later on she devoted most of her attention to Jack and Julia. (She was an old schoolmate of Julia's, and so exactly like the one in Jeeves and the Old School Friend that it was ridiculous.) We played charades and the drawing game. Your father was adamant about the charades, but finally succumbed to one round of the drawing game. Later to the Summit, which was jammed with a football crowd, including Dr. Carter, who was accompanied by a lady who declared she loved him for his marvellous touch. A phrase that I fear will never be applied to me.

Friday night I went out to the country for dinner. Mother better than in a long while, and everybody looking forward to the return of Douglas Jr. on Monday. I have asked Gwen and Douglas and your father and John to Three Men on a Horse next Thursday evening.

The children are now asking "Where's Mummy?" several times a day. At least Linell asks "Where's Mummy?" and Isabel asks "Vare's Mummy?" I don't know how long the promise of those Paris dresses will keep them satisfied.

Darling, I adore you, and I am so damned lonely. And I try to lose the loneliness in seeing a lot of people, and the more people I see the more I ache for you. Blessed, blessed angel, once you are home we have *got* to be together for ever. And five minutes. No more goodbyes. I worship you.

Ogden

October 28, 1935

Dear Blessed Sweet —

A good day today; two poems well begun, and the plot of the first act nearly completely outlined. I think it's fair; as soon as I get it the way I want it, I'll send it to you. A nice note from dear old Bergman, now in Philadelphia, praises the Mussolini poem in the American.

Yesterday afternoon I went to a house-warming cocktail party given by Kitty and John Stinson. They are in one of those courts off 39th Street, really an awfully nice little house, though rather jammed at the time. Their baby is a good baby, but they made my flesh creep, throwing it around like a football. Phil and Eveline Goldsborough were there, Eveline still jubilant over the Huey Long affair; John and Ellen Bordley; Martha, Ed and Eleanor; Jack and Julia and their ———s, and various people unfamiliar to me.

I was discussing the football game with Miss Summers in Isabel's room today. Knowing how she feels, I said what a pity Nôtre Dame had won. Out popped Delia's head from the bathroom. "Not a pity at all, Mr. Nash!" she said indignantly. "They're fine devout boys."

Peggy has asked John and me to dinner tonight, and I shall try to see what I can see.

I love you, darling.
Ogden

P.S. Darling Frances, I adore and worship you. Write to me, darling, and have you still a lipstick?

October 29, 1935

Darling love —

I'm afraid I shan't get used to this emptiness. Do you remember how often I used to tell you that I never really believed I had you? Every morning when I woke up it was a glorious amazement to find that I really did, and to see your head on the next pillow, and to stretch out my hand and touch you. Now it's just the opposite. When I wake, I can't believe that you aren't there; I can't look at a doorway without thinking that you must presently walk through it, I can't enter a room without hoping to find you sitting in it waiting for me — reading, or even knitting. And at the same time I know it can't happen, and darling, darling, that's an appalling knowledge.

I miss you in my work. I'm getting along quite well, really, but most of the fun is gone without you to show it to and discuss it with. You know that your praise is the only praise, and your disapproval the only disapproval, that mean anything to me. The only way I have of showing off to you is in my work, darling. The marked passage in the enclosed cutting from the Reader's Digest caught my eye today, and I send it along because it expresses something I feel so strongly.

Well, the show progresses. Three pages written today, and I think it's gathering headway. Ideas seem to be breeding ideas, and my confidence and fluency are being built up as I settle down to it.

Dinner at Peggy's last night with John and a girl named Elizabeth Stewart, no relation, from Boston. Afterwards we went to the movies in Reisterstown, and saw Diamond Jim. You were quite right in wanting to miss it — it's mostly preposterous and tedious, with only a few flashes of interest. Peggy looked very well indeed, but I'm afraid she and John will never be anything but brother and sister.

Douggie Gorman came to lunch today, and talked well about his trip. He's off for New York in a couple of days to try to get a job out of Dan or Malcolm or Charlie. I'm sorry to say that a letter from Noble says that Lucy Anne's heart is pretty bad. Also a letter from George Elliman which I shall send to you as soon as I have answered it, as rich in unconscious humor as Daisy Ashford — except that I have always doubted Daisy's unconsciousness, and shall always believe in George's.

I got the new Babar and the new book by the Brave Mr. Buckingham lady for the children today. They were delivered so late that I only had time to read the new Babar before bed time. They both loved it —

incidentally, they can now be read to both at once, so long as Isabel has a book of her own to clutch. And we'll investigate Mrs. Ticklefeather tomorrow.

Oh, my lovely girl, I live only in you. Perhaps I shall feel better when I get your first cable, which should be tomorrow, and your third letter, which can't be until about a week from tomorrow — but darling, darling, what are words? I want *you!*

> *Good night, my adorable sweet.*
> Ogden

November 11, 1935

Darling glorious blessed angel —

Four letters this morning — really ten, as the boat letter amounted to about six. I adore and worship you, and the letters are marvellous, and I am a new man, the newest man I will be until December tenth. Thank you, sweet. I am so glad the trip is doing you good, and I think it is wonderful about the rash. And you feel just the way I want you to feel; homesick, but not homesick enough to ruin your enjoyment. *And* you love me. Oh, my very darling girl, be good to my heart.

Stuart called up yesterday afternoon and asked me to supper. I had planned on supper at home, so went out there afterwards and met a strange conglomeration of people. A Mr. and Mrs. Piles. Yes, that was their name, and I have been wasting sympathy on people named Pyle. An old gent named Heinecken who sat on the edge of his chair all evening growing steadily tighter and never making a sound except for one ten minute interlude when he sat down at a parlor organ that Stuart bought for ten dollars and played Silent Night. And a strange woman in red named Mrs. K—— who comes from Easton and runs a dress shop on Charles Street and said "I adore your poetry." And I said I did too, and she said "I have to go to New York next week, why don't you come with me?" And I said I was sorry, I had to work, and she said, "I must be slipping." So you see Towson has perils to equal those of Paris.

The more people I see the more I thank God for you. And thank you for God, for you have given Him back to me. Darling, darling, Frances, I adore you. Sweet!

> Ogden

Hollywood turned out to be a strange detour in my father's life. He had been summoned there by Irving Thalberg, who had a special assignment in mind for the East Coast humorist. However, he never revealed his plans for Daddy either to MGM or to Daddy himself, and, in an ironic twist of fate that was to typify any and all of my father's dealings with Tinsel Town, died just after Daddy arrived on the coast, leaving a group of very puzzled studio execs to deal with the new writer in the stable. I now think that since Thalberg had the idea of what eventually would become "A Day at the Races" in the hopper of work to do, he might have had Daddy in mind for this effort. The fact that Daddy was a great Marx Brothers fan and the fact that his humor would have fitted Thalberg's vision of his movie make this a reasonable guess. However, any plans he may have had for the venture went to the grave with him, and Daddy was to languish for two and a half years on Writer's Row at MGM, waiting for the phone to ring with something of substance for him to do. He was given many different assignments during those years; his first was to work up a screenplay for an old operetta the studio had acquired — *The Firefly*. He could do anything he wanted with it; all that was to be kept from the property was the music. Jeannette MacDonald was to star. An odd task for Daddy, it would seem, but he went to work with a will. Having completed a scenario that set the movie in New York in the 1890s, he was informed that a decision had been made to place it in Mexico. More writers joined the project, including one of Thalberg's contract writers, Claudine West. Then he was lifted from *Firefly* to work on something called *Maytime* for a month only to be shuffled back to *Firefly* with a new collaborator, Alice Duer Miller. *Firefly* was by now set in Napoleonic Spain.

I offer the *Firefly* odyssey as an example. My father must have felt like a literary Sisyphus — pushing story ideas partway up a hill, being yanked away to another hill with another script to push while the first story rolled back to the bottom again — and so on, ad infinitum. He never reached the top of a hill with a story, and it almost destroyed him.

Another frustration that plagued him in Hollywood was the fact that he could write and sell nothing for himself. All his work belonged to the studio. In 1936, before he went to Hollywood in August, he had sold eighty-four verses; from that time till 1941 he produced only six verses and one short story, which he sat on until his contract ran out. The studio infighting, the multitude of writers assigned to single scripts, the uncertainty of contract renewals (contracts were picked up every five months) — all these things were anathema to my father.

So why did he stay? First of all he wanted to make his mark in the medium. Daddy from his earliest days had loved theater and cinema. He wanted to be successful in those fields. Secondly, only a millionaire could have belittled the weekly salary. And Daddy, who had his own family to support, was by now also contributing to the growing medical bills that Granny Nash was incurring, as well as chipping in here and there to help his brothers, who were both in and out of work. There was one thing that made Hollywood a bearable experience, though — the friends my parents made there. Daddy was almost immediately befriended at the studio by Albert and Frances Hackett, who were writers at MGM at the time. The Hacketts took the Nashes in tow, entertaining them and introducing them to others who would become lifelong friends. The core group over those years included the Hacketts, Edgar and Jane (Wyatt) Ward, Ben Ray and Frieda (Innescourt) Redmond, Tony and Laura Veillier (she later married Alan Rivkin), the Joel Sayres, the Sid Perelmans, George Oppenheimer, and Corny Jackson. There were many happy times spent with these people, and their presence in Daddy's artistic limbo kept him from being totally miserable.

Daddy, though he had begun to do some radio work and was by 1938 involved in scripting a Joan Crawford picture with Jane Murfin, had become desperately unhappy with his West Coast existence. His health, both physical and emotional, was beginning to deteriorate. He constantly ran an inexplicable low-grade fever (about 99.9) and once woke Mother in the dead of night, asking her frantically, "Frances, who am I?!"

By the spring of 1938 Mother, as she observed him falling into a state of deep depression, felt that something had to be done. While she understood his need to make a success of his California venture and appreciated the lure of the amazing salary, she saw him unable to write his own poems. His considerable talent was going to waste and subsequently dying. The cost of Hollywood gold was far too high. She urged him to give it up. That of course was all he needed — a graceful out. He wasn't quitting — he was doing it for Mother. So he gave the studio notice that when the current option ran out he wanted to go back East.

During this time Isabel and I departed for Baltimore, where I had been enrolled in Calvert School. Our parents didn't want me to have to make my debut there when the other children in the class had already gotten to know one another since I had inherited the family disease of shyness.

The "Spangle" of my father's letters was a Bedlington terrier that my parents — actually, my father — had acquired during our first year in California. Daddy thought the lamblike creature a real charmer and brought her home on an impulse. Charmer she was, lamblike she was not. By the time she set out for the East Coast with Isabel, Delia, and me, it was a mercy she had not been lynched. She had chewed up two sofas, bitten a plumber, a mailman, and a gardener, and made us suffer through a false pregnancy. Daddy, the acquirer, was not the keeper. Poor Mother was. I am sure she heaved a sigh of relief as Spangle departed, probably just ahead of the law for her third offense. I'm also sure she must have worried about future lawsuits from the porters and baggage-car men the little dog might assault on her eastern journey. However, Spangle became civilized the minute she shook the dust of sunny California from her paws. All that she approved of from her former life would be with her in her new one, including a squeaky rubber toy made in the image of *Popeye*'s Wimpy.

No children could ever have felt more loved than Isabel and I did. We were so very lucky. Whenever we were separated, our parents kept us eagerly watching the mail, and we were never disappointed, for their letters came regularly; but most of the time we were together, and Mother and Daddy created a magic world of books and games, songs and stories, and hugs and kisses that made the big outside world less ominous and helped to heal hurts real or imagined that occurred there. I once came across some notes on being a parent that Daddy had jotted down on one of his ubiquitous yellow legal pads, which read as follows:

> Try to understand your children, particularly
> the things they don't want to tell you.

and,

> First you woo your sweetheart; years go by,
> then you're wooing your children; true love
> and kisses are different, and differently important,
> but just as hard to come by. Don't compromise.

I don't believe he ever did.

September 15, 1938

Darling girls,

It is a dark evening, it looks as if we should have rain, but the Japanese gardener is outside the house watering away just as if the sun were burning things up. Mummy is sitting on the sofa reading the evening paper, and I am at the card table writing a letter. Can you guess who I am writing the letter to?

The Good Humor man has gone tinkling by; I think he must be a little surprised that nobody asks him to stop at our house any more; I expect the man who sells ice cream at the Owl Drug Store misses you, too.

Mr. and Mrs. Lee only brought one of their three dogs over on Sunday, but he was as big as six Spangles put together — and he is only a puppy, not yet full grown. His name is Captain, because he is a Newfoundland, and supposed to rescue people from drowning, like Captain Watkins. But actually he is afraid of the water; at least he ran away from the pool whenever I did one of my dives. Nobody else's dives seemed to frighten him. He looks very funny when he runs away, because he is nearly as big as a bear, but not so graceful.

Mummy and Astrid have been getting your books ready for the express man, so At the Back of the North Wind and Water Babies and lots of other old favorites will soon be with you again.

I love you both enormously.
Daddy

September 23, 1938

Darling Linell and Darling Isabel —

Thank you for your interesting letters, which Mummy and I were so glad to get. We are very pleased to have such thoughtful daughters.

I wonder if Spangle has caught a squirrel yet. I'm sure she is trying very hard. I saw a squirrel on our lawn yesterday, the first I've ever seen in California. I expect it only dared come to our house because it had read in the squirrel newspaper that Miss Spangle Nash had left for Baltimore.

We saw Junior the other evening as we were driving along Sunset. He was dancing on top of a huge pile of rubbish, but he stopped dancing

"She's as much a part
Of the house as the mortgage;
Spangle, I wish you
A ripe old dortgage."
California, 1938

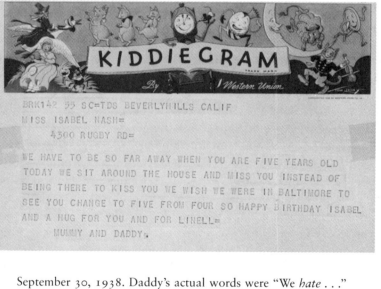

September 30, 1938. Daddy's actual words were "We *hate* . . ."
but we all agreed that Western Union did very well with the rest of it —
especially in spelling "Isabel" and "Linell" so faithfully.
(*Courtesy of Western Union Corp.*)

long enough to wave to us, so that was all right. There was a little boy in a cowboy suit at the foot of the pile, and he threw a handful of mud at us, but it didn't hit us, so that was all right, too.

I love you both tremendously.
Daddy

P.S. Six kisses for Linell xxxxx
Six kisses for Isabel xxxxx

September 28, 1938

Darling girls —

First of all, I want to wish Isabel a very very happy birthday, and then I want Linell to give her a huge kiss and pretend it's from me. You know how I wish I could be there to do it myself, and to see how grown up Isabel looks when she is five years old.

On Sunday Mummy and I went sailing — to Catalina Island on an enormous boat. The masts were much taller than our house, and when the sailor was putting the sails up he climbed the highest mast like a monkey — but coming down he didn't bother with the mast at all; he just slid down a rope.

When we got far out on the ocean the captain got out a fishing line with a big hook on the end. He tied the other end to the rail, and we all waited to see what would happen. Nothing did happen for so long that we forgot all about it. Suddenly the line gave a jerk and we all ran to pull it in. There was something very heavy at the other end. We pulled and pulled, and pretty soon we saw an enormous fish. He was so heavy that we could hardly pull him into the boat. He was three feet long and weighed about thirty pounds, and had big goggle eyes. A sailor cut him up and gave us a piece to take home, which José cooked for our dinner the next night; it was delicious. The name of that fish was an albacore.

We anchored off Catalina, and after supper we flashed a light on the water, and hundreds of flying fish began to fly. They really did, and they were beautiful. They were about eighteen inches long, and you see them swimming like all the other fish. But they have two fins just like a bird's wings, and when they get excited, or when some big hungry fish is chasing them, they spread them out and rise out of the water and skim through the air very fast. Mr. Mankiewicz, who owns the boat, gave me a long stick with three barbed points on the end and asked me to try to spear one. I did try, and I did spear one, much to everyone's surprise. My surprise, too. But I was sorry after I had done it, because flying fish are not good to eat, and I don't like to kill anything uselessly.

Last night we had dinner with Mr. and Mrs. Lee and we saw their little girl, who is ten years old. Her name is Cynthia. We longed so for our own girls.

You'll never guess what we are going to do on Saturday night. We're going to the dog races. Just like the horse races, Linell, but with dogs instead of horses. I'll write next week and tell you if it was fun.

Once again, happy birthday, Isabel, and I love you both so much and miss you both so much that I may burst at any moment, but I'll try not to.

Daddy

My parents returned to Baltimore on November 18, 1938, and we had our usual three-generational Christmas at Rugby Road, which was now to become our home. Christmas in our family was almost Dickensian — preparations for the great day were taken very seriously and the household was filled with weeks of building excitement. I cannot remember ever believing in Santa Claus, and, to me at least, the joy of Christmas was greater because we children participated in the giving as well as the receiving. We were aware that the wonders of the myriad gifts in the stockings and under the tree were born more of the loving generosity of our parents and grandparents than that of a chubby man in a red suit. We were taught early that the celebration of giving to one another was to commemorate the ultimate gift to us all, the Christ Child. So, mixed with the very real acquisitiveness children do feel at Christmas, was a feeling of wonder and awe as Christmas Eve dawned. In the evening after supper, we would go to the living room and Boppy would play carol after carol on his 1910 Steinway. We would sing all the verses of every one. As we grew older, we used to take parts, but in the early years only Daddy, harking back perhaps to days at St. George's, would harmonize. We always ended with "Silent Night" and then would troop into the library, where we would hang stockings with great ceremony — six of them and one for Spangle. Then Daddy would open Kipling's *Rewards and Fairies* and read what was our traditional ending to Christmas Eve, "Eddi's Service." He was a wonderful reader and year after year one could almost see the Chapel at Manhood End on that stormy Christmas Eve and feel the wonder of the little priest at the creatures who celebrated mass with him.

Filled with the secret promise of the night, Isabel and I would be bundled off to bed. Delia would hear our "God blesses" and "Now I lay me's" and we would fall asleep at last, while the flickering of the flames in the fireplace threw patterns on the ceiling that danced with the shadows in the corners.

The great day itself was always full of joy. From the stockings before breakfast and the presents under the tree before church, to the visits to relatives after the huge holiday feast, all was a kaleidoscope of sights and sounds, tastes and feelings that fulfilled the expectations. And in the evening after more caroling, Daddy would read *A Christmas Carol* or *Pickwick Papers* while Isabel and I, by now in our nightclothes, would draw or cut out paper dolls. We never wanted the day to end, and there would be a chorus of groans when Daddy closed the book. But sleep came easily that night.

January 1939 marked a wish fulfilled in my father's life. He, of all the Nashes, had never been to Europe. Gwen, Eleanor, Ted, and even Aubrey had traveled the Continent extensively during the years of plenty, but he, who surely would have enjoyed it most of all, was fated to miss out. Going abroad had always remained one of his fondest dreams. Of course, Mother's affinity for the Old World and her wonderful descriptions of its sights and sounds made it all the more tantalizing to him. But now they were going to those magic lands — together. They planned a trip of six weeks in the off-season, thus making it more economical. This was Daddy's first real vacation since the honeymoon, and both he and Mother had felt a certain sense of urgency about seeing those places that she loved so well. While they were in Hollywood they had followed first with dismay and then with horror the march of events overseas. In 1938, they had listened with their friends to the wireless broadcast of Jan Masyrk's speech to Parliament following the rape of Czechoslovakia and had sent him a telegram of support signed "10 Americans." They knew that time was short. So the trip may have held a bittersweet taste of "This is the last, this is the last," but as can be seen from the following letters, it was nevertheless a great success.

January 27, 1939

My darling girls —

This is just a short letter to tell you that I love you both enormously; indeed I love you so much and I am so proud of you that I am almost bursting out of my clothes, and everybody in New York looks at me and says, "Goodness, he certainly must have two beautiful and sweet and clever daughters to be proudly almost bursting out of his clothes like that!" We had a quick train trip to New York and ate a delicious luncheon as we rolled along. I suppose you will eat on the train on Sunday as you whizz to Atlantic City. I know you will have lots of fun, and I wish I could see you talking to the ponies and giggling at the way you look in the magic mirrors.

Be good girls, darlings, and have a lovely time.

I adore you.
Daddy

January 27, 1939

Once there were two delightful daughters
And their parents sailed off across the waters,
And they said to each other
We think we'll miss our mother,
But when it comes to missing our father,
Well, let's not bother.
And they were so clever and so pretty
That they took the next train to Atlantic City.
And they went to the Hotel Marlboro-Blenheim,
And they told Miss Summers stories about Dr. Grimesby Roylott
Who had a ventilator and a bell rope and a serpent
Brimming with serpentish venom,
And they ate in a delightful dining room filled with eggs and
Ice cream and chicken and macaroni,
And they made friends with a pony,
And sometimes after meals,
Why they bundled up and rode around in chairs on wheels,

And after a while they said we wonder what's happened to our
   cough;
Our cough's gone off!
These refreshing ocean breezes
Have removed our sniffles and sneezes!
So that's what happened to their Atlantic City visit —
It was exquisite.
And when I get home I will give them each an enormous kiss
If they can guess who wrote this.
                          The End

                          With Love,
                          Daddy

February 6, 1939

My sweet girls —

I wish so that you were here with us. The next time we must surely bring
you along, so remember to practice your manners and learn to eat all
sorts of food. Paris is full of children. There are lots of parks, and every
park is full of boys and girls on bicycles and roller skates, or playing
football and other games all day long. Also, I think everybody in Paris
has a dog, but none of them are as pretty as Spangle. A beautiful river,
the Seine, runs right through the middle of the city, and Mummy and I
have already counted 22 bridges that cross it. Don't you think that you
could have fun here? The French children are very polite, as everyone is
in France, and I am sure you would enjoy playing with them; so, Linell,
you must pay great attention to your French teacher and learn very fast,
in order to be able to understand well when you come here. You might
teach Isabel some of what you learn, too.

   There are many, many interesting things to see here. Paris is a very old
city, and today Mummy and I saw a beautiful building that was started
by the Romans more than 1600 years ago. It is called Cluny. We have
also been to the Louvre, a museum now full of the most beautiful paint-
ings and statues; but years ago the kings and queens of France used to
live there, until the French people got angry with them and chopped off
their heads.

   This afternoon we went to a beautiful cathedral on an island in the
middle of the river. It is called the Cathedral of Nôtre Dame, which

means the cathedral of Our Lady the Virgin. It is more than 900 years old, and so high that you can hardly see the top. The windows are of gorgeous stained glass, red and blue and yellow and green and purple, so that they cast light like a rainbow on the walls. A very good king of France who lived 700 years ago and later became Saint Louis was buried (from) there. Tell Delia that we offered a candle to the Virgin Mary for each of you there, and that we are bringing her back a rosary from there also. Mummy and I climbed the tower later. We were very tired when we got to the top, but it was interesting. Some hideous stone gargoyles were looking right into our faces, so *we* looked down at Paris lying at our feet, and it was beautiful. We could see miles of river, and the bridges and the lovely old buildings. — It is warmer here than at home, but sometimes the fog is so thick that even the taxi drivers get lost; last night three of them ran right off the street and into the fountains on the Rond Point on the Champs Elysees, which Boppy can tell you about. It must have been very damp and uncomfortable for the passengers.

I think you would like the French trains. We rode on one from Le Havre to Paris just like the one that Gaston et Joséphine took when they were leaving for America. When the engine whistles it says tweet tweet instead of toot toot, and the porters are very polite.

You would like the boat, too. There is a little theatre where there are puppet shows for children every afternoon, and there is plenty of room to run and play on the decks. Sometimes, when the wind blows hard and the sea is rough, the boat joggles a little bit, but that is good fun, like being in a swing. On our trip there was a little girl only 14 years old who is already famous because she plays the violin so beautifully; her name is Guila Bustabo, and she played for us one night, at the gala concert, where everybody gave money to help the old sailors. French sailors have very pink cheeks indeed, and speak very fast, and I don't think they ever get old, really, so I am not sure who got the money.

I must tell you that whenever you walk along the banks of the Seine you see dozens of old men fishing with long, long poles. I don't think they ever catch anything, but they have a lovely time thinking about what they *might* catch just supposing there *were* any fish there. We'll try it when you come here with us; perhaps we'll catch the first fish ever to be caught there.

I adore you both, my darlings,
and don't forget me.
Daddy

February 17, 1939

My darling Linell —

I found your letters and your valentine waiting for me when I reached London yesterday, and I was delighted to get them. I love *you* so much that it makes me very happy to know that *you* love *me*. And such beautiful handwriting! And the lovely pictures of you and Isabel on your ponies!

London is a very old city, and its streets are like a puzzle. Also, all the cars here drive on the wrong side of the street, and you must be very careful crossing. We haven't seen the king and queen yet, or Princess Elizabeth or Margaret Rose, but maybe we will; and tomorrow we'll walk by Sherlock Holmes' house.

I adore you, sweet.
Daddy

February 23, 1939

My darling girls —

This is the last letter you will get from me, because next week Mummy and I will get on the boat and sail for home, and a week after that we will really see you again. I am very excited at the thought of kissing you and talking to you and playing with you.

We went past Sherlock Holmes' place today, but I am sorry to say that it has been changed since he used to live there, so it is really nicer to read about than to see. Also, I went to the Tower of London, where they used to chop people's heads off, and I even saw the axe they used to do it with, so I think the Tower is nicer to visit than to live in. But I want to take you both there some time to see the jewels, because that is where the crowns of the kings and queens are kept, and they are very beautiful and sparkling indeed, and I think you would enjoy seeing them.

Would you like me to grow an enormous moustache? I hope not. There is a gentleman in the hotel who is called the Laird of Fotheringay, and his moustache sticks out so far on each side that he has to turn sideways to get through a door. I think myself that he is very tired of it, but is too silly to think of cutting it off.

I know you will be glad to hear that we got taken to the greyhound races, and that I won quite a lot of money. I think that maybe Spangle had written to a friend among the dogs here and told them to treat me kindly.

We have seen lots of children riding in the park, but they are not as pretty as my girls. The horses are very pretty, though; lots of white ones, and lots of charming ponies.

Don't forget that I love you, darlings, and I'll see you a week after you get this letter.

Daddy

Soon after they returned from Europe, Daddy was summoned back to Hollywood for a radio show that his good friend and agent, Corny Jackson, had engineered for him.

That March venture spawned more radio performances — on the *Bing Crosby Show* and the *Chase and Sanborn Hour*. So Daddy set out for the Coast again for a three-week stay. Mother was supposed to go with him, but was taken ill the day before they were to leave, and subsequently had to spend some time in the hospital, thus making the trip an impossibility for her.

The mention of Dorothy Lamour in one of the letters recalls a story told by Corny Jackson about an incident that occurred at a rehearsal for one of the Chase and Sanborn shows. Always suspicious of Nash verses, which she found peculiar and unfathomable, she was totally outraged by the verse assigned her for this particular show. She accused Corny of trying to sabotage her career. The verse in question was "The Egg," which goes as follows:

> Let's think of eggs.
> They have no legs.
> Chickens come from eggs
> But they have legs.
> The plot thickens;
> Eggs come from chickens,
> But have no legs under 'em.
> What a conundrum!

Corny, puzzled, tried to calm her. "What's the problem, Dotty? It's just a funny poem . . ."

But she became even more furious. "Well, if you think I don't know what *that* word means — and that I'll be fool enough to say it on the air — you're crazy! I wasn't born yesterday!" "Eggs" was not included in the format. As Corny remarked later, "Who knows how many Dotties might have lurked in the radio audience? Discretion seemed the better part of valor."

The Garden of Allah
Hotel and Villas
Hollywood, California
Tuesday
April 11, 1939

Dearest darling —

After our talk last night — and a *good* talk, sweet; we're improving — and your letter this morning, I am a new man; still lonely, still furious with Fate, but cured of that awful sensation of being marooned in a vacuum, and able actually to believe that time isn't standing still and that the days will pass.

What a horrible time you have had! I feel like a skunk not to have been with you. Even in my ignorance it was hellish having to leave; if I'd realized exactly what was coming I could never have left. I adore you, angel, and I hate every world there is when you suffer.

The income tax situation looks very good, though I won't know exactly for a day or two. But I think, considering the income involved, it will be as pleasant a surprise as an income tax can be. Also — cross your fingers — the man called me up this morning to say he had been going over your last year's return and had found what he thinks is grounds for a refund of seven or eight hundred dollars.

I spent the morning getting straight on the insurance of my rented car, then went to the studio for lunch with Frances and Albert. I saw Joe Mank[iewicz], who told me he's going to make nothing but *good* pictures in the future, and has a *good* picture in mind he wants me to do for him. But Tony gets in this week, and I'll make no commitments before talking to him.

At four, I am due at the J. Walter Thompson office for a preliminary script conference; I am eager to make this next broadcast a really good one; they liked the last, but I was quite dissatisfied. However, I was in such a miserable frame of mind at the time that it's lucky it wasn't worse. Now I know you're getting better, and also know I'll get home nearly a week earlier than I'd feared, things are quite different.

A quiet dinner with the Hacketts last night; George Oppenheimer, Scott [Fitzgerald] and Sheila Graham. Scott looking very well, and sent his love to you all.

The previous evening, dinner with the Lees, me the only guest. Cynthia very excited, as I had given her and Dorothy tickets for the broadcast. I'm dining with them again tonight, with instructions to squire Dorothy to the movies while Leonard does some homework.

My week here will be up on Friday, so I then pack up and move to the Hacketts; anything you write or wire from now on should go there. Will you tell Gwen 711 N. Canon?

I'll be glad to leave here, which with you would have been great fun — pool, ping pong, badminton court, etc. — but under the circumstances is just a mopery. I take bachelorhood sullenly.

Don't forget Sid [Perelman]'s broadcast; either 8 or 8:30 Friday on WOR. I hear he's extremely good.

Dave is in the Northwest and won't be back before I leave.

Two years ago you were East and I was West on your birthday; that's about enough of that, don't you think? I hope you like the watch; if not, we'll exchange it. In the meantime, please use it to help me count the minutes.

I adore you forever, darling.

Ogden

P.S. Kiss the children for me, if you've had mumps. I love you.

———

The autumn of 1940 brought the last of my father's attempts to break into the glamorous kingdom of successful Hollywood screenwriting. Joe Mankiewicz had sent word he had a story for him to do and Daddy was very excited by the summons. He and Mother were saddened, though, by the fact that it would mean spending Christmas away from us. The thought of that magic time at Rugby Road without the star magicians made Minnie decide on an alternative. After all, she was something of a magician herself. So by the time my parents left for the Coast on November sixteenth, we were almost ready to depart for Minnie's farm, Rider's Trust, outside Salisbury, Maryland. An excited pair of children, we were taken out of school for the occasion, and off we went, a merry troupe — Minnie, Boppy, Miss Summers, Delia, Isabel, Spangle, and me.

What a time we had that Christmas! Minnie's idea was completely successful. The farm, with its ducks, geese, goats, baby chicks, and wonderful workhorse, Dan, took our minds off the fact that we missed our parents. And Minnie kept us busy with the making and wrapping of presents to send to California. Many letters and specially planned phone calls kept us in touch.

But the Hollywood experience turned sour once again. This time the problem wasn't the work; it was Daddy's health. What was at first thought to be a bout with the flu lingered with no explanations to be found. The persistent fever, experienced once before in 1938, reappeared, and the patient was finally hospitalized in mid-January for a battery of tests. From the week before Christmas when the illness struck until the end of January, Daddy felt completely miserable and yet had been given no diagnosis to explain his discomfort. But at last a verdict came in — he showed positive on a tuberculin test. As far as the doctors could determine his lungs were not involved, and they also opined that there was no danger of his infecting anyone else. Their advice was to go home to Baltimore to his own doctors, to take tuberculin shots once a day for a prescribed period of time, then to be tested again. A sad end to a venture with so much promise. George Oppenheimer, who had begun collaborating with him on the script when he became ill, took over the task entirely and in late February 1941, Mother and Daddy returned home to Rugby Road.

I can vaguely remember the electric hot plate topped by a small saucepan for boiling Daddy's tuberculin needles and syringes. It sat in my parents' dressing room at Rugby Road, and I hated thinking about poor Daddy's having to give himself those shots. To a child who lived in dread of yearly inoculations at the doctor's office or hid a cut for fear that a tetanus booster would be in order, the fact that one's father should be subjected to a shot a day was appalling. Yet he never complained about it and my already high opinion of him was reinforced beyond belief. His health improved through the spring and we gradually settled back into our routine lives. On the surface it was as if the California debacle had never happened.

Recollections of life at Rugby Road begin really with the house itself. My grandparents planned it with great care, and it was completed in 1927 after several years of work. It was stone, with a slate roof and casement windows with lead mullions and hand-blown glass panes. Many of

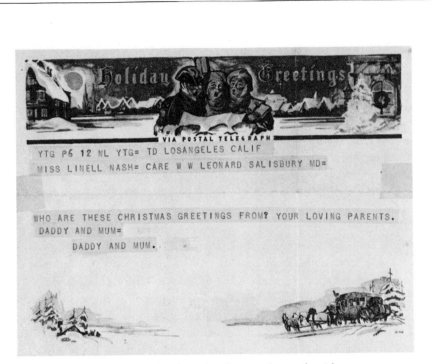

One of many communications that kept us in touch with our parents
during the Christmas we were apart.

the fittings were specially ordered, including beautiful marble mantels in the living and dining rooms and a dining-room chandelier of great elegance. The library was paneled in lustrous wood brought from an old colonial house on the Eastern Shore that had once belonged to the family but had been abandoned in the late nineteenth century and had deteriorated till it was good only for salvage. The downstairs hall was of black and white marble squares — to the children of the household it invited hopscotch, which was permitted — and roller-skating, which was not. There was a lavatory next to the library that had black fixtures, most fascinating to all our friends from school. The kitchen domain was vast, including pantry, "cold" pantry, enormous kitchen, and maids' dining room.

It was peopled with some constants — Carrie Custis, the queen of all cooks, a Salisbury native who had come to work for Minnie after Nannie Jackson's death, and Clarence Collins, who had joined the Nash household in 1933 at Isabel's birth as cook, butler, and chauffeur, and who had transferred to Rugby Road in the last two capacities. A number of live-in maids came and went over the years, and when Clarence left to do war work in 1942, there were some other butler-chauffeurs. But there was no one like Clarence, and when he returned to us after the war there were universal feelings of joy and relief. A laundress and a gardener came by the day.

The cellar contained a laundry under the kitchen and a room for flower pots and outdoor equipment, located beneath the library. Both rooms had doors and windows and lay at opposite ends of the house. Between them was a vast expanse of cellar presided over by the huge ominous furnace that glowed and glowered at all comers. It reminded me of a sleeping volcano, for it occasionally executed its own form of eruption — exploding suddenly and blowing off its door with a clang and clatter as loud as the explosion itself — its preferred time the middle of the night.

The second floor was reached by a great curving stair with easy, shallow steps and a banister of satiny wood created for sliding down. A hall ran the length of the house. At the west end, over the library and garage was my parents' suite — bedroom, dressing/sitting room, and bath, and a little upstairs porch where they fed birds in the winter. At the east end over the kitchen and maids' dining room was my grandfather's room and bath. Three other bedrooms opened onto the hall from the south side of the house: Minnie's, Delia's, and the one Isabel and I shared. Each room was separated by a full bath and there were fireplaces in three of the

rooms — Boppy's, Minnie's, and ours. On the north side of the hall was
an office/sewing room whose walls were actually closets lined with drawers where linens were kept. Mother's desk was there and the typewriter
on which she typed many of Daddy's poems. The house-long hall itself
was one great expanse of bookshelves. Three generations of beloved
books provided a wonderland for rainy days or days with sniffles or
stomach aches.

The third floor contained three maid's rooms, a bath, a number of
storage closets, and a big playroom where Isabel and I spent many happy
times. Our first Victrola, the kind that you wound, and all our toys were
there, including a wonderful rocking horse with huge glass eyes and flar-
ing nostrils that I was sure came to life when I wasn't looking. I was told
that the creaks and scuttering noises over my bed when the lights were
turned out were probably chipmunks in the walls, but I knew better. It
was "Dapple-Grey" roaming his pasture by night.

The grounds were created for enjoyment. A walled flagstone terrace
ran the full length of the house. In warm weather we often had breakfast
there, sitting under an arbor of wisteria and climbing roses. The garden
below was also walled. There was an aquamarine-tiled fish pool, replete
in summer with large, lazy goldfish who, at the first touch of frost, were
brought indoors in bowls for winter comfort. Two contemplative white
marble cats sat primly at either end of the pool; again, as with "Dapple-
Grey," I believed that they had another life when humans retired for the
night. This front garden was the formal cutting garden; to the east was
another enclosed yard with apple trees and several pines. To the west lay
the wilder shade garden. Hundreds of my grandmother's prizewinning
daffodils nodded from periwinkle-covered slopes that ran down to the
end of the property. Huge oaks stood in this area as well as one cherry
tree, which was solemnly covered each year with a bridal veil of cheese-
cloth to save the precious crop from greedy birds. There were two things
that my grandmother had planned for Rugby Road that were unusual.
Where the western cellar door from the gardener's domain opened there
was an area closed off from view by a stockade fence. In it were many
cold frames and a huge concrete compost pit, which Minnie utilized to its
fullest potential. The other piece of planning was far more interesting to
Isabel and me. Each section of the property had its own set of under-
ground sprinklers, and on hot days we would beg and agitate any and
all grown-ups in sight to turn them on so we could run through them,
giggling and squealing as the cold spray pattered on our squirming
bodies. The sun turned the spray into rainbow mist, and when we were

exhausted from our self-indulgent antics, we would flop onto the wet grass and watch the shimmering colors dance above us.

But every memory of Rugby Road contains a memory of my father. Other fathers went off to work in the morning. My father's work was all over the house. While his official workplace was either the library (before and after the war) or his upstairs sitting room (during it), his yellow legal pads would often find their way to the living-room coffee table. His notes to himself would be on scratch pads by telephones or on market lists or old envelopes. He always gathered these things up, and sometimes years later, when its time was ripe, one of those ideas or funny rhymes would suddenly appear in print.

When we were in the early grades, and in bad weather, Daddy drove us to and from school. Later we walked, feeling very grown up indeed as we slung our book bags over our shoulders and set off on the twenty-minute hike. From the time we were school-age, we ate with our parents and grandparents and our meals were full of games that Daddy initiated. There were the usual spelling games, a geography game, a history game, and a wonderful game called "Who Am I." Isabel and I took turns choosing the games for the meal.

Almost every evening when homework was finished, Daddy read to us. The family would gather in the library, and while Daddy made Dickens or Kipling or Dumas come to brilliant life, we children drew or painted in coloring books or struggled with beginner's samples of tapestries that my mother and grandmother were working for dining-room chairs. This reading hour almost exempted us from "summer reading lists" for our entire childhood. We simply read other books and wrote the required book reports from memory, occasionally doing some for friends, if pressed.

In leisure times there were many games he taught us — Sardines, Red Rover, Red Light, Kick the Can. We learned to play darts and mumblety-peg — much to my grandmother's horror. And then there was baseball. Baseball was one of my father's true passions. He took us to ball games at old Oriole Park to watch the International League Orioles. We saw old class players on their way down and young class players on their way up. The taste of a ballpark hot dog, the smell of peanuts, and the electrifying cry "Play Ball!" will always remind me of those hot summer days when Daddy would help us comprehend the game and taught us the significance of the *K*'s and *B*'s and 6 to 4 to 3's that he scripted so industriously on his scorecard. Mother was almost as great a fan as he was, and when the team was on the road we all listened to the games on the radio. When the Orioles won the "Little World Series" in 1944, I don't think the Nashes could have been any happier had it been a big-league championship. At home, Daddy taught me to pitch and to catch fly balls. I had an aptitude that pleased him, I think, for he would spend hour after hour with me in the garden, setting my fingers properly on the ball for different pitches and snappily fielding my sometimes erratic efforts. By the time I went off to boarding school at fifteen, I could throw a blazing fastball, a solid curve, and a zinger of a slider, but my knuckleball still left much to be desired. My father's first love was the New York Giants, and his favorite Giant was Mel Ott. He took me to the Polo Grounds once to see Mel Ott play, and I was properly impressed.

Actually, all of our family was sports-minded. My grandfather traveled regularly to Princeton for football games, always happy to take any and all along with him; we listened to other college games on the radio, as well as to the championship fights. Racing was also part of my childhood. I was wild about horses from the time I was tiny, and what more wonderful place for a horse-crazy child to grow up than a spot fifteen minutes' drive from a major racetrack? Daddy loved to go racing. Mother was only lukewarm about the sport, so Minnie and Isabel and I were his more frequent companions at Pimlico. I will never forget my first Preakness, nor the horse who won it. It was 1941, and in my nine-year-old eyes, the sight of Whirlaway blazing from last place to first was never to be forgotten. I have seen greater horses since, but "Mr. Longtail" will always hold a special place in my heart. In racing, as in baseball, Daddy taught me the mechanics of the sport. I learned to read the *Daily Racing Form* and to understand the odds board. He also influenced me against betting the favorite — albeit unconsciously, I think. He always played the long shots at the track, and in one other aspect of his life — Broadway. He tried to make calculated risks of both, recognizing them for what they were, reaching for the stars.

My parents and grandparents always attended our school "assemblies" whenever Isabel or I appeared in any of the playlets held each Wednesday. Spangle attended once too, much to my chagrin, as it turned out. I was to take part in a second-grade French play in which my assignment was to walk across the stage, leading Spangle and declaiming, "Vendredi, je me promène avec mon chien." Daddy had quarreled with the gender of the line, remarking that "ma cheinne" was what I should say; but on the great day, I was too nervous to worry about that. When my moment came at last, I grasped Spangle's leash firmly and started on stage. She came willingly enough at first, but one glance at the sea of faces beyond the footlights gave her pause. She tried to retreat, but, unable to do so because of the death grip I had on the leash, she opted to do the next best thing. She lay down, her head averted from the audience. "Vendredi," I began, my voice squeaky and shaking. "Vendredi, je me promène . . ." — a wave of giggles swept through the hall — ". . . avec . . ." — here I tugged futilely at the prostrate dog and only succeeded in dragging the oh-so-pathetic creature's body as far as center stage — "mon chien." At this point the house was rocking. As I stood frozen in place, I saw my father quietly leave his seat and head for the stage door. Seconds later, though it seemed an eternity, I saw his familiar form in the wings and heard him say sotto voce, "Spangle, biscuit."

Such a resurrection was never before seen! In a trice the dog was up and in high gear. Across the stage she flew, barking joyously, giving me a Nantucket sleigh ride in her wake. When I reached the blessed wings, I threw myself sobbing in mortification into Daddy's waiting arms, while the merry miscreant jumped gaily around us. I remember he said something funny that turned my sobs to giggles, and by the time the school marched out my life was back together again.

That was Daddy — always there when feelings were raw or disappointments seemed insurmountable. We never doubted for a minute that Daddy could "fix it" in those magic times at Rugby Road.

Nineteen forty-one was our last summer at Little Boar's Head until after the war. Though America was not yet involved in the conflict, it was much on everyone's mind. Mother, with the other young women of the community, joined the Red Cross and took first-aid courses, led by the sculptress Malvina Hoffman, who was a perennial summer resident. And with Minnie and Delia, she knitted socks and balaclava helmets to send to England. The sound of the radio was a constant background to our daily lives. In the fall, after we returned to Baltimore, Daddy set out on a lecture tour that had been arranged during his ill-fated Hollywood stay of 1940–41. These letters are from his first experience with the vicissitudes of the lecture circuit.

Life at Little Boar's Head before World War II.
The Nash girls share some light
summer reading.

Picnic on the rocks — Little Boar's Head.
Isabel in hat, Linell beside her.

Hotel Statler
Buffalo, New York
Tuesday, 9:30 A.M.
November 11, 1941

Darlingest —

You have further to walk in the Buffalo station than in the Santa Fe at Los Angeles. You emerge on Paderewski Boulevard and drive through two miles of Poland; it's like spending the weekend in the Fordham backfield. However, on reaching the hotel I asked for a room with a view of the city, so I am now on the 16th floor with large windows South and East, from which it is apparent that Buffalo is quite a city. I can see the lake about half a mile away. Happy thought: find out *what* lake. I have had breakfast, bath and shave, and am now awaiting a gentleman from one of the papers. When I finish with him, I'll begin digging into the lecture. I'm a little worried about my Rochester connection, as I'm speaking here from one to two, and my train leaves at 2:29 from the other end of town. Still, if anything slips, that's Mr. Peat, not me.

I was glad to find Orphan Annie in the paper here. You must follow her while I am away, and then, just as the same moon looks down on us both, so will we be linked by our sharing of Annie's daily misadventures.

The reporter has come and gone, a kindly young man. The water I see is the Niagara River on its way to Lake Erie. Also, it seems that my talk is to be broadcast, locally, and needs last only half an hour. Unhappy thought: Can that "scarcely a small touch of chastity" go out on the air? I'd feel lost without it.

I must now start trimming the piece down to the half hour. Let us say that I whittle as I whistle in the dark. Incidentally, Buffalo is ankle deep in melting snow — I hope the storm will spare Maryland until you have reached Salisbury.

My heart is yours, darling. All my love to the children, and I adore you.

Ogden

Somewhere in Ohio
4 P.M.,
Wednesday, November 13, 1941

Dearest darling —

This is written very much en route, with the pad perched on my knee, in the mid afternoon of a day that has so far lasted for a week or even a leap year.

Yesterday of course was pretty tough. After writing you I went downstairs and performed, let us say with moderate success. All the members of the club had big badges with their names and businesses written large. I didn't expect a group of New Yorker addicts, but I don't think those boys had ever worked up to the sports page, much less the Saturday Evening Post. Still, there was a fair amount of laughter, and whenever they were puzzled I got the impression that they thought maybe it was their fault; particularly as the entire theme of the gentleman who introduced me was the vast quantity of money I earned by my specialty. I did have a few minutes pleasant chat with the head of the school board or something, who was a fraternity brother of Charlie Brackett's. At luncheon I sat next to a dentist who knows Dr. Brun and is mad at him for making money. All this business lasted so long that I almost missed the train to Rochester, but the four bags and I finally scrambled into an extra small daycoach seat and covered the 35 miles in an hour and a quarter.

I was surprised and pleased to be met at Rochester by the man in charge of festivities, who turned out to be friendly and helpful. He has a cousin in Baltimore who is, I think he said, superintendent of art in the public schools, named Leon Winslow; does that mean anything to anybody? At any rate, he took me to the Sagamore Hotel, and they were full up — a radio convention we hadn't known about. We tried two more with no luck, and I finally landed a room in the place where the Orioles stay, so you might tell Linell that I slept in Hal Sieling's bed; who can say that it wasn't? My engagement was for 5:30, so I expected to be through and back on the telephone by 7, but that was my mistake, as dinner and a floor show preceded me on the program. I caught a slight inkling of my problem on the way out to Kodak Park (the main Eastman plant) when Tozier (my pal) pointed out the site of the house, now torn down, where Dickens' wife was born. I was so humbly surprised at this little item that he reconsidered and finally said, oh no, I mean the other one, Kipling; of course that was long before Dickens' time. — So I skipped the floor show and revised the talk as drastically as I could.

The audience consisted of 600 foremen of the Eastman Co. and was oddly mixed, as some of them are highly cultivated college post-graduates while others are simply mechanics. Actually, I was better pleased with the way this job went than with the Buffalo one, though both were far behind Worcester.

Afterwards I met a fellow I used to work with on streetcar advertising for a drink at the hotel, left a call for 5:30, heard your lovely whispered voice on the telephone, and collapsed. But not indefinitely. I was worried about the call, and woke up at 4:30 to remain awake until 5:30, when I rose and dressed, leaving my shaving and tooth brushing for the train. At 5:50 I asked the clerk for my bill, and telling him not to bother to wake me at 5:30, dashed off to the station to climb into my compartment, perform my toilet, and get another two or three hours' rest. Well, it seems that a freight train ahead of my St. Louis train had just gone off the track, killed the engineer, and tied up all traffic East of Rochester; my train couldn't get in. The only official in the station spoke almost no English, must have reached here since the war. Nobody knew what to do, but eventually I was advised to go to Buffalo and ask somebody there.

So unshaven and unwashed, I piled me and still my four bags back into the Buffalo day coach. In Buffalo they were more alert and a helpful station master hustled me onto a train bound for Cleveland. Day coach again, my beard sprouting assiduously. Four hours later got to Cleveland, and I am now luxuriously installed in a compartment speeding toward St. Louis. I have had a shave, a wash, a clean shirt, a drink, soup, broiled chicken and crackers and cheese, and now look forward to revising my speech for Tulsa. I'll call the Warrens tonight between trains in St. Louis if it isn't too late, but my chief desire is 10 hours' sleep.

I adore you, darling, and I miss you horribly. The picture gets more important all the time; thank you for thinking of it.

All my love, sweet.
Ogden

Hotel Fontenelle
Omaha, Nebraska
Saturday evening
November 15, 1941

Dearest darling —

I feel much refreshed after your letter and our telephone conversation. I love you very much indeed.

Nobody has approached me here yet, so I hope I may be permitted a quiet Sunday to myself. Tulsa was kind, but kept me on the dead run, which I shall now describe.

As I told you, I was met by a gentleman and a lady, whisked to the hotel and photographed before clean shirt, shave, or any sort of orientation. He a Mr. H——, but we parted as S—— and Ogden, she a Mrs. Conhaim, and we parted as Mrs. Conhaim and Mr. Nash. After the photographing and interview I was granted two hours to arrange my affairs, and was then taken to the Tulsa Club — very elaborate indeed, like the Baltimore Country Club in a skyscraper, only richer — and given a very good luncheon. I had asked to be allowed to get right back to the hotel to work on my talk, as I wanted to correct some of the Buffalo and Rochester dead spots, but S—— H——, a rich realtor, insisted on showing me the city, so I sight-saw for half an hour, and was really glad to have done it; nothing special to see, really, except the Frank Lloyd Wright house, but I was pleased to have a look at that, as we never discovered that one on Green Spring Avenue, and also I could get some idea of the city, which seems to be richer than Oyster Bay and Sewickley combined. When I finally got back to my room, the revising was interrupted by telephone calls from booksellers about autographs and an incursion of twelve girls from the Creative Writing Course, who pleased me with their frankness; all they wanted was to show me what they had written and be told it was good, and also have me give them the formula for making money by writing. Having disposed of all this, I finished my work, dressed, and went with S—— H—— to a high ball party, after having met his wife and four children en route. At this party I met a lot of men whose names I don't remember, but I liked them, as at least half a dozen were thoroughly familiar with my stuff, a sure road to my cockles. From there to the dinner at the Tulsa Club where I had lunched. About three hundred men, the, as Fortune would put it, high-income group of Tulsa. The talk went better than fairly well — not a triumph, but a long way from disaster. After that, the evening really turned odd. Several of the men who had enjoyed the verses asked me to come and have a drink with them (by the way, I was quite wrong, Oklahoma is dry, though the Tulsans all have good cellars, and Nebraska is wet; I was precisely wrong) but S—— H——, my sponsor, took me by the arm, winked at me, whispered that we didn't want to sit around with a lot of men, and led me to a back stairway. I thought we were going back to his house, but he drove me to a bungalow on the outskirts of town, explaining on the way that we were going to call on two girls named Dorothy and Catherine. Well, those are very nice names, but I began to wonder a little. Then he told me they ran a superior dress shop and went to New York all the time, and were fine girls. I drew a deep breath and followed him into the bungalow, and was presented to Dorothy and Catherine, who turned out to be pleasant, medium attractive, and not very bright, especially Dorothy, who had been given a ticket to the third game of the World Series and went to Belmont Park instead, not even handing her World Series ticket over to her father-in-law. I sat stiffly in a straight chair with my brief case at my feet trying to figure things out, and S—— H—— asked for a bottle of champagne which he had left there earlier in the day, which we solemnly drank, and then either Dorothy or Catherine said had I seen my picture in the paper, and I said no, and she said she'd get it for me only she couldn't because the paper was in her grandmother's room and her grandmother was ninety and she didn't want to disturb her, and then S—— H—— said that his father had given him an allowance of $200 a month when he was at the University of Illinois and in four years he had saved $2,500, after which he produced a bottle of sparkling Burgundy, which was also drunk solemnly, and then I said I'd have to get up early, so we said good night to Dorothy and Catherine, who showed me a photograph of their grandmother, who looked rather like Granny Ingersoll, and S—— H—— took me home, and I don't know whether to devote my future to solving the Mystery of Edwin Drood or the non-sequitur of Dorothy and Catherine.

Next morning I was up bright and early to revise my talk all over again for the ladies, as I was due at 11:30 at a store to autograph books. I thought I'd have ample time, but I was interrupted by batches of books to autograph from two other stores where I couldn't appear, plus the chairman of the Red Cross, complete with another photographer, whose achievement I enclose. I finally finished my work in time to be only ten minutes late for the autograph party, which turned out to be very successful. One of my clients turned out to be the D.A.R. lady who had written me the indignant letter last winter about some slighting remark about the D.A.R. in Free Wheeling. Fortunately, hers was one of the letters I had answered, and apparently satisfactorily, so we met and parted as friends. I think she really probably came to see for herself whether or not I was a Jew. So far as I can tell, we sold about 150 books. Most of them were the dollar reprint, but even so, I think that's a valuable spreading of the gospel.

Now I must tell you about the Magic Empire Women's Forum, the group I addressed that afternoon. But it is late now, so I'll wait till tomorrow to go into that, and content myself at the moment with saying I adore you.

Sunday morning

I love you today, too. The Magic Empire etc. is the brainchild of Mrs. Conhaim, who is a Scotch girl married to a Jewish geologist, and very bright indeed. Its membership consists of women living *outside* of Tulsa; no Tulsa ladies allowed. Members pay $1.00 a year, for which they get ten lectures a year, including such attractions as Dorothy Thompson, Quentin Reynolds, and me. They love it, and in two years have grown to a horde of 2,300, and they drive in from a radius of as much as 200 miles. The ingenious trick is that it is backed by the merchants of Tulsa to bring the women there for their shopping rather than to Kansas City or Oklahoma City. So that's what the Magic Empire Women's Forum is or are, and I love them dearly, because they laughed steadily, and kept me reading request poems for fifteen minutes after the talk. No, I haven't slipped back to see Dorothy and Catherine, I just ran out of Omaha paper. Mrs. Conhaim took me home for dinner, and her husband turned out to be an old pal of Allen Rivkin's, and we listened to Information Please, which I thought very poor and the transatlantic business just an elaborate and silly trick, and then I went back to the hotel and packed. I had an interesting and easy trip to Kansas City, about 5 hours, yesterday morning on the streamliner. In Kansas City, I encountered possibly the most flattering example of interest in me of my career. Some woman in Tulsa had asked me when I would reach Kansas City; I told her, and thought no more of it. But I was met there by her son, a student of some special kind at the University of Missouri, who is writing his term paper on me and had hitch hiked 120 miles to interview me, forsaking the Missouri-Oklahoma game for the championship of the Big Six. I must say I was touched. So I talked to him for half an hour, boarded the Burlington Zephyr, and here I am. The weather continues perfect, as it has been ever since leaving Buffalo; straight Indian summer, with thermometer in the seventies all day, and cool at night. From my window I see the Missouri River and a Sunshine Biscuit warehouse. This hotel most elaborate, with, truly, a radio playing in every elevator.

In looking over my schedule, I notice that I am expected for an interview and luncheon tomorrow noon, so I may have from now till then to myself. I shall breathe easier with this one behind me.

Now darling, cross your fingers, because I've had a brilliant idea and I think it will work. From Ft. Worth I go to St. Louis, arriving there the morning of the 20th. The schedule calls for my going from there to Chicago, remaining in Chicago until the 24th. But I noticed a lot of beautiful B&O trains in the St. Louis station when I passed through the other day. I could catch one of those, be in Baltimore the morning of the 21st, with you that afternoon and Saturday, and drive back to Baltimore and catch the Liberty to Chicago Sunday afternoon. This would not be as expensive as it sounds, since four days in Chicago would cost a good fifty or sixty dollars.

I'll have to investigate trains etc., but I'm very excited at the idea, and hope it appeals to you. One necessary thing would be for Ollie to be in the house early Friday morning to let me in, give me some breakfast, and the keys to the car. I'll let you know definitely from Ft. Worth.

Kiss the children for me, and don't forget that I adore you.

Ogden

Omaha, Nebraska
November 16, 1941

> Darling Isabel, Sweet Linell,
> This is the tale I have to tell.
> I travelled to Buffalo, New York,
> And there I delivered a humorous tork,
> But I found the audience rather dreary,
> And would rather have trudgeoned in Lake Erie.
> Rochester next, on Lake Ontario
> High-ho the Kodak, high-ho the dairy-o!
> Rochester, dears, and your daddy, who's me.
> Somehow or other just couldn't agree,

And then next morning, to cap the clim-*ax*,
I couldn't depart, as my train left the tracks;
But *I* was not on it, to Rochester's fury,
And that night I arrived at St. Louis, Missouri.
I travelled from there on a train named Will Rogers,
Who was loved in the West like your ma loves the Dodgers.
I wakened in Tulsa, where folk do not toil,
As everyone there owns a well full of oil.
Think sweetly of Tulsa, if not too much bother,
Since the whole population was kind to your father.
They harked to his words and they purchased his books.
And they laughed at his jests instead of his looks,
And asked for poems about Linell,
And sent their love to Isabel.
I found only one flaw in Oklahoma,
Their water has a chlorine aroma;
Though clear and plenteous, pure and cool,
It's rather like drinking a swimming pool.
Now to continue my lilting ditty,
I went from Tulsa to Kansas City,
And then to here, on a train called the Zephyr,
Whose cowcatcher caught not even a heifer.
So now I sit in the state of Nebraska,
On the way from Salisbury to Alaska,
And I tell you, darlings, that here in Omaha,
The water *still* has a chlorine aromaha.
How different the water in our abode
At 4300 Rugby Road!
So now I'm wondering what on earth
The water will taste like in Fort Worth.
Darling Isabel, sweet Linell,
I hope you're happy, I hope you're well.
When I am away from you, I miss you.
This row of x-es . . . xxxxxxxxxxxxxxxx
    means I kiss you.

Lots of love —
Daddy

P.S. Don't whisper it, even to your Didey-babies,
    But with luck, I will see you on Friday, babies.

Hotel Oliver
South Bend, Indiana
Tuesday, 10 P.M.
November 25, 1941

Darling sweet —

As I talked to you three hours ago, and shall talk to you again before
this letter reaches you, I am writing mostly because I want to tell you
that I love you. Through our years I have spent a good deal of time in
wondering whether I love you more every day when I am with you just
because of being with you, or whether I love you more every day when I
am separated from you because I miss you so terribly, and I have finally
come to the conclusion that I just love you more every day, and would
rather be with you than separated from you. I hope this is all right.

This evening, I am glad to say, went very well; another warm and responsive audience which sat and applauded for a minute or more even
though I had got carried away by my own charm and run well past my
hour. But individually they are funny people here; good hearted, but with
the graciousness and aplomb of Uncle Howdie. I was met at the station
by a Mr. F——, accompanied by his six year old daughter, who won my
heart immediately because it seems that she always goes with her father
to meet the visiting speakers, and dearly loves the sight, sound, and smell
of a train, but has not yet ridden on one. Mr. F—— dumped me gruffly
at the hotel, returned to guide me to the auditorium, and when all was
over, walked stiffly up to me and said he had enjoyed my talk but hoped
I didn't mind his having gone out in the middle of it to throw up. I said
No, not at all, I hoped it wasn't anything I had said, and he said No, he
didn't think so, probably his wife's pecan pie, good night. — A dozen or
so men and women came up to me, obviously with the most tremendous
effort, to tell me they had had a good time, and every kind word had to
be wrenched out, as if they were presenting me with one of their lungs or
kidneys. It interested me for several reasons; it accorded with my previous thoughts about Indiana, and also was in such strange contrast to
their group behavior, which was so generous and without self-
consciousness.

This particular room is the first really dismal one I have encountered
on the trip, and the most expensive. If I was a little despondent when I
talked to you, I think it was the wall paper, the National Casket Co. furniture, the dripping faucet and the athlete's foot carpet that flavored my
mood. Also the fluttery stomach that precedes every performance. But

now, with nothing but Bucknell University between us, I feel much better. Allowing for the change in time, my calculation is that 65 hours and 8 minutes will put my hand in yours, if you come to meet me, otherwise 65 hours and 23 minutes unless you are with Mr. Charles or Mr. Pierre, a contingency with which I simply refuse to cope from here.

An interesting point about Decatur. There were about twenty-four people at the party I went to last night after the talk. In the course of conversation it developed that all but two had cancelled their subscriptions to the Chicago Tribune, which has heretofore been even more of a Middle Western Bible than the Sears Roebuck catalogue. Just more America First than they could swallow.

I am now casting a chary, or wary, eye upon the bed, which I like to presume is fit for human consumption. The thought of an eleven hour train trip tomorrow, topped off by a night in Buffalo, has a truly soporific effect. By the way, I'm not due in Buffalo until 9:40 P.M., and there is that long safari to the hotel, so it may be 10:30 or later before I call.

All my thoughts are with you, and all my heart is with you. I adore you. Good night, my own truly beloved.

Ogden

Wednesday Morning: Hi, sweet, I feel much more cheerful, and why not? Day after tomorrow — Here's my heart, darling.

———————

When he came home at the end of November there was only a short time left before the historic Sunday that changed our smooth-running world. We had gone to a noon movie with our parents that day, and when we got in the car to come home, Daddy turned on the radio. As the news sank in, I can remember Daddy's saying "Dear God!" He turned to Mother, and then, wordlessly, they embraced, her face hidden against his tweed coat; his eyes straining into the growing dimness of the December afternoon. Isabel and I were terrified. We knew something awful had happened but we didn't understand what it was. Mother spoke to us then gently, inviting us into the front seat with them, where we sat, their arms encircling us as they explained the meaning of what had happened at Pearl Harbor.

Daddy applied to the Navy immediately but was turned down because of his eyes. So he did what he could — he became an air-raid warden at home, made war-bond tours across the country, and wrote slogans for the war effort. Mother did hospital work for the Red Cross and Minnie and Isabel and I used to make flowers to sell at war rallies out of war-savings stamps — each stamp a petal. There were flowers fashioned of ten-cent stamps and twenty-five-cent stamps and dollar stamps, and each flower was priced accordingly. We faithfully observed blackouts and ate Spam (which I loved, much to my father's horror) and Minnie grew a victory garden. Miss Summers joined the Army Nurse Corps, but because she was too light (eighty-five pounds) was refused overseas duty. Instead, she was assigned to work with Japanese Americans in a California internment camp.

Rationing of oil changed some things at our huge house. The living room was closed off for "the duration," as was the library. The dining room did double duty and Daddy worked upstairs. The piano was moved into the curve of the hall stairwell so piano practice could continue. Fireplaces were utilized often, as were electric heaters and hot-water bottles.

The St. Anthony
San Antonio, Texas
Wednesday afternoon
February 4, 1942

Darling angel —

I arrived here at 7 this morning and got your first letter in time to wallow in it before my talk, which was at 10.30 — A.M. I hope you are as proud of your First Aiding as I am, but I'd love you just as dearly even if you were helpless in the face of shock or snakebite. I'm afraid you must resign yourself to being my girl forever.

I spent a truly quiet day in Waco yesterday, arriving at noon and not stirring from my room till 8 in the evening; lunched and dined on sent-up sandwiches. I don't think I missed much by not roving, as I could see vast stretches of the town from my 9th floor window, and it looked decidedly dreary; but in any case, I had a lot of work to do on the lecture. At 8, I got picked up by a couple of about our age, a Mr. and Mrs. Clifton, who took me to the arena and also informed me that they were expecting me for a drink after the lecture. There wasn't much time for this party, as my train left at 10.52, but I played the game, dashed upstairs and packed, came down and asked for my bill, and got it: 36 cents. I protested; so did the clerk; said the charges were for three telephone calls and an air mail stamp, and they couldn't take a penny more. So I told him I had taken two baths and used up all the towels, and he finally agreed to accept $1.50. Then, off to Southern High School. The talk really went awfully well, and gave me fresh confidence, which I fear may be shaken in Coffeyville. Very pleasant people at the Clifton's party afterwards, including a Mrs. Brenstedt who had known Ted in Cedarhurst, under what circumstances I didn't ask, and a Mrs. Um-um, whose name I never caught, who is a friend of the Howard Smith's, and is bringing her husband to the Hopkins some time soon. It developed that everybody in the room had been at the Hopkins at one time or another. I couldn't break as much ice as I'd have liked to, for they were all very kind and very attractive, as I had to mount my cab and drive six miles to a lonely little hut on the railroad tracks where the taxi-driver turned on the lights and left me to hope that the train would stop. It did, and I stepped out of the prairie resplendent in my London dinner jacket and escorted myself to my suite.

I snatched an hour's nap after arriving this morning, and faced my thousand ladies in fine style. I'm glad to say it was an enormous success with nearly three minutes of applause after I was through; a marvellous audience. Then who should come back stage but a hither to unseen and undreamed of cousin, a Mrs. Corning, who was originally a Burgwin, and she and several friends took me to a Mexican restaurant for luncheon; a place which is said to be so good that the rich Mexicans drive up from Mexico to get Mexican food at its best. They all eyed me with malicious anticipation as I added hot sauce to the hottest dishes, but thanks to Carrie's cuisine I disappointed them, not yielding even a single hiccup. After luncheon I was taken to the Alamo, the old cathedral, and the Spanish governor's palace, as well as through the Mexican quarter, and enjoyed myself thoroughly. Texas has been good to me, and I appreciate it.

The hotel here has electric-eye doors, like Read's Drug Store or the Pennsylvania Station in New York; furthermore, it has Kleenex in the bathroom and no radios in the elevators. The weather is incredibly balmy, a soft, moist 75 or 80.

It is now 5 o'clock, and I think I have the rest of the evening to myself, which suits me very well. — I had a note from my Army-Crime Club friend; he has been transferred to Galveston. — My train leaves for San

Marcos at 9 in the morning and I address the teachers in the evening, then rush for the midnight to Wagoner and Coffeyville. I am surprised and delighted to find that the days really are passing.

I adore you always.
Ogden

The St. Anthony
San Antonio, Texas
Wednesday evening
February 4, 1942

Beloved darling,

If you can bear a second letter from San Antonio, this is it. When I opened my bags to get a clean shirt to drive in, it reminded me of something that I have thought of every time I've changed my clothes, but have so far forgotten to thank you for. Your packing was perfect, and I have never had such an easy trip so far as clothes are concerned. Anyone else could see that I have been packed with skill, but I know more than that; I have been packed with love. It may be odd to find romance in an undershirt or a pair of socks ready to the hand — but after all, that is just one of the reasons I adore you; the way you transmute the most ordinary, prosaic things into your own shimmering self.

I am grateful, and entranced forever. And incidentally, I love you.

Ogden

This 1942 Valentine verse metamorphosed a year later into the song "How Much I Love You" for the Broadway show *One Touch of Venus*.

To My Valentine
More than a cat bird hates a cat,
Or a criminal hates a clue,
Or the Axis hates the United States,
That's how much I love you.

I love you more than a duck can swim,
And more than a grapefruit squirts,

I love you more than Ickes is a bore,
And more than a toothache hurts.

As a shipwrecked sailor hates the sea,
Or a juggler hates a shove,
As a hostess detests unexpected guests,
That's how much you I love.

I love you more than a wasp can sting,
And more than the subway jerks,
I love you as much as a beggar needs a crutch,
And more than a hangnail irks.

I swear to you by the stars above,
And below, if such there be,
As the High Court loathes perjurious oaths,
That's how you are loved by me.

Book-Cadillac Hotel
Detroit, Michigan
Thursday night
February 19, 1942

Darling love —

It is a great relief finally to be free to sit down and write to you, as I have felt rather like a white slave ever since leaving New York, with neither will nor body of my own. This branch of the trip, at least until this evening, has turned out to be by far the most exhausting, with nothing but the vaguest traces of privacy. When I spoke to you last night there were three adults and a baby with their ears cocked, with the result that when we talked this evening I had a feeling that everybody in the hotel was crouching at my keyhole. But now my lights are turned down, and I've got a Do Not Disturb sign on the door, and a bathroom and clothes closet to myself and nothing but my own beck and call to answer to, and I am able to think again of my soul, as my own — and yours. I love you.

I arrived in Endicott without much sleep, as you know. The trip was a beautiful one, first through our Delaware Water Gap, then along the Susquehanna, but I was hoping for a nap of at least two hours before speaking. My host, very pleasant, but a sort of publicity man for International Business Machines, had other plans, and I spent the afternoon being shown and told things — all most interesting, and I'll tell you about them when I get home, but at the time I was dead on my seat — and was eventually installed in the Company club and entertained at a supper of company big shots, wives, etc., at which I was introduced and had to make a speech. After all this, I was astonished to find that my main performance went off so well, but it did; really received with great enthusiasm; many books sold and one stolen. Then back to the Company club for coffee and cake; then the drive to Binghamton and the two hour wait for the train, which finally came through at 1:45.

Sharon, Pa., I am sorry to say, is a dump, in spite of the overwhelming and jealous hospitality of its inhabitants. Sight-seeing, God knows why, in the morning, luncheon of fourteen committee ladies and gentlemen until 3.30, then, miraculously, one hour of repose before dressing for 6 o'clock supper, then off to the auditorium through a minor blizzard, then the talk, well but not extra-well received, then, not bed, but a trip of five miles into the country for a party where I signed and wrote sentiments in sixteen books and drank five cups of punch whose base was lime sherbert. Bed at 2.30 and up at 8 this morning; reaching the breakfast table to find two more people asked in to meet me. Do you wonder that a 2500 room hotel seems like temporary heaven?

I have so much more to write you and tell you, but I am just too tired tonight, and I want to get this letter off to reach you tomorrow. On other trips I've been able to reach out to you with my thoughts and words, and I resent having been deprived of that solace this time. I'm not really as cross as I sound, nor have I had so dreadful a time; I think it's just the cumulative effect of too many one night stands and the constant effort to be nice to everybody at all times. I'm tired of smiling.

Beloved angel, I adore you, and your face and voice are always with me. These days are crowded, but hideously slow, and it seems as if I'd been away for years and had further years to undergo before seeing you again.

You are my true love and life.

Good night, and I adore you.
Ogden

Book-Cadillac Hotel
Detroit, Michigan
Monday, 7:30 A.M.
February 23, 1942

Darling angel —

Have you ever been adored by a man about to take the train to Saginaw?
This is it.

> *All my heart, sweet, always.*
> Ogden

We spent the summer of 1942 at Rider's Trust, where Daddy taught us to
fish for the bass and sunfish that inhabited the "pond" (eastern-shore ter-
minology for what would be designated a "lake" elsewhere). He also
taught us to row the little boat that we fished from as well as to paddle
bow in the canoe. By summer's end, he entrusted us to paddling stern occasionally, which made us feel very grown-up indeed. We sometimes used
to take picnic lunches up to the little family graveyard overlooking the
pond. It was very peaceful and pretty there, and Isabel and I would wonder about the long-dead relatives whose journeys' end had been marked
in this quiet spot. The grown-ups would try to identify them to us, but
even Minnie and Boppy could remember only a few inhabitants. Some
markers dated back to Colonial times and were unfamiliar even to the senior generation, save by name and family lore.

By summer's end, the prospect for writing a Broadway musical with
good friend Sid Perelman became very real indeed. The fall found Daddy
commuting to New York a great deal. Sometimes he stayed in an apartment hotel, sometimes with his sister, Eleanor. The show that eventually
would become the smash hit *One Touch of Venus* was going through
horrific growing pains. One set of authors coming in (Daddy and Sid) as
another set went out (Sam and Bella Spivak). The incomparable Kurt
Weill shepherded my father through his first venture in lyric writing —
Weill's distinctive and haunting music touched a responsive chord in my
father that produced such songs as "Speak Low," "Foolish Heart," and
"That's Him." The show survived the early tug-of-war and marched forward steadily, with producer Cheryl Crawford firmly handling the reins.
Elia Kazan was engaged as director and Agnes de Mille as choreographer.

The cast was headed by Mary Martin, with John Boles, Kenny Baker and Paula Lawrence in supporting roles. A young dancer, Sono Osato, was electrifying in de Mille's dance sequences.

Wednesday noon
October 14, 1942

Darling sweet —

I am now engaged in trying to write a song for Vulcan the theme of which is, work is not a satisfactory substitute for love. I feel so deeply on this subject that I don't know whether I'll produce a masterpiece or a mouse.

I got home last night from a pleasant supper with Eleanor and the girls just before I called you; then Allan came over to pick up Bella's script, as I thought it wise for him to be familiar with it, for tactical reasons. — Kurt is laid up with a cold, so I am to go out to his place tomorrow, up the Hudson.

I tried to get the Hacketts to eat with us, but no luck — they've got their cook back and insist that we go to them Friday evening — don't dress. They're trying to get Sid and Laura, and possibly Jane Murfin. — Breakfast at the drug store again; I'm becoming quite a man-about-Liggetts.

I enclose the front cover of the current Publishers Weekly — looks as if Little Brown might really go to work.*

> *I adore you darling, and*
> *wait for Friday.*
> Ogden

*This refers to the publication of *Good Intentions* (November 1942), his third book of verse for Little, Brown. His first five (excluding Doubleday's *Cricket*) were published by Simon & Schuster. — Ed.

Sunday, 4 P.M.
October 18, 1942

Darling angel —

I am back in the room alone and not liking it; I've got the Cleveland Symphony, but it's not quite the same as what I left on the train. I love you.

I came back on the top of a 5th Avenue bus and saw a parade — a regiment of the State Guard on their way to services at St. Patrick's. It made me feel young and healthy just to look at them. — I shall work on the crossword and ponder lyrics for half an hour, then walk down to the news-reel before meeting the Perelmans. The news reel is fascinating, but not quite the same as what I left on the train.

Tell the children I love them very much, but don't tell anybody how much I love you.

Ogden

As 1943 brought *Venus* to Broadway, we spent the summer on the New Jersey coast, close enough for Daddy to commute easily. He was on the *Guy Lombardo Radio Show* that summer too, and we used to listen to him every week. After the double set of blackout shades had been drawn and snapped down tight, we would sit in the dimly lit living room listening to my father's voice come to us from New York, reading verses that he often first tried out on us at home.

That summer the beaches of New Jersey were black with oil and tar from shipping sunk by the U-boats that prowled the Eastern seaboard. Between our summer cottage and the sea lay a row of sand dunes; on the top of the one directly in front of us was a coast guard call box. I can even now feel the sense of comfort and safety that enveloped me when I would peep from my bedroom window at night and see the reassuring figure of a young coastguardsman mounted on a dark horse and silhouetted against the sky as he scanned the empty beach and whispering sea from his watchtower of sand. He was my own private symbol of America on guard, standing silent and ready between me and the fearful enemy who lay hidden off the coast.

In September when we children returned to Baltimore and school,

Daddy was off to Boston for the road opening of *Venus*. Mother joined him after settling us into the fall routine.

The Ritz-Carlton
Boston, Massachusetts
September 16, 1943

Darling —

The Shubert Theatre. I am fairly certain the front doors will be open. If not, knock on them until someone answers, and tell them who you are. If that fails, you'll find the stage door down the alley to the right of the theatre. If you use the stage door, take the left hand door on entering. All these directions because I may not be able to get back to the hotel.

Scenery situation improving. Orchestrations from the residential section of Heaven.

> *I adore you.*
> Ogden

The Ritz-Carlton
Boston, Massachusetts
September 29, 1943

To Isabel,

> My sweet, although you were divine
> When you were just a child of mine,
> I'd be the happiest of men
> If I could see you change to ten.
> I do not like to be away
> On such a stupendiferous day.
> Now that you're old enough to caddie,
> I am a very happy daddy.

> *Many happy returns,*
> *and I love you.*
> Daddy

Guy Lombardo and Ogden Nash, summer of 1943.

Nineteen forty-four seems to have been letterless, perhaps because we were all together.

The annual birthday poem to Mother leads off the 1945 letters.

April 12, 1945

I'm glad you're born, I'm glad you're mine,
And doubly glad you're thirty-nine.
If you were twenty-one again
I'd be the miserablest of men,
For twenty-one could only laugh
If wooed by forty-two and a half,
While as it is, I have a chance
To forge a permanent romance,
Since yearly God has kindly granted
You more enchanting, me more enchanted.

The success of *Venus* was a double-edged sword. On the one hand it brought a kind of super-recognition and remuneration to Daddy that his years of steady work had not attained; on the other, it created an addiction that my father had to wrestle with for the rest of his life. That lightning strike of beginner's luck shaped much of his existence for the next decade, sending him on one wild goose chase after another as he sought to recapture the magic.

The summer of 1945 was spent on Martha's Vineyard, working on a new show with Sid Perelman. The composer, Vernon Duke, also visited, and Isabel and I were fascinated by the creation of songs and story lines. We also loved to listen to Daddy and Mr. Perelman as they swapped puns and skewered clichés. I remember one exchange on a deep-sea fishing jaunt that began with the phrase "No stone unturned." Mother and Isabel and I giggled helplessly as it became "No tern unstoned" and then "No stern untoned."

But those happy times that summer, topped off by V-J Day, when the whole island went wild in celebration, marked the summit of the year. The fall saw mounting problems with the show. The truth was that it was not a good show, but those involved were too close to see the forest for the trees. Mother, while thrilled by *Venus*, was never thrilled by the world that *Venus* represented. She hated the auditions for "angels," she was appalled by the risks of show business, and most of all she felt that Daddy was pursuing a dangerous, destructive tangent that was leading him away from the hard-won place in American letters that he had built with year after year of solid, dedicated work.

In 1945, much to Spangle's horror, the family unit expanded to include Krag, the biggest German shepherd ever born. Poor Spangle. She had put up with cats, guinea pigs, canaries, and chameleons at various points in her life. But these other creatures came and went — only she endured. Undoubtedly she felt that Krag would go the way of the guinea pigs, but she was wrong. He would outlive her by two years. He worshipped the ground she walked on; she tried her damnedest to pretend he didn't exist. Their relationship brought forth the 1947 poem "Two Dogs Have I."

By the beginning of 1946, Mother had become resigned to the fact that come hell or high water, Daddy was determined to pursue the task of bringing another show to Broadway. Everything in her considerable sense of critical appreciation told her that this was a lost cause. The show, now titled *Sweet Bye and Bye,* was a dud and not worth a fraction of the unhappiness it was to cause. This musical, whose name would come to represent a malicious omen, eventually died an ugly death in Philadelphia, leaving in its wake a sea of damaged friendships and raw nerves. In the struggle to sustain its life, Daddy was asked to tap friends and relatives for transfusions of money, since the "angels" had long since flown. This was indeed proof of the sense of desperation he felt at the time. Nothing could have been a greater punishment to him than to go to such people for monetary help. Asking for money was anathema to him; the sort of thing he had been brought up to feel no gentleman would ever do. For instance, when he left Farrar & Rinehart in 1933 to embark on a full-time writing career, he had signed with an agent rather than dealing directly with the selling of his verse.

Beyond the agony of *Sweet Bye and Bye,* though, 1946 was a difficult year all around for the Nashes. In June, Mother had a hysterectomy after the discovery of a tumor; while she was still in the hospital, I had an emergency appendectomy. Daddy's brother Ted had been fighting terminal cancer for almost a year and after a colostomy was struggling gallantly to make the most of the time he had left by trying to help Daddy raise money for the show, but was in rapidly failing health. My father must have felt beleaguered by the Fates. But he did celebrate his love for Mother in the following verses — the first her birthday poem, the second marking her return from the hospital, and the last a heartfelt acknowledgment of the love that kept him going in very trying circumstances — and, incidentally, commemorating the anniversary of her acceptance of his first proposal on that long-ago Morley weekend in 1929.

———————

Harvard Club
27 West 44th Street
Wednesday, 8:30
October 17, 1945

Darling. What am I to do? Am I faced with the bald alternative of having you angry and unhappy, or lying down on the job? I am miserable and bewildered; deeply, deeply in love, and therefore all the more hurt and disappointed to find your hand withdrawn from me when I most need it. What's the use of my saying I wanted to get back tonight if you don't know it, that if I stay over it is because I myself feel that I must? At 10.45 tomorrow morning the songs are to be played for the music publishing house owned by Warner Brothers. That session will affect not only the publication of the songs but a possible Warner Brothers investment in the show. Mild and Mellow is not right yet; almost, but not what it should be. It is the one love song in the show. If we can have it right by tomorrow our position will be much stronger. That is why I am now going to work with Vernon.

I am sorry I couldn't reach you sooner. My call was in for an hour or more but the circuits were busy; arrival of the fleet, I suppose. I am also sorry that I now feel that perhaps I could do a better job tonight if I had telegraphed instead. My heart is sore; but I think not as sore as yours would be if I took the easy road to mediocrity. I am following my road — not Vernon's, not Sid's or Kurt's or anyone else's; I am doing the work I know how to do, and doing it the best way I can. My course will leave me tonight on a cot in a cubicle in the club gymnasium instead of beside you as I want to be, but it's these present and temporary miseries that will let us both lie more peacefully later on, and once again I beg you to help me.

I love you.
Ogden

For Frances
April 12, 1946

Love is the lost dimension, a realm of time
Where seconds lag and years slip by unheeded;
The precipice to drop, the cliff to climb;
Love is to need, and needing, to be needed.
It is the patient architect that builds
Misunderstandings into understanding;
The sunrise, and the waking sea it gilds;
The far new shore, and the precarious landing.
Love is to hold the moon in solid fingers
And find it lovelier so than in the sky;
To seize the silver echo as it lingers,
Know beauty was born to grow and not to die.
Do not deny me; every year has proved
That this is love when you are the beloved.

Ogden

More Than Ever for Frances
July 9, 1946

I wish the room were daintier,
I wish the walls were paintier,
I wish that I were saintier,
But even though I aintier,
Praise God, you're home.
I've gone from gloom to gloomier,
My thoughts have been too doomier,
Our room has been too roomier,
I've lost my sense of humior,
Praise God, you're home.
My arms were getting emptier,
My dreams were all undreamtier,
My life was too unkemptier,
Temptations too untemptier,
Praise God, you're home.
Though Britons look askancier
As Russians woo romancier,

And Frenchmen ask it fancier,
Praise God, I've got the ancier,
Praise God, you're home.

Ogden

For Frances
August 29, 1946

Geniuses of countless nations
Have told their love for generations
Till all their memorable phrases
Are common as goldenrod or daisies.
Their girls have glimmered like the moon,
Or shimmered like a summer noon,
Stood like lily, fled like fawn,
Now like sunset, now like dawn,
Here the princess in the tower,
There the sweet forbidden flower.
Darling, when I think of you
Every aged phrase is new,
And there are moments when it seems
I've married one of Shakespeare's dreams.

Nineteen forty-seven was a year that found our family together until the fall, when Isabel and I were dispatched to boarding school. This was a decision that did not please us — for most of our friends were not similarly routed. The majority of Baltimore girls graduated from local schools; only a few set off for the prep schools of New England. But both sides of our family had been raised in the boarding-school tradition, and after much researching, it was determined that we should go to Miss Porter's School in Farmington, Connecticut. Daddy pictured me very accurately in the following poem written shortly before my fifteenth birthday, and also in the published poem, "Tarkington, Thou Shoulds't be Living in This Hour," written in the summer of 1947 and, much to my anguish, published in the New Yorker for all the world to see. Acquaintances were only too aware of some of the incidents mentioned in it, and my pals on the beach at LBH quoted portions of it unmercifully for days.

What is a tall young girl to do?
She grows three inches and crouches two.
Her only slipper is a ballerina,
And she huddles together like a concertina.
How I wish she would just uncurl.
There is nothing as lovely as a tall young girl.

What is a quiet young girl to do
When the faces of friends are thick with goo?
She smears her cheeks like the Queen of Trumps,
And wonders why she blossoms in bumps.
I will see the meeting one day I hope
Of a feminine face and a cake of soap.

March 26, 1947

I propose the health of Linell Chenault.
She's lived fifteen years without a fault.
With possible parents so numerous,
I'm glad she agreed to be born to us.
So whenever I see her radiant face
I light up like a firefly but not in the same place.
She rings in my heart like an Easter bell,
So raise your glasses in praise of Linell.

The story "Victoria" appeared in *Harper's Bazaar,* and I still think of it as one of the best tales of terror that I know. Daddy had a vast collection of Blackwood, Dunsany, and other authors of that genre. He was fascinated by lore and legend as well, and would tell us Gullah stories from his childhood that would leave our hearts thumping and our scalps prickling.

Baltimore, Maryland
September 30, 1947

Dearest Isabel —

Happy birthday, many happy returns and all my love. Mummy and I are sitting in the living room wishing you were with us as the line-ups for the first World Series game are coming over the air. Krag has been whining to get out and whimpering to get in, and now lies in front of the terrace door with his paws crossed for the Dodgers. I am still rooting for the Giants. We saw our Baltimore Colts in action against New York in the Stadium on Sunday — a crowd of 51,000 and half an hour to find a place to park. The Colts lost 21–7, but put up a wonderful battle, and we look forward to seeing them against San Francisco next Sunday. — Then last night we went with Minnie to see Bobby Clark in Sweethearts and I regret to report that we spent the evening screaming with laughter. A silly operetta, but what a gorgeously ridiculous man. At one point where all was confusion about who was the princess and who was the milliner and who was whose adopted father he stepped forward and remarked confidentially to the audience, "Never has a thin plot been so complicated."

We had a wonderful visit to Little Boar's Head and seem certain to have the Mackay cottage again next summer, and what about those three sailors who serenaded you in the General Putnam Hotel? — I enclose a Literary Crypt — do you want any more? I also enclose $5.00 and hope you will write me about money — whether you draw an allowance from a school bank, or would like me to send it to you weekly, or what.

Your tennis racquet and shorts get off to you today — Peter and Francise are having a baby. Niku left for school in the best of health and asked me to autograph a book for him. I hope you are starting to do some writing again. — A cable from London says there is a good chance that Venus will be produced there by Christmas. Maybe if it makes a million dollars we should all go see it in the spring vacation. Krag just went out again. — I send you herewith a freight car full of love.

Daddy

October 5, 1947

Dearest Isabel —

What a weekend of sports this has been. Mummy and I crouched over the radio keeping score and rooting the Dodgers in, at which I think we have done a surprisingly good job. I have never heard such a series, establishing all sorts of butter-fingered records — most wild pitches, most bases on balls, most players used, longest 9-inning games — but very exciting. I don't know whether you saw that our old friend Sherman Lollar has got 3 hits out of 4 times at bat for New York. I had a hard decision to make today, as I had seats for the football game, but finally chose the Dodgers and gave my seats to the Waterses. I missed a good one there, as our Colts played the mighty San Francisco team to a 28–28 tie. — I look very like a purple pincushion now, as I have gone to a new doctor to try to clear up my rash and every day he punctures my arms with some new substance trying to find the cause, and every evening I bathe my feet in a purple liquid he gave me. — I have started to write the story of Victoria, and am halfway through, almost too scared to go on. — Spangle needs a bath. — Aunt Anne spent Friday night with us, looking very well, but tired after 3 weeks of 24-hour duty with her new grand-child. — The N.Y. Herald Tribune of October 2, 1947, gets around to announcing that the mocking bird was chosen Mississippi's state bird in 1929. — Krag is still looking for you, and now sleeps at the foot of the little steps just outside our bedroom door. — Our apple trees are laden with fruit, and we eat apple float for breakfast with apple sauce to sweeten it. — I enclose $5.00 in case you need it, but would still like to hear from you about the arrangements up there for your pocket money. — I love you enormously.

Daddy

In the next two years Daddy became enmeshed in another attempt at a Broadway show. But, unlike in 1945 and 1946, he did not neglect his own work. He sold a good number of poems as well as coming out with another book, *Versus*. The dearth of letters until the summer of 1949 reflects the fact that we were together as a family during that time.

The musical *He and She* was a focus of our 1948 summer at LBH; Vernon Duke was a frequent houseguest and the tinny piano in the living room of our rented "cottage" was in constant use as he and Daddy worked over new songs as well as the resurrection and restructuring of old ones from *Sweet Bye and Bye.*

Isabel and I were at the age where we were falling in love almost weekly, and since the objects of our affections generally did not return them, we were in a constant state of unrequited love. The torch songs were therefore our favorites and I can remember singing "Roundabout," "Just Like a Man," and "Red Devil Blues" with great feeling. Though they never saw the light of day in *He and She,* they would resurface in *Two's Company* in 1952, at which time "Red Devil" metamorphosed into "Haunted Hot Spot."

----

400 East 50th Street
New York, New York
March 14, 1948

Dearest Isabel —

Love and thanks for your first letter, which arrived this morning. It gave Mummy and me strength to do this week's Double Crostic, which turned out to be a jaw breaker, tooth-puller and brain baffler — but we conquered it amid moans of, why isn't Isabel here? And yesterday you should have been here, too, aside from the fact that we miss you. There was a whopping 5-alarm fire, nay, a conflagration, directly across the river from us, and we could stand at the window and watch the fireboats in action as they held the flames back from a 3-million gallon oil storage plant. Never a dull moment, including my luncheon on Thursday with the one and only Vernon, who has hired a publicity agent and greeted me rising from a surf of press clippings like old What's-his-name rising from the sea; and regaled me with the detailed saga of his European triumphs, musical and amatory. You can have him, I don't want him, he's too luscious for me. — Felix and I are reasonably happy about our project which is slowly rounding into satisfactory shape. We have now heard from Mary, who seems to be interested and appreciative, has some reservations and wants to see more before deciding; not bad for this stage of the game. But keep your fingers crossed and your tongue in your cheek. In between, I am revising poems for my new book, which Mummy is typing away at like mad, and people keep taking us out to French and Italian restaurants so that we are bloated with frogs legs, snails and garlic eclairs — I have ordered a birthday cake without garlic, a small one, as we're asking only the Longwells; dinner at home, and then a toot to a nightclub. Tomorrow night we're taking the Redmans out; her play is closing in two weeks which I think is a shame, but I expect she'll find a new one shortly. And on Tuesday we're having an evening with the Perelmans, so Sid can tell me about his trip around the world and I can tell him about my trip around Vernon.

All my love —
Daddy

For Frances
Christmas 1948

Next year, my dear, next year
The envious world shall note
The rubies on your wrist,
The emeralds on your throat.
The hall shall look like Cartier's,
The bathroom look like Kirk's,
The library shall blossom
With all of Trollope's works
Next year, my dear, next year,
We will not be austere.

No tawdry bourgeois Buick
Shall bear you up and down
But a Jeepster for the country,
A Jaguar for the town.
And Vogue shall marvel monthly
At the splendor of your furs,
And Mrs. William Paley
Shall wish that they were hers.
What wonders shall appear
Next year, my dear, next year.

That you may not know winter
Nor yet the summer's heat,
The decks of many liners
Shall sound beneath your feet,
And when, the journey over,
Agnes unpacks your bag,
You shall have television

On a screen as big as Krag.
I swear it loud and clear,
Next year, my dear, next year.

This year, my dear, this year.
I cannot offer much,
My gifts are all of tinsel
And all my treats are Dutch.

This year, my dear, this year,
I've little to bestow
I cannot even give my heart,
You had it long ago.
And therefore till the billions
Roll in from He and She
I bring you but this dubious gift;
Another year with me.
So be my only dear
This year as every year.

By late spring of 1949 *He and She* was looking very iffy, and when some family property was unexpectedly sold, Mother used her share in the proceeds to take us abroad. A description of our trip was recorded faithfully in the following letters to Minnie in which Daddy was much more charitable to his offspring than the facts might have warranted. Another view was wryly recorded in his poem "My Trip Daorba."

When I contemplate today the impossible behavior that I (often) and Isabel (occasionally) displayed, I marvel at my parents' forbearance, which was almost saintlike. They put up with complaints and rebellion from me almost constantly, and Isabel's going into deep mourning for a lost love toward the end of the trip, as well as our various illnesses. In Florence, I remember the night that Mother never left my side, changing cold cloths on my head one after another until my 104-degree fever finally broke, while Daddy read aloud from one of the many books always available from our "traveling library," which was contained in a good-sized suitcase. Mother spent hours packing and repacking for the four of us, and Daddy was constantly tested by wagon-lit strikes and changes of plans and reservations due to our indispositions.

They had to endure such things as my demanding ketchup in a five-star Paris restaurant, my refusal to get in a carriage in Rome because I felt the horse was being overburdened, my deliberately getting lost in the Forum, and both Isabel's and my tearful, resentful attitude when we were removed from Venice, where we had both fallen in love with a tall, dark stranger. This last episode presented a twofold problem for Mother and Daddy — for, while their daughters shared a united front in their unhappiness over leaving Venice, once they were wrested away, they spent many ensuing hours arguing violently about which was the object of their hero's affections. I'm afraid that once it even came to blows (mea culpa) on the boat going home.

There was another tribulation that I burdened Daddy with that summer; one of the very rare instances in our relationship that resulted in his being unable to help me. It had to do with Latin. Because I had missed a term at school due to a bout with hepatitis, I had to make up Latin among other things, and Daddy had offered to coach me over the summer. To my credit, I had warned him that even if I had not missed that term I would still have failed the course, but Daddy couldn't believe that a daughter of his could be a dolt when it came to Virgil, and so he set out with enthusiasm to help me comprehend the travails of Aeneas. After perhaps five sessions, his cheerful attitude was dampened. He began to realize that to make me a Latin scholar would entail beginning back at "amo, amas, amat," which is a long, long journey from "Arma virumque cano." He was outraged in defeat. "How could you have been getting A's and A minuses in Caesar at Bryn Mawr School? You are a Latin illiterate! What were they doing? Couldn't they tell that you didn't know basic Latin?"

I confessed my deep, dark secret. It was that the vocabulary built by my literary upbringing had given me the ability to recognize Latin words and accurately translate the straightforward sentences in Caesar. This allowed basic sloth to take over and I never bothered to learn how the language was built. The headmaster at Farmington, on seeing my grades from Bryn Mawr, had decided to let me skip Cicero and go straight to Virgil. It was a disaster of the first magnitude and one never to be set right. I still shudder when I think of Aeneas, but my real heartbreak over the whole thing was knowing how much I had disappointed Daddy by not doing well in something he loved. Isabel, a much better student than I, was able to make the transition from Caesar to Virgil with distinction and her excellence made up for my failure.

When we returned to the states, Daddy soon set out on a lecture tour, for *He and She* was dead in the water.

French Line
a bord le Ile de France
Tuesday
August 2, 1949

Dear Mrs. Leonard —

All sorts of changes since I wrote you on Sunday. First, I must gratefully
mention the weather. We woke up yesterday off the Grand Banks to find
ourselves bathed in the most magnificent cool mist, and out came tweeds
and sweaters that we had been on the point of jettisoning. It is the same
today; Frances lies beside me on deck in flannel dress and blue coat. We
were happy to see in the radio news that your heat wave was lifted, and
hope your ordeal is over — apparently all the people we saw the first day
have been sent home and replaced by a superior grade. The girls now
have young men; Isabel a very serious one named M—— H——, from
Boston, Linell one named Joe (that's all I know so far) from Colorado.
M——'s grandfather is a minister, his father is a minister who has been a
missionary to the American Indians but not an impoverished one I
gather, and he is at Trinity (where he knows Manning Parsons) getting
ready to be minister. A most attractive boy, very earnest and determined,
particularly determined that Isabel keep her engagements with him. They
talk interminably and at the moment the fascination is mutual; her eyes
are aglow, and I suspect a slight flutter of the heart. We think she
couldn't be in better hands — More on Joe later if he stays in the running. He has loose hips, dances well, looks a little like wicked Georgie
Hambleton, has pleasant manners and is going to be a doctor. Here my
information runs out. — Do tell Mr. Leonard that we have spent some
time with Joseph Wechsberg, whom he will remember as having written
those delightful articles in the New Yorker on the Vienna opera clacque.
He is covering the maiden voyage for the New Yorker; came over on the
Ile from Havre and is now on his way back. He is a charming man, a
Czech, and we have enjoyed seeing him, particularly as he once played in
the orchestra on this ship and has put us onto various things that
wouldn't have occurred to us. — A gala dance last night, balloons to pop
and paper balls to throw; we had a table for six, and each girl danced
steadily with her own swain from 10.30 to 1.45, which had become 2.45
because of the time change, on the energy of youth and a half glass of
champagne. They are playing shuffle board at the moment, then are es-

corted to the movies. I don't know when Virgil will squeeze his way in.
I close with all my love, crying, Peace, it's wonderful.

Ogden

Hotel George V
Paris, France
August 8, 1949

Dear Mrs. Leonard —

It is now 3 o'clock Monday afternoon and we leave for Nice at 7. This
first Paris stay has been rather different from what we planned, as we
have had to keep the girls in their rooms the last two days — sore throats
and a temperature just over 99. Dr. Bailey has most kindly come every
day; tells us the bug was all over the ship, many passengers now in Paris
with the same symptoms. Nothing serious, and responds to rest, liquids,
aspirin, and the passage of time. The invalids have been happy enough,
sleeping, eating like mad, and making friends with the waiters and the
very sweet French husband and wife who do our rooms, from which they
have learned that Frances and I are sleeping in a bed once occupied by
Louella Parsons. We have been somewhat restricted in our exploring, as
Frances has also had the unpacking and repacking to attend to, but we
got out for a stroll yesterday afternoon and again this morning, getting
pleasantly lost and enjoying working our way through this fascinating
and unpredictable maze of streets. There is always something to look
at — The girls are quite fit to travel; the agency tells us it is very warm in
Italy now, so they should not be long in rounding into top form. Your
first letters arrived today, a great pleasure to us all. I hope you note the
Gallic thriftiness of the stationery pilfered from the boat.

All my love —
Ogden

P.S. Dr. Bailey just came in, gave us a clean bill of health on girls, and
presented us with paregoric, bismuth, and penicillin lozenges for the
Italian adventure. A wonderful man.

Hotel Negresco
Nice, France
August 9, 1949

Dear Mrs. Leonard —

I am writing while poor Frances continues with her career of packing,
this time to get us off at 8.45 tomorrow morning in the car for Genoa.
Our trip down was fascinating but rather beyond our anticipation. We
arrived at the Gare de Lyon 10 minutes before train time to discover that
a wagon-lit strike had just been called, with the result that we sat up
from 7.45 last night in Paris till 11.20 this morning, 15 hours that really
tested our love for one another. We at least had a compartment to ourselves and could take turns lying down on the seats, but this privilege
went mostly to the girls as convalescents, and with two people stretched
out there was not much room for the other two to sit, so Frances and I
spent some cramped and crouching hours. The compensation was a clear
full moon shining on some of the most beautiful country I have ever
seen. We came miles down the Rhone valley and I can now tell you just
where to find Dijon, Chambertin, Vougeot, Beaune, Lyon, Avignon and
Marseille, particularly Marseille, as there was of course no food or water
on the train, and it was at Marseille that I finally, at 8.30 or so this
morning, found on a platform wagon some croissants, Evian, beer and
wine. I've never before had beer and wine for breakfast, but this was nec-
tar after the drought. The girls behaved really beautifully, were also
awake a good deal of the time to see the poplars forming dance figures in
the moonlight and the sharply outlined fields always hedged or tree-d in,
and the churches and villages, while they listened to the silly little whistle
of our locomotive. The conductor was a darling, most upset about our
difficulties; and our dear Dr. Bailey and his wife were in the same car as
far as St. Raphael. A night we will remember for years, and now that it
is over, one we would not have missed. But if my handwriting straggles,
you will understand. — Here we had baths, lunch and two hours sleep —
then a trip through the town and a delicious dinner in a small out-of-the-
way restaurant. As you will remember, this is a town of garish color and
unrestrained architecture — everything in the most extraordinarily suitable and successful bad taste. The girls are again agog, as am I. The people, — taxi drivers, porters, maids etc. all so heart-warmingly helpful and
pleasant. Our rooms are facing the sea; the temperature must be in the
nineties, but we came in to find our beds covered with blankets and com-

forters. The French must be a thin blooded race, or do they do it for the English?

My mind is gone and I must sleep. I am babbling, but babbling happily.

All my love,
Ogden

Hotel Excelsior
Rome, Italy
August 17, 1949

Dear Mrs. Leonard —

As you can see, I am still one hotel or, in this case, two hotels — behind in my stationery, but they are rather stingy with it in these parts and when I can snatch a handful I do so. — I think my last letter was written in Florence just before the latest and please God the last of our tribulations tumbled out of the cupboard on us. Isabel had recovered from her cramps and Linell had begun hers, so we took Isabel out to see things and left Linell in bed with a bottle of mineral water and two books. We returned to find her shaking with chills, and frightened because she had vomited. In the next hour her temperature went up to 102, so we threw out the nets for a doctor. Came up with a sweet little man named Aschkenassy, English-speaking, who I feared at first was a Turk or Hungarian but to my relief turned out to be a German Jew, booted out in 1936. Of course his diagnosis was the same as ours, Italian summer stomach, and he told us there were several other cases in the hotel. He prescribed for her; and next day her fever was gone, but she remained very uncomfortable and queasy so that she was in bed for the rest of our Florence stay, poor kid. Yesterday when we started driving she began to feel better, and tonight she is full of beans, not to mention a perfect filet of sole with white wine sauce that she ate with gusto. But don't think my tale is over. The night before we were to start our drive to Rome we put them both to sleep with normal temperatures and congratulated ourselves. At 4 in the morning Linell waked us to say that Isabel had what she had had. We rushed in to find Isabel hot with fever of nearly 101, stomach ache and nausea. Gave her aspirin and ice packs and got good old Dr. Aschkenassy at 8 A.M., one hour before we were due to leave.

But Isabel had decided she was going to get well fast. Her temperature was down to 99 and her stomach had stopped hurting. The doctor said she could go if she stretched out in the car and kept warm. He gave her some kind of stimulant. It was wonderful. She dressed, walked out into the marble hall, threw up the stimulant and everything else in her tummy and felt much better, slept nearly all the way to Perugia, had a good night and woke up this morning fit to play three sets against Cochet. So much for the health situation. It has been rather tough, and Frances and I felt for a while like Florence Nightingale and Father Damien, but surely the pendulum must now swing the other way. — Our drive down was of course beautiful. The car was comfortable and the driver competent and helpful. We couldn't stop much the first day, being anxious to get Isabel to bed in Perugia, but did get a few minutes in San Gimignano, which lost no towers in the war, and a view of the cathedral in Siena, though we didn't go into it. Then that extraordinary gray-brown landscape below Siena, and on to Perugia. Frances and I took a walk there while the girls were having supper in bed; saw some enchanting old buildings, and leaned over a terrace wall to watch little men three hundred feet directly below playing that incomprehensible Italian form of bowls. The view and the sunset colors would have been unique except that every sight here is unique — Today both girls were alert during the drive. We loved Assisi and spent a fine hour in the cathedral, aided and impeded by a young student monk, if that's the phrase, from Louisville. Then a good luncheon on an arbored terrace high above the valley, and later mile after mile of walled towns and old fortresses; finally our first glimpse of Rome, shining white some twenty miles away, just as the earlier barbarians must have first glimpsed it. — The hotel here is perfection and tonight's *prix fixe* dinner, at about $2 apiece, was a delight. The girls are full of plans. We have a car for 2 days of sightseeing; they want to see the Sistine Chapel and the Vatican, and after that mostly the old Roman stuff, what a word, it's mine, not theirs. We have written to Donna Beatrice Theodoli, Katharine Meyer's sister but I don't imagine she will be in Rome at this season — Frances and I are both extremely well, our only regret being that the girls, one or the other have missed seeing some of the things they had been looking forward to. I never cease marveling at their accurate and intelligent knowledge of everything in the churches and galleries, and hope to write to their history of art teacher to tell her so. Florence badly hit where the bridges were mined, otherwise untouched, and Lord, so beautiful. But Siena and Assisi fascinating, too. Ten years wouldn't begin to be enough to see them in. We have now had two wel-

come batches of letters, Florence and here. Thank you. All my
love —

Ogden

Hotel Excelsior
Rome, Italy
August 18, 1949

Dear Mrs. Leonard,

Even though the stationery says we are at the Excelsior in Rome, we *are*
at the Excelsior and Rome, but I am now in the good graces of the hall
porter and have access to his secret hoards. It is now six o'clock, the end
of our first afternoon here. We were waked at 9 this morning by the arrival of a car complete with guide, but as the girls needed rest after their
2 days of nurturing convalescence we dismissed it, though with difficulty
and only after Frances and I made a special trip to the agency office to
explain matters. Our schedule had simply called for 2 days of car and
guide, and we had thought we could notify them when convenient. The
manager was very helpful, and we now take the treatment tomorrow and
Sunday. Frances and I strolled around for an hour or so on the Via Con-
dotti which is apparently the best shopping street; very tempting, and we
must come back some day, as well as to Florence and Paris, with a hogs-
head of spending money. — The girls ate a fine luncheon, with Linell
really beginning to take notice of the spaghetti. After luncheon we taxied
to St. Peter's for a preliminary look, and thanks to a thunderstorm that
came up as we started to leave, we visited it twice, even unto the papal
treasury. We spent most of the time gazing at the Michael Angelo Pieta,
which I suppose you could look at forever, and the girls found their Raphael and several other things that were on their minds. Then back to the
hotel for tea, toast and honey, and presently baths. We have tickets for Tra-
viata tonight outdoors; the air has cleared after the storm and it should be
beautiful. — We have finally found an up-to-date guide book, and are planning our remaining days with eagerness and possibly intelligence. Your
thoughtful birthday cable came today; thank you both for remembering me.
Now that the girls are well again I don't feel a day over 46.

All my love.
Ogden

Hotel George V
Paris, France
Monday
August 29, 1949

Dear Mrs. Leonard —

We got here at 11.30 last night to find a wonderful batch of mail waiting
for us, *and* the cable with the good news of the Battle of Baetjer's Run. I
suspect this to be the first time any member of the family has come out
ahead in a law suit. I also got Mr. Leonard's letter with the money for
the ties and shall try to avoid hand-painted jobs, naked ladies, champagne glasses and Clan MacGregor jobs for him. — Venice was almost
too much of a success, as the girls are apt to burst into tears whenever
they think of it, and we dare not mention such words as piazza, canal, or
gondolier. And it seems they both lost their hearts to a young Italian who
used to walk around and smile at them, once lit Linell's cigarette when
her lighter failed (the modern equivalent of the dropped handkerchief)
and to whom they managed to say goodbye on the bridge in front of the
Doge's Palace the night before we left. Isabel is looking for a letter from
him in every mail, serenely disregarding the fact that he doesn't know her
name, and Linell is in a comparable state. It's too bad Tarkington only
wrote about boys. There is considerable difference of opinion as to which
of the two he loves. Isabel saw him first.

   We have emerged from two long days of travel in very good shape.
On Saturday we had a ten hour bus trip from Venice to Milan. Not
really as long as it sounds, as it included several very pleasant stops. First
a half hour at Vicenza, where we saw a perfectly magnificent sight hitherto unheard of by Frances and me, a theatre built by Palladio in 1580,
which we will tell you about when we get home. Then two hours in Ve-
rona, where we had a delightful luncheon at a hotel Frances thinks you
and she once stopped at, the Colombo d'Oro, saw some buildings and
later stayed in the bus while our fellow travellers trudged off to see Ju-
liet's tomb, which would have the authenticity for me of Mr. Pickwick's
or Falstaff's. We stopped for tea at Gardone on Lake Garda, again beautiful, arriving in Milan too late for anything but a glimpse of the cathedral from the bus, then a late dinner and early bed. We were up at 5.15
yesterday morning and got places on the 7 o'clock train. This time all the
customs were easy, Italian, Swiss and French, though the various halts delayed the train for a couple of hours. We had several hours of Switzerland where the mountains and valleys and waterfalls filled us with joy

and awe, and a Swiss dining car filled us with one of the best meals of
our trip. We passed the time looking, reading, dozing and eating, and
condoling with an American lady and her daughter whose husband and
father had got off at Belfort to adjust an error in the tickets and been left
behind, with money, passport and tickets in his possession. The railway
people sprang into action, saw them across the border without a passport, etc., and at every stop we received news of the progress of Mon-
sieur, whom they got on another train two hours later. They were from
Santa Barbara, so nothing really disturbed them. — We now have our
trunks back and are all unpacked. — Frances and I spent the last two
days in Venice covering the city on foot while the girls dreamt of love;
covered miles, and loved every foot. — We are all well and I trust the
emotions are subsiding.

All my love.
Ogden

Hotel George V
Paris, France
Tuesday
August 30, 1949

Dear Mrs. Leonard —

This is the weary letter of a male who has spent 8 hours with 3 females
on the Faubourg St. Honoré and other streets with windows on them
with things in them. What is more, I spent the last 3 hours at a fashion
show for jeunes filles where 26 dresses were exhibited, with only one
model, who, though charming, wasn't able to change costumes under 5
minutes. However, the results were good and both girls have now spent
all their money on smart looking clothes which I shall wait for you to see
rather than attempt to describe. We are delighted that they are now pen-
niless, as they approached us this morning with the eager, beaming suggestion that they pool their money with ours, and we then turn in our
passage on the DeGrasse, go back to Venice and the young voiceless
troubadour, and fly home. I walked into the girls' room this evening and
found Isabel on her knees by the bed praying for a letter. — But Paris is
getting them in spite of themselves, and they keep bursting inadvertently
into gaiety before they remember their tragic roles, so I'm not too disturbed — just 47 and trying to remember and understand. — We got Mr.

Leonard's ties today, three rather sombre ones which I hope will be right; Veron has changed management and didn't seem quite as of old. — Tomorrow we start on museums etc. — The girls take great pleasure in the French press, which is full of wonderful unauthenticated horrors, couched in the most florid and ingenuous terms.

All my love —
Ogden

———————

Back home at last, Mother and Daddy spent very little time recuperating from their "travels with *two* donkeys." After packing us up and seeing us off for our last year at Farmington (Isabel had skipped a year and would graduate with me in 1950), plans were made for an autumn of lecture tours. While Daddy did take a short solo trip South in October, they traveled together to the West Coast in November, returning before Christmas.

———————

Just out of McBee, S.C.
Saturday October 15, 1949

Darling Frances —

Forgive the writing, which is not mine, but that of The Seaboard Air Line, which is now apparently trying to make up the hour and a half it kept me waiting in the McBee station, perhaps the least palatial building in South Carolina. — After my visit to Hartsville I am furious that we decided that you were not to come. I stayed with perfectly (this is another whistle stop and I can write again — no, here we are pulling out) delightful people who treated me royally, and I was so cross over your not being there that my enjoyment was half irritation. — The talk went wonderfully well, it was a really good one, for me, and they sold 75 of my books afterwards, all they had, leaving a dozen or more would-be buyers disappointed. The J—— C——s, with whom I stayed, are of the family that owns the town, where they have had mills since just after the Civil War. They are about our age, with a 17-year-old daughter now in school in Washington and going to Sarah Lawrence next year. She is in love

Daddy in the library at Rugby Road, 1949.
(*Reprinted from the* Baltimore Sun; © 1949 *the Baltimore Sun Co.*)

with a 38-year-old roué from Virginia and they hope it will pass; we are really not alone in our afflictions. They have also a ten-year-old boy with an accent thicker than molasses (this is another station, so you can see I am not on a streamliner); a tortoise shell cat like Simba except that he liked me, jumped into my lap and licked my face; and two fascinating toy dogs that are half rat-terrier and half Chihuahua which sounds revolting but works out very well. Samuel Stoney, forgive me, Samuel *Gaillard* Stoney, the Charlestonian who tells the Gullah stories (here we go again, this train is like the old Number 11 streetcar) was also staying in the house, complete with Al Hirschfeld beard but without his wife, the poet Frances Frost, who divorced him because she got tired of listening to him. I got there in time to hear him speak in the afternoon; he is most interesting but quite exhausting, and won't stop when he is through. In fact, he never stops, and also prides himself on being outrageous. — The C——s had about a dozen people in after my performance, and a negro quartet from the mill sang spirituals. Harrison Smith was there, having stayed over an extra night just to hear me, I was told, though I suspect it was the hospitality of his C—— hosts, cousins of my C——s, that held him. — I have been feasting on hominy grits, sweet butter, rice, black-eyed peas and another one that was new to me, lady-finger peas, which are to the black-eyed peas what the French pea is to the regular pea. This morning I went through the mill — literally, not figuratively — with J—— C—— and discovered what happens to yesterday's papers. He makes them into tubes and cones on which the yarn, cloth, etc. are wound in the textile mills. — I encountered a cousin, a very pleasant older woman, and was told of several more. — The weather the last two days has been perfect, true early autumn. The country resounds with mocking birds, and the camellias are coming into bloom. This is just on the edge (this is another station stop, as you may have noticed) of the gray moss country, a few wisps here and there; cotton and peaches side by side. Good race relations and good labor relations, a great relief. — All of which simply makes me miss you more and more; things I can't share with you lose so much of their value. Please love me, because I adore you.

Ogden

Herring Hotel
Amarillo, Texas
Wednesday midnight
May 3, 1950

Darling Frances —

I finally made it, but it has been a rough trip. The Santa Fe can act just like the Seaboard or the Southern when you get off the main line, which I definitely did. I had to wait an hour and a half in the Wichita Station, and after getting on the train lost time slowly and inexorably. I was on the wrong side, with the sun in my eyes, but from what I could see of Kansas, Oklahoma, and the poor relation part of Texas, I feel that I didn't miss too much. Flat, flat, flat — I'd guess that the natives have to be married men or roués to see the faintest sign of a hill — The main thing that bothered me was the railroad towns, where the women and even their husbands had tried hard to put up a little white fence and do some planting. Unfortunately their neat little bungalows and yards are right along the tracks, and this is a line where diesels are only hearsay. They get to hear the romantic whistle of the steam engine, but they also get a smokestack of soot on the petunias and the drying wash.

The temperature has been going up and down like Spangle begging for more sugar. Very hot all day, but about 40 when I got in. No lull in the wind, however. I noticed how the rivers were being blown away and turned into sterile dunes. Edna Ferber's Cimarron was just two miles of trestle over a ten-foot trickle.

I used special delivery on my last letter from Wichita in hope that it would reach you before you took off for Farmington; I feel badly that I didn't arrange your trains for you. I am trying to time this to reach you up there. I think that perhaps you can talk better to Mr. Johnson than I could have. I do feel that this year he has completely failed in his proper job of understanding what they (Linell and Isabel) had on their minds, and that he and the teachers are penalizing them for the sin of having been literate before they reached Miss Porter's — However, this is all late and irrelevant; I should have caught it a year or so ago.

I almost wired Cook to send flowers to Linell, but finally decided it might embarrass her, so I'll content myself with a telegram.

I miss you madly, and miss being with the girls this weekend. I'm sure that Isabel as a sister is as tense as I am as an absent father.*

> *Darling sweet, I love you.*
> Ogden

*The occasion that had brought Mother to Farmington was a performance of *The Mikado* in which I had a role. Daddy's decision about a telegram rather than flowers showed how well he knew me. — Ed.

Hilton Hotel
Lubbock, Texas
Thursday night
May 4, 1950

Darling Frances —

Every demon out of the Arabian hell is howling at the windows. I have been privileged to undergo an extra fine Texas Panhandle dust storm, and it is an experience — The wind was blowing hard when I got off the train this afternoon; as Dean Allen, who met me, was opening the car door his hat took off like a kangaroo, and he retrieved it a hundred yards away. I had a quiet afternoon at the hotel after an interview with a cozy middle-aged reporter whose sister is now married to the first husband of Zasu Pitts. A sandwich, a nap, then my talk with you. I can't write about Ellen Daniloff, it is too much, but I have their address and will try to get something off to Serge. The wind right now must be 80 miles an hour.

My talk was at 7:15, in competition with an intercollegiate rodeo that Texas Tech has just started. They are in the middle of a vast building program here, so I spoke in a makeshift one-story building (edifice, structure, shack) put up during the war. About 800 students, faculty and townspeople, and just about the best audience I have ever had, full of constant warm laughter. I heard a good deal of flapping and banging while I was talking — they were so good that I went 10 minutes over — but didn't realize what it meant till afterwards, when we were walking to the car, leaning forwards against the wind with our eyes, ears and throats full of Texas and Mrs. Allen said you can be sure they enjoyed it, because they stayed and wanted more when they were expecting that building to take off at any minute. — After our drive home, with dust and sand and heaven knows what sifting into my tonsillectomy, cars creeping in low gear with fog lights, and a real hurricane in process, I wondered why I hadn't got the hell out about the time I started my public wondering about the two Jackies. Anyhow, it was a great success, with a good meeting with the honor students afterwards. Dean Allen's wife turns out to have been a secretary at Doran before the Doubleday merger, and still remembers what a sweet guy Dave Bramble was, which I was able to tell her he still is.

Darling, after talking to you this is my plan. I get into Baltimore on the B&O about one o'clock daylight time Wednesday. I'll go to the house and get some clean shirts and catch the next Pennsylvania train putting me in N.Y. in time to take you to a late dinner, around 7:30 or 8. I may have to see Vernon later in the evening. Then the audition with Lee Shubert on Thursday. — Home to Baltimore Thursday evening if possible, but we'll stay the extra night if necessary, as this thing seems hot. In any case we have to leave before noon on Friday, as I am speaking for Mr. Callard's group at dinner Friday night. — I assume that your mother will be going to Baltimore Wednesday afternoon and we can just keep the room on — will you speak to Mr. Schoenhardt about it? And darling, if you get a chance, do call Simsbury house about a graduation reservation.

How I love you in the middle of a dust tornado — I wish you were here to realize it.

All my heart, sweet —
Ogden

P.S. I had meant to airmail this to you at Farmington, but I distrust the weather and your time of departure. So it goes to N.Y. as I shall do because you are there. You are my girl.

The lectures continued, and the year gave rise to yet another musical in the works. This one, subsequently titled *Wedding Day*, would also fade and die, though it kept struggling till mid 1951.

Isabel had chosen to wait a year before "coming out" since her friends in Baltimore were still in school. When Daddy's friend and agent, Alan Collins, suggested that she join him and his wife and daughter on a trip to England and Italy in the fall, she accepted with alacrity. In the course of her visit to England she found herself pursued by an older married man and wrote home describing his attentions. Her news brought this response from Daddy. It is a letter that has taken its place as an icon in our family and has been passed on to the next generation.

———————

Baltimore
October 19, 1950

Dearest Isabel —

Please don't burn your fingers again. Apparently you got through this one all right, and Reggie was there to butter the blisters, but I am not pleased by the episode and I trust that by now you aren't either. The propensity of old men for fooling around with young girls has been the object of coarse merriment since primeval days, as I should think your reading, if nothing else, would have told you. I must say, that even knowing Mr. C—— B——'s reputation, which is less that of a Don Juan than of an under-the-table groper, I was somewhat taken aback to find that the same man who had made passes at my wife in a London taxi in 1939 had transferred his attentions to my daughter in 1950. Where was your sense of humor? Where was your sense of fastidiousness? And where, if I may use an old-fashioned phrase, was your moral sense? You should be intelligent enough to know that in various eras of history it has been fashionable to laugh at morals, but the fact of the matter is that Old Man Morals just keeps rolling along, and the laughers end up as driftwood on a sand bar. You can't beat the game, because morals as we know them represent the sum of the experience of the race. That is why it distressed me to find you glibly tossing off references to divorce. You surely have seen enough of its effects on your friends to know that it is a tragic thing even when forced on one partner by the vices of the other. Read the marriage vows again — they are not just words, not even just a poetic promise to God, they are a practical promise to yourself to be happy. This I know simply from looking around me.

It bothers me to think that you may have sloppy — not sophisticated, sloppy — ideas about sex. I have never tried to blind you to any side of life through any form of censorship, trusting in your intelligence to learn of and to recognize evil without approving or participating in it. If you want a case history of what the purely animal approach to life can do to a fine talent over the years look at the new Hemingway book. It isn't glamorous to be a push-over, as five minutes of eavesdropping on any group of men would convince you, and don't think that you can be messy with just one; the word gets out and you are thereafter the helpless object of dirty conversation, leers and confident insults. The hell with it. Throw Iris March and all the golden doomed Bohemian girls away and be Isabel; there's more in it for you.

So much for that. Reggie sounds like perfection and I hope you can hang on to him across time and space; or has he already been replaced in Rome? You're a little hard to keep up with, though I must say that your letters keep us wonderfully close to you. We are having Indian Summer here, warm and hazy, air full of smoke from burning leaves. Aunt Fay and Uncle Everett are giving Linell the Thanksgiving dinner dance. She is off tomorrow for a weekend at the U. of Virginia with Dom, after many speculations as to how M—— will take it. You may be interested to know that my verses for the Columbia-Kostelanetz recording of Carnival of Animals have been narrated by Noel Coward. What fun.

Keep on having your gay time, but keep yourself in hand, and remember that, generally speaking, it's better to call older men Mister.

All my love —
Daddy

For my family, 1950 was a year involving the old tradition of "coming out" — when a girl made her debut in society after her graduation from school. There was a set pattern of functions for the debutantes then. June began the ritual with its series of tea dances, dinners, and balls. It was followed by the "little season" in September, which was a modified version of June. On the Monday after Thanksgiving one's official debut took place at the "Monday German," or Bachelors Cotillon. The girl wore a traditional white ball gown and long impossible opera gloves, which took forever to don or shed, and was escorted to the occasion by a phalanx of white-tied partners made up of her father and his friends. Poor Daddy, who had begun to suffer from a progressive muscular constriction of his fingers, had even more trouble with the tight white kid gloves than I did, but it did not cramp his style that long-ago evening. He twirled me around the huge floor of the Lyric Theatre with verve, and led me in one of the two obligatory figures in which we girls were presented to the Cotillon Board. It was a magical evening that included a bouquet from Battle, the Philadelphia florist that sent debutante bouquets in fancy white hat boxes with the recipient's name elegantly scripted on the lid.

Lines to Accompany a Cotillon Posy

All of your partners are bald and married;
Some of your partners may have to be carried.
Should one expire of senile zest,
Place this bouquet upon his breast.

Ogden Nash

At the beginning of 1951, Daddy had scheduled a six-week lecture tour. Mother was supposed to join him in Florida for the last part of it, but did not start out with him because Minnie was having a double cataract operation in mid-January. Mother's decision to be with her was a good one, for while the first operation went well, the second was a disaster and Minnie nearly died. She went into shock and began internal hemorrhaging that would call for many transfusions and a very guarded prognosis on the part of her attending doctors. Mother was at her side throughout the crisis, which lasted almost three weeks. I can remember her exhaustion when she would come home for a brief respite, only to set out for Johns Hopkins again after a bath and a quick bite to eat.

Hotel Faust
Rockford, Illinois
Monday evening
January 15, 1951

Darling love —

I've just settled down in this first of the new series of hotel rooms; washed up, and mixed my drink of Scotch and chlorinated water. It occurs to me that I adore you and miss you, and my eyelids hold a breathtaking photograph of you standing on the Mount Royal Platform. It's exciting to know that after 19⁵⁄₁₂ years you are more entrancing than ever, although the realization does not greatly alleviate my loneliness. I now find that there is much to be said for Florida. — I got to sleep about 12.30 last night after the Washington shuntings were over, and lay abed until 11.30 this morning, rising fresh as a daisy or perhaps, alas, a bachelor's button. — Two dull hours in Chicago unable to get in touch with a Scott or a Stone, then a mild hour and a half on a commuter's train, and here I am. — Off now for supper before the Coffee Shoppe closes. — A

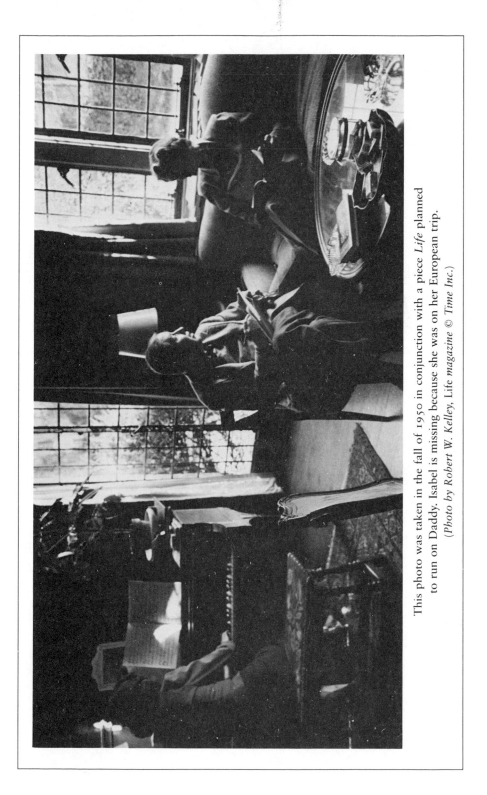

This photo was taken in the fall of 1950 in conjunction with a piece *Life* planned to run on Daddy. Isabel is missing because she was on her European trip.

(Photo by Robert W. Kelley, Life magazine © Time Inc.)

dull letter if ever I wrote one. But it raises my spirits to talk to you even in this unsatisfactory way. My love to the girls, and never forget that you are my world.

> Ogden

Postcard to Miss Linell Nash
from Rockford, Illinois
January 8, 1951

> Here I sit, in Rockford, Ill.,
> My elbows on the window sill,
> Watching traffic, even in Rockford,
> Move one foot forward and two feet
>   bockford.

> *Love,*
> Daddy

Postcard to Miss Isabel Nash
from Kansas City, Missouri
January 17, 1951

> As to Venice is the
>   Gritti,
> The Muehlebach is to
>   Kansas City,
> So I should be
>   more enthusi-
> Astic, but I am not.
>   Scusi.

> *Love —*
> Daddy

Postcard to Miss Isabel Nash
from Des Moines, Iowa
January 1951

> I test my bath before
>   I sit
> To keep my stern from
>   tingling,
> Then the moment I
>   lollop into it
> The telephone starts
>   jingling.

> > *Love —*
> > Daddy

Postcard to Miss Linell Nash
from Des Moines, Iowa
January 1951

> I talked on the local radio
> But no one ever mentioned dough.
> Somewhere I'll find a stack of coin
> But not, I fancy, in Des Moines.

> > *Love,*
> > Daddy

Hotel Muehlebach
Kansas City, Missouri
Wednesday, January 17, 1951
11:30 P.M.

Darling Frances —

I've already written you one quite dull letter today, from Des Moines, but
I arrived here a couple of hours ago and found your words waiting for
me, so I can't resist telling you again how much I love you. I would have
done so an hour and a half sooner, except that I was virtually followed

up to the room (fluorescent lights and a bed that comes out of the wall with arms like Mae West's) by a reporter, and found myself undergoing my third interview of the day, having already submitted to the press and the radio in Des Moines. I have developed a very pretty automatic deprecating simper. — Then after the interview I had to wash my nylons. — Don't bother about my lack of dinner jacket in Fulton, I'll just be the simple homespun Baltimore boy fresh from a coon hunt. Fulton is where Winston Churchill made the famous Iron Curtain speech, and he probably wore rompers. I'm still wincing, or flinching, slightly at the thought of three days in Oklahoma City, but why anticipate anything except Florida?

Large pieces of my love to everyone at home, and all of it to you. I truly adore you.

Ogden

Postcard to Miss Linell Nash
from Kansas City, Missouri
January 17, 1951

> I've never seen the Terrace Grill,
> I do not think I shall or will.
> My hours in all these gay resorts
> Are spent in washing socks and shorts.

Love,
Daddy

Palaco Hotel
Fulton, Missouri
Friday
January 19, 1951

Darling Frances —

Your telegram finally caught up with me this morning, delayed overnight because my hosts here moved me, wisely, I understand, from the Seminole Hotel to this one. I do hope all continues to go well with your mother; at best the strain must be a heavy one, and I hate not being there.

This is a very pleasant community, 30 miles from a railroad. Settled by Kentuckians, and strongly Southern in feeling; great local country pride, as on the Eastern Shore. This is known as the Kingdom of Calloway. The college consists of about 300 girls. They were all dressed up last night as if for the German, and among the male faculty members there were even two white ties, and I felt very plebeian indeed. However, I started out by telling them that a debutante season had worn out my evening clothes and I wouldn't be able to afford new ones until after six more lectures, so they sympathized with me, and my regular presentation ran ten minutes over time because of extra laughter and applause. A really good evening. Afterwards I went back with some of the faculty for sherry and crackers and cheese and a couple of hours of thoroughly enjoyable conversation. I've just now returned from luncheon with some fifteen of the girls who are working in literature and the drama, attractive and cheerful to talk to.

I enclose the Kansas City interview together with a photograph that should reconcile you to my absence. It had an odd sequel. Just as we were about to go in to dinner at the college last night I got a message to call the Kansas City operator. I had had your mother on my mind and put through the call with some anxiety. The caller turned out to be a man I had worked with at Barron Collier in 1923 and hadn't seen or thought of since. He had caught the newspaper piece and wanted to buy me a dinner, so I am to meet him between trains this evening, if I can remember what he looks like.

This letter paper is deceptive, having been stolen from a previous hotel with fortunate foresight, because there is not a scrap in this place, which is adequate but distinctly one-horse. — Tell Tommy I thought of him yesterday. Just as the train moved out of the Kansas City station the woman across from me opened her bag and gave a yeep as if she'd found a tarantula. It was her car keys, and she had left the car blocking her sister's driveway.

The weather is unbelievable, sunny and over 70, with people walking around in an incredulous daze.

I must now pack for my trip to Kansas and Oklahoma cities. Do give your mother all my love, and remember again that I adore you.

Ogden

P.S. I'm sorry there are no pretty post cards available here for the girls.

Biltmore Hotel
Oklahoma City
Sunday
January 21, 1951

Darling Frances —

Two letters from you and one from each of the girls have brightened my
Oklahoma City life. It also cheers me to realize that now one full week
has evaporated and that I will see you either in 14 days in Winter Park
or 13 days in Jacksonville, my mind being very much on that extra
day. — As I told you, I really enjoyed my stay in Fulton, then had a good
trip back to Kansas City, though the train was an hour late. For that reason I ate on the train, thinking that my old Barron Collier friend, Al
Woods, would have given up. But not so; he and his wife and two
friends, a Mr. and Mrs. Miner (he an editor of the Kansas City Star)
were waiting for me, and I spent a pleasant hour with them before taking
the Oklahoma City train.

The summer weather has passed; the temperature now in the upper
twenties, and the sun shining vigorously.

I settled in here, sent my clothes to the laundry, and had breakfast,
noting in the paper that it was the last day of King Solomon's Mines at
one of the theatres. About eleven I was called up by a man named Dean
Richardson, who runs not only the Town Hall here, but the three Texas
meetings at which I am speaking. Asked me for dinner, and I accepted
without much hope of any sort of evening. After luncheon I went to the
movie and had a wonderful time with Deborah Kerr's jungle hairdo and
the crocodiles and two bags of popcorn. Dean (he is Dean now, and his
wife is Becky from Savannah) picked me up at six, along with the town's
top bookseller, Hollis Russell, whose sister, it turns out, had lived for
some months with the Redmans in Hollywood and had met us there once
around 1937. The Richardsons have a miniscule apartment (three grown
children and a daughter in school in Texas) and we had cocktails in the
kitchen while she whipped up a really Cordon Bleu dinner, after which
we talked pleasurably till midnight, when they brought me home. Several
interesting points came up during the evening. I learned that the bookseller is giving a party for me following the lecture where 200 of my
books will be on hand, with apparently no guest allowed to leave until
the last book has been sold. The other point was Dean casually mentioned that I would be 5 days in Corpus Christi. This hadn't occurred to

me before, but of course is so. Before I could express my bewildered dismay he went on to say that that is the King Ranch country, and the Klebergs, who seem to be close friends of the Richardsons, had written them to say how pleased they are that I'm coming, and wondering if I'd care to see something of the ranch and maybe do a little boating and fishing. I controlled my emotions and said yes, I would care to. I don't know what it will amount to in the end, but it's an enticing prospect and I wish more than ever you were with me. So, I have asked the Richardsons over here at 5.30 for a hotel room drink from my meager supply of Scotch. I like them very much, and they have certainly given me the most practical kind of hospitality.

Who is this 28-year-old friend of Linell's and Lucy Davis's? Has anything been heard of the disgruntled Mr. S——? And how much time is Ned spending around the house; I shouldn't like to find another J.W. situation on our hands.

I am glad your mother is coming back to the house, as a matter of fact, I had been about to write suggesting it. And when she is stronger I wish you could persuade her to get hold of your Aunt Margaret or Mrs. Tutherle(?) or some other pal and take a Florida trip or a cruise — I'm sure Miss Einstein could whip something up. I speak of course without knowledge of finances, but I do feel that something of the kind, if at all possible, would help bring her back much faster.

I dreamt of you last night and was not pleased to wake up. I miss you and I adore you.

Ogden

Hotel Adolphus
Dallas, Texas
Tuesday
January 23, 1951

Darling Frances —

These are really the words of an exhausted man; I feel as if everything had been happening, as indeed it has. To begin with; I needn't have worried about the reception of the talk in Oklahoma City — Hollis Russell the bookseller *did* sell 200 of my books at his 3–7 soirée, and I signed them all. The only trouble was I wrote a little verse in the book for the first buyer, and before I got through I had done nearly a hundred little verses for other buyers. The effect on the public was sensational, and why not? I've never been through anything like it. At any rate, Oklahoma City is now mine. — When I finished, at 7.30, I staggered back to the hotel to pack and get my bags out of the room, for which I would have been charged another night after 8. I was so weary that not till I undressed on the train did I realize I had left dressing gown, pajamas and slippers in the closet. I've wired the hotel to send them on to me in Mc-Allen, and can only hope for the best. — After packing I went back to Russell's house where he had a few leading citizens in for drinks and I wrote in some more books, and then he took me out and bought me a badly needed steak dinner, and took me down to the station. I went right to sleep in my underclothes, too tired to struggle with the big suit case for my other pair of pajamas. — I got in here at 8 this morning, another beautiful day, sunny and temperature in the 50's. After breakfast and bath I got myself out to the Women's Club promptly at 10.15, my envelope under my arm, only to meet a blank expression on the face of the secretary when I announced myself. The lecture is not today, but tomorrow. Someone in the Leigh office slipped up, because my itinerary distinctly calls for the 23rd, in addition to which my rail and Pullman tickets to McAllen are for this afternoon. Such fun. I came back to the hotel and persuaded them to let me have my room for another 24 hours and got the porter to exchange my train reservations for tomorrow, so all ended well, as I'm not due to speak in McAllen till Friday. As a matter of fact all ended better than well. I dropped in on the biggest bookstore here and found a magnificent display of my stuff. The manager fell on my neck, and the next moment I was engaged in the happy task of signing another 150 books, this time fortunately without little verses, except a few for employees. Then the manager, a delightful man named Albright suggested that I stop by a small bookstore run by an enterprising girl named Elizabeth McMurray, inviting us both to lunch with him later. Oh, to diverge for a moment — at the first bookstore I met a fellow author, a local gent named John William Rogers, whose book, The Lusty Texans of Dallas, has just been published in Dutton's Cities of America Series. He presented me with one of his books, copies of which are on display all over town, from Nieman Marcus to the smallest barber shop. I'll try to persuade one of my bookseller friends to mail it home for me, as it's a massive $4.50 job. Then he, Mr. Rogers, invited me to a dinner being given in his honor tonight, which I accepted with pleasure. — I

One of many postcards
from Daddy's lecture tour
in the winter of
1951.
(*Courtesy of Oklahoma City
Chamber of Commerce*)

THIS SPACE FOR WRITING MESSAGES

Jan 22

The citizens of
       Oklahoma
Adore this oily, rich
            aroma.
There seems to be a
       well for each,
But I've got nothing
       but a speech.

Love - Daddy

Miss Linell Nash
4300 Rugby Road
Baltimore - 10
Maryland

AIR MAIL
6¢

PHOTO BY COURTESY
OKLAHOMA CITY CHAMBER OF COMMERCE

next enjoyed curried shrimp with Mr. Albright and Miss McMurray, who turns out to be a friend of Dan and Mary's and has promised me a snap-shot of Dan in a Texas 10-gallon hat and shorts. — Both of them know lots of my old friends in the publishing world, so the only word for my luncheon is *plaisant*. — Margo Jones's Dallas Theatre is a great institution, and I am to have luncheon with the theatre group tomorrow and see as much as I can of the play before leaving for a 5 o'clock train — While I was signing books I found myself being interviewed over the tele-phone for an afternoon paper with a noon deadline, and I have just fin-ished a tape-recorded interview here in the room for the radio, so I feel that Dallas has really opened up for me. In spite of which I am still cross with the Colston Leigh office, because it might have been a real mess. I am charging them for wasted taxi fare out to the Women's Club, tip to the porter for changing the tickets, and telegrams to the hotel in McAllen.

I think I have now told you about my last 24 hours except that the shower wouldn't stop running and the plumber has been constantly in and out of the room.

I love you with all my heart, and count the days until Florida.

Ogden

Oh, P.S. — The last copies of Family Reunion I signed were 5th print-ing — 2 in November, 2 in December, now 1 in January. Nice?

Postcard to Miss Isabel Nash
from Corpus Christi, Texas
January 27, 1951

> Laborers from below the
>   border
> Do not respect our law
>   and order,
> And heading for this
>   Promised Land,
> Illegally swim the Rio
>   Grande.
> They suffer jail and other
>   setbacks,

And locally they're known
as wetbacks.

Love —
Daddy

Postcard to Miss Linell Nash
from Corpus Christi, Texas
January 27, 1951

Last night I ate a Mexican meal
Which would have melted a throat of steel,
But being used to Carrie's soups,
I finished it without hiccoups.

Love,
Daddy

Robert Driscoll Hotel
Corpus Christi, Texas
Sunday
January 28, 1951

Darling Frances —

I have now been in Corpus Christi nearly 48 hours and this is the first
chance I've had to start a letter. — McAllen went very well, and they disposed of about 100 books, after which I got taken to luncheon by two
elderly ladies at 11.30 A.M., went back to my room and packed up everything, including my pajamas and slippers which arrived from Oklahoma
just in time, and got on the bus, landing here about 8, after six hours of
driving on perfectly straight roads through perfectly flat country, all pow-
dered with the drought. I was really tired, and asleep by 10. Next morning — yesterday — Corpus Christi hospitality began. I was supposed to
go boating but the wind was too high, so my hosts took me back to their
house instead for Texas stories and luncheon. In the afternoon I was
taken for a three hour tour of the city, its industries, waterfront, Naval
Air Base and goodness knows what not; back to the hotel with just time
enough for a bath, then out to dinner with another group and more
Texas stories. I tore myself away at 11 and again flopped promptly into

bed. The weather here is exhausting; a temperature of over 80, with a forty-mile dusty wind blowing, and all my clothes are far too heavy.

This morning I rose at 8, and was driven out 60 miles to the King Ranch, to be welcomed there by Mr. and Mrs. Richard Kleberg, who were tremendously kind. He is a man in his middle sixties, and a glowing ball of fire. Mainly interested in genetics, improving the breed of everything he sees, from grass to cattle and game cocks; a facile, fascinating, and non-stop conversationalist. I don't think I spoke a dozen words while there. First they gave us coffee in the house, a huge white old Spanish structure built around a court, then Mr. Kleberg took us out to see what we could see. We rode in a Buick specially built for him by General Motors for hunting and inspection trips; gun racks with 3 guns apiece on the front fenders, 2 detachable seats on the bumper for shooting, special steering and wheel design for getting through sand, 2 way radio plus long distance telephone in the glove compartment and fixtures of hand tooled silver. In a word, quelquechose. We drove cross country first to see the cattle he has developed, known as San Gertrudis, a cross between the Indian Brahma and the short horn; shaped like elephants and nearly half as big. Then the horses. Linell would really have gone mad. About a dozen 2 year olds of illustrious ancestry, perfectly beautiful, and friendly as puppies. Then I met two really noble ones — Bold Venture, who is now past 18 but is considerably more chipper than Spangle, and Assault, back from Santa Anita where he won his first race but later bled and has been returned home. I took care to stroke him so I could say I had. He pranced and capered and paraded and played games with the ranch vet in the most charming way, and was enjoying life to the full. — Radios play music all day in the barns and Mr. Kleberg encourages people to speak to and fondle the horses on the reasonable theory that it prepares them for the tumult of the race track. — There were quarter horses, too; a mare that holds 5 world records up to $5/8$ of a mile, and an elderly stallion named Wimpy whose clowning ability makes him a combination of a sea lion and a panda. The quarter horses are heavily built, like a bull through the chest and shoulders, and Wimpy has squirrel cheeks, like me. We were joined at luncheon by a Kleberg nephew named Armstrong, whose 4-year-old son fell off a horse yesterday onto a rock and fractured his skull and broke his ear-drum, but nobody seemed worried, they say he's doing fine. Armstrong apparently finds either too much family or not enough land in Texas and is moving to Alabama, which I didn't know was cattle country, but it is, and he has bought a ranch there and will start introducing Kleberg methods. He told me, by the way, that one of the best undeveloped potential pieces of cattle territory is on the Eastern Shore, Albermarle. He said Maryland, but my hunch is it must be Eastern Shore of Virginia. Shall we become cattle kings nearer home than Stuart and Preston? At the moment I am about in the state Isabel was in when she got to Paris — I've seen and heard too much to assimilate any more, but I am to be picked up in an hour and taken to dinner at the Country Club. Tomorrow, luncheon and the talk, and a dinner again tomorrow night. I hope to have Tuesday free, but there is talk that if the wind dies I'll be taken out on the bay. This is the roughest trip I've ever had as far as extra-curricular activities go; it's been wonderfully interesting, but I simply can't get down to any work. Darling, I didn't write poems for all those Oklahoma people, just made up rhymes for their names.

Dr. Clifton apparently did a good job and my feet are fit for anything; also my back is holding up well in spite of having had to do a spot of heavy lifting here and there.

Today marks the begining of my third week out, and it hasn't seemed any shorter, either. All my thoughts and longings are for you, and I'd feel too far away and too long away even if things were normal at home. As it is —

You know how I want you to come to Florida, and I know you want to come, but it certainly doesn't look too hopeful at the moment. If it's obvious you can't make it, better call or wire James MacMartin at Leigh by Wednesday or Thursday to cancel tickets. I adore you —

Ogden

Postcard to Miss Linell Nash
from Corpus Christi, Texas
January 29, 1951

Like others of the forty-eight,
Texas is a Baptist state.
I've been long enough in the
    Hotel Driscoll
To come home Baptist instead of
    Episcal.

Love,
Daddy

Postcard to Miss Isabel Nash
from New Orleans, Louisiana
February 1, 1951

> If this weather continues,
>   New Orleans
> Will be eating codfish
>   cakes, and beans.
> I will not heed the Mayor's
>   excuse; it's
> Just like Boston,
>   Massachusetts.

> *Love* —
> Daddy

Postcard to Miss Isabel Nash
from Chicago, Illinois
February 20, 1951

> On the shores of
>   Lake Michigan
> I cut into
>   whitefichigan.
> It's simply
>   delichigan.

> *Love* —
> Daddy

Postcard to Miss Isabel Nash
from St. Louis, Missouri
March 9, 1951

> As American towns and cities
>   I wander through,
> One landmark is constant everywhere
>   I roam:

While lecturing in the Chicago area in March 1951,
Daddy attended a *Quiz Kids* radio show.
(*Photo by Toivo Kaitila*)

The house that the Banker
    built in nineteen-two,
Dim neon tells me is
    now a Funeral Home.

Love —
Daddy

The Park Plaza
St. Louis, Missouri
Friday, 10:30 P.M.
March 9, 1951

Darling Frances —

I have met my first Christian Science audience, and they are mine, about
1200 of them; tumultuously enthusiastic even in spite of dandy candy
and reference to such non-existent things as itching and the common
cold. — This afternoon, as I wrote you, I climbed into my evening clothes
at 4; tomorrow I am to be picked up at 3 in the same uniform and
driven 40 miles to the Scientist college for meetings with the students and
faculty before the main event.

    Charlton's party this afternoon was pleasant enough; I met Gutzon
Borghum's niece; a woman who had missed us in Milledgeville, Georgia,
last spring; and a chemist who was out to prove himself funnier than me,
which as you know is not a difficult assignment. — After the talk a hitherto unknown first cousin presented himself — Edgar Nash, a very cute
name, I think; son of my father's brother Henry; he is Assistant General
Freight Agent of the St. Louis San Francisco R.R., and seemed a very nice
man; an interloper, I trust, among the Scientists.

    Edmund wants to take me to the Vienna Art Exhibit tomorrow morn-
ing, but I don't know; it's been a rough week. — Preliminary and tentative inquiries have turned up no Schmitz information, which proves
nothing, but I'll keep probing. There are hundreds of them in the telephone book here, but I gather that this is a heavily German city; Edmund
knows a lot of Schmidts but no Schmitzes.

    In an hour I can think that I'll see you a week from tomorrow.

I adore you.
Ogden

Fort Marion
Little Rock, Arkansas
Noon
March 15, 1951

And this my darling, Frances, is the last letter; it should reach you Saturday. It is now only 26½ hours until I board the train for Baltimore, and I
am in a mixed state of ecstasy and disbelief. — I got here about ten minutes ago after a very tedious 6 hour trip; I stay here until 5.30, then set
out on another 6 hour trip to Monroe, La., where I spend the night; then
an 8 A.M. bus to Ruston, the talk, a conference with the students, a
luncheon with the students and faculty, a radio interview, and, at 3.05
P.M. (if the train is on time) homeward bound. — My room here is agreeable enough, overlooking the broad and muddy Arkansas River. The
lobby is filled with racing folk, as we are near Hot Springs, and legisla-
tors, as this is the State capital. Not much to choose between them in
charm.

I had a nice time in Ft. Smith, quite an old town for these parts
(1833) and a Confederate garrison during the Civil War. A good audience that really seemed to enjoy the talk, and a coffee session afterwards
where my childhood favorite, Creole kisses were served.

Wonderful looking boys and girls here and in Texas, there is much to
be said for the pure American stock.

The Creole kisses remind me that Cousin Ethel Kingsland brought
some pralines for us out to Edmund's house in St. Louis, but said she'd
mail them if I couldn't conveniently carry them, which I couldn't, so if a
strange package arrives, that's what it is.

I am very tired and hideously lonesome, but I am also fairly content
because I can honestly feel that I have done a good job under circumstances very difficult for a man as much in love as I am. I adore you. Regardless of whether anyone buys them I have completed five solid verses
and hope to finish the sixth this afternoon if I am not too restlessly excited by thoughts of home. There is a Hotel Frances here; I'm glad they
didn't book me into it, as it would have been more than I could bear.

All my heart, darling —
Ogden

By this time, I was seeing more and more of my "28-year-old friend," and Mother must have been anxious about it. John Marshall Smith (Johnny) was a World War II vet and very different from the college boys I had been dating. The ten-year gap in our ages was a concern to my parents, as was my own immaturity. While neither of them tried to influence me in any way, they did point out the fact that a thoughtless flirtation was not in order with Johnny. It was neither fair nor right. I had been accustomed to playing at life while he had been living it. He had survived the Pacific campaign and was trying to plan the rest of his life. Their words caused me to do some very hard thinking and in early May I went to stay with friends at LBH for a week to try to sort things out.

Those seven days away from Johnny told me what I wanted to know and I came home with no cobwebs of doubt in my mind. Daddy could understand the pain of being separated from the person who holds one's heart, and he and Mother welcomed Johnny warmly into the family. Daddy wrote in a June letter to Vernon Duke, ". . . Frances and I like him enormously. He is ten years older than Linell which is all to the good as she can do with a steadying hand, being a very immature nineteen. They hope to be married in October . . ."

And indeed we were. Daddy contracted to write a poem for *Life* magazine entitled "Father-in-Law of the Groom," which was a sequel to the one he had written about me when I was a baby, "Song to Be Sung by the Father of Six-Month-Old Female Children." It ran the week after our wedding, replete with pictures. Daddy presented us with *Life's* check to be used for our New York honeymoon. He also set us up with tickets to Broadway shows, a day of racing at Belmont Park, and luncheon at 21.

Nineteen fifty-two marked the end of an era, for early in the summer 4300 Rugby Road was sold. So much had changed for its family during the two preceding years. Minnie and Boppy had moved to an apartment. I had married, and Isabel was off to college. Darling Spangle was no more, and Krag was failing fast. The house, born to host a way of life that was almost obsolete, seemed forlorn; its large elegant rooms a stage set waiting for a cast of characters that had moved on. Daddy was now committed to many months of lecturing, necessitated by two debuts, a wedding, and the gradual drying up of the magazine market. For weeks at a time the house held only an arthritic cranky Krag and a lonely Delia, whose "babies" were grown and gone. The kitchen wing, once so full of

"Oh, let the girls get on with the trousseau
Here's a man Friday at last for Crusoe,
To chew the fat and exchange the dope with,
And a simple masculine mind to cope with."
Daddy and Johnny in the library at Rugby Road, September 1951.
(*Photo by Halsman,* Life *magazine* © *Time Inc.*)

"Father-in-Law of the Groom,"
October 12, 1951
(*Photo by Mark Kaufman,*
Life magazine © Time Inc.)

"*Linell, though I can't read you clearly*
You know I love you long and dearly . . ."
(*Photo by Mark Kaufman,* Life *magazine © Time Inc.*)

hustle and bustle, was occupied by Clarence alone aided by occasional day help.

These circumstances, combined with a number of interesting possibilities for Daddy that were beginning to bubble up in New York, made it evident that the time had come to say good-bye to the big stone house in Guilford.

On our last evening together there as a family, Daddy cooked a farewell steak on the terrace. Johnny was on his annual two-week Maryland National Guard duty at Camp A. P. Hill in Virginia, so it was the original cast that gathered on a warm evening at the end of May for the curtain call. Only Spangle was missing, but Isabel and I swore to one another afterward that we could hear the click of her toenails behind us in the marble hall. We reminisced about bygone days and speculated on the future as the twilight deepened. Part of that future was my daughter Nell, who would be born in September, and I remember the pang I felt when I faced the fact that my baby would never be a part of the magic of Rugby Road.

After supper was over, Isabel and I wandered the familiar grounds as a glimmer of fireflies began to rise from the lawn. We said good-bye to the marble cats who would stay here, enigmatic guardians of the now-empty fish pool. As we strolled through the gardens, we remembered times past; we noted the hiding places, the climbing places; all the symbols of our childhood. Here was a flowering tree we had helped Minnie plant, there, the site of our games of mumblety-peg. With each step we were bidding farewell to the two little girls we were now leaving behind us with the marble cats, destined to play forever in those gardens, which would always remain unchanged in our dreams.

Too soon, it seemed, darkness drew its curtain down and, wordlessly, we turned together and walked back to the welcoming house, our eyes filled with unshed tears. "*Partir, c'est mourir un peu.*" There was a last evening of reading in the library. Daddy chose for the occasion several chapters from P. G. Wodehouse's *Young Men In Spats*. He knew how close we all were to tears and he wanted us to leave this part of our lives with a smile.

My parents had rented another house in Baltimore to fill the gap between leaving Rugby Road and finding a suitable New York apartment, but they went to LBH as usual for the balance of the summer. Minnie and Boppy went with them as did Isabel. I visited for two weeks over Daddy's birthday, and Johnny made whirlwind weekend trips.

By the time September rolled around, the musical revue *Two's Company* was really under way, and Daddy spent much time commuting between Baltimore and New York, where he worked feverishly on lyrics for the Duke tunes.

Soon Daddy was off to Detroit, which was to host the road opening of *Two's Company*. His work from this point on was of such intensity that he noted on the margin of one of his worksheets, "Why am I going through this hell instead of the simple life in Hollywood?" which, considering his horror of Hollywood, indicated the depth of his despair. Songs were added, songs were subtracted, songs were changed. But finally, on Sunday, October 19, *Two's Company* opened to a packed house. Almost immediately an electrifying incident occurred that would be an omen for the future. Its star, the one and only Bette Davis, appearing in her first musical, fainted dead away four bars into her opening number, to the astonishment and horror of both cast and audience. The shock was so great that, as the revue's conductor, Milton Rosenstock, recalled, "She just lay there. Here was this woman lying on the stage. I kept going 'um-pa, um-pa.' Finally after a while I just stopped. You never heard such silence in all your life. And then I heard Ogden who was sitting with Vernon say 'Oh my God.'"

At last a stagehand had the presence of mind to bear her off to the wings, from which she emerged minutes later to announce to the house, "Well, you can't say I didn't fall for you!" She went on to deliver a marvelous performance that night and the three remaining weeks in Detroit played to sell-out houses while the New York advances built to more than a million dollars.

While Daddy struggled with the show in Detroit, he was able to write two short letters to Mother and a longer, serious one to Isabel, who had fallen in love again.

Tuesday night
November 4, 1952

Darling Frances —

I thought everything had happened to me, which was a mistake. The last two nights have proved that there is always something lurking around the corner. However, there is no question about the show's being a hit; the

The last family cookout at Rugby Road — late May 1952,
Daddy presiding; his audience (*counterclockwise from right*): Boppy,
Isabel, Minnie, Mother, and me. My maternity wear for
the occasion was my great-grandmother
Jackson's pongee duster.

"Now I'm counting, the cycle being complete,
The toes on my children's children's feet . . ."
Fall 1952. Four generations: Johnny, Daddy with
Nell, and Boppy.

melodramatic but unfortunately honest publicity has built up the New York advance orders by another $100,000. The problem is for the producers to weather the next three non-performance nights, on which they will have to refund about $18,000. Meanwhile, I am working earnestly on stuff that I know should go into the show; at least two songs that are *songs* rather than preludes to a ballet. The internal politics are beyond belief.

I love you.
Ogden

The Sheraton-Cadillac Hotel
Detroit, Michigan
November 5, 1952

Dearest Isabel —

I am heart-sick and profoundly distressed not to be with you at this time. I have talked to Mummy as much as I can and she has told me as much as can be conveyed over the telephone. I am naturally disturbed at the thought of an engagement, as distinguished from opposed to it — please understand that. I feel that it demands earnest consideration. — As you know, I have seen very little of ———, but I like what I have seen, and should he end up in the family I am sure I could have as happy a relationship with him as I have with Johnny. I know nothing of his financial situation, this again does not disturb me too much; money is important, but not all-important. Having seen him so little, I know nothing of his plans for the future, what his ambitions are, what kind of life he wants. You are familiar with all this, I am sure, but I think some one should communicate it to Mummy or me.

I am also sure that you must realize how deeply concerned I am about ———'s unhappy family history. Emotional instability, melancholia, depression are material, practical, frightening things, and torture to live with. This point should be thoroughly explored. — Again, being so far away, I have no method of determining the quality of your feelings; whether this is really it, or whether — forgive me — it is another passing fancy which has been made to appear the real thing by the very real drama of the situation and other outside factors.

My heart would be lightened if you could bring yourself to withhold any final decision until we talk together.

```
      PA562 KB126
K=LLK128 BDA PD=KANSAS CITY MO 26 1050A=                26  PM 12
MRS JOHN MARSHALL SMITH, DO NOT PHONE=
      5113 FALLS RD BALTO=  A  31

WE ARE SORRY WE ARE ABSENT WE ARE GLAD YOU'RE
CUTE AND HERE'S OUR TWENTY ONE GUN SALUTE FROM
THIS DAY ON YOU CAN VOTE LIKE A MAN SO REGISTER
QUICK REPUBLICAN LOVE AND HAPPY BIRTHDAY=
      DADDY AND MUMMY=
```

In 1952, the age of suffrage was twenty-one — a source
of frustration to me as I had worked hard for the
Eisenhower ticket in Maryland and by election day
had become a mother as well as a wife. I used to mutter
that childhood phrase "It's not fair" quite a bit, to which my
father would automatically respond "Life's not fair" —
as he had for twenty years. This 1953 birthday telegram reflects
his acknowledgment of my
former discontent.

I love you enormously and I am enormously proud of you, and your happiness is all I want. Always know that I am devoted to you.

Daddy

The Sheraton-Cadillac Hotel
Detroit, Michigan
November 7, 1952

Darling —

Here's the check I spoke of, a happy indication of Harms' faith in the score and in me. A wonderful show last night, benefiting from many changes; of which more go in tonight and tomorrow. Only one worry — that voice! She was very hoarse, but wants to rehearse today anyhow. Her spirit is fine, but cross your fingers.

I love you more than ever —
Ogden

———————

Daddy's concern proved prophetic. "That voice" gave out in the fourth week after the December 15 Broadway opening. The show closed; advance ticket sales, which guaranteed a year of sellouts, had to be refunded. Months of hopes and dreams and, above all, exhausting work, were down the drain again, when the prize had been almost within my father's grasp. It was a staggering blow. As he wrote in a June 1953 letter to Vernon Duke,

> God knows the collapse of Miss D. left me speechless; I learned of it in Charlotte, North Carolina, at the beginning of my lecture tour. The lecturing, which I had bitterly resented in advance, turned out to be a Godsend in view of the Davis fiasco, as it brings in a few dollars. I gather that there is no chance of our ever seeing the back royalties, so I'm just trying to forget the whole bloody mess . . . I can't bring myself to contemplate any further theatre ventures at the moment, but passage of time may heal bruises and restore ambition to be a lesser Loesser.

Five-month-old Nell did attend the February 21, 1953, golden anniversary of my grandparents' wedding, but she let Daddy do the talking.

———————

Golden Wedding Poem for Minnie & Boppy

You'd scarce expect one of my age
To speak like an actress on the stage,
But though I know it's wrong to boast,
I also know I'm brighter than most.
So rise and join me in a toast.
I wish to salute my great grandparents,
Who show no sign of wear and tearance.
I don't run to the bakery for Koester's,
I run to embrace these two ancestors
Who planted a little family tree
That produced that gorgeous blossom, me.
I'm told they spoil me, but I don't blame them;
I haven't decided what to name them.
Should I say with elegant éclat
Great grandmamma and great grandpapa?
Or should I my loving mother copy
And say, Great grand minnie and Great grand boppy?
Perhaps, till I switch from bottle to mug,
I'll simply call them P-r-r and Glug,
For by any name I'm proud of they
Upon this golden wedding day.
So bottoms up with the foaming jug,
Here's all the best to P-r-r and Glug
And years as merry as a marriage bell
From their loving descendant, Little Nell.

In between lecture trips in the spring of 1953, Daddy took time out to have chicken pox. He noted this fact in an inscription on the flyleaf of his new book, *Private Dining Room,* which he presented to Boppy on his birthday:

Who can trust calendars and clocks
When grandpapas get chicken pox?
I hope the *great*-grandparent group
Escapes the whooping cough and croup.

It was an affliction he joked about with great good humor but he was really quite ill, and by the end of the lecture series in May he was very tired and profoundly thankful to be able to look forward to a summer in LBH.

A piece of cheerful news was that he was engaged as a panelist on the weekly NBC television show *Masquerade Party.* That lifted his spirits considerably, and when he and Mother found a perfect apartment in New York, prospects really began to look up. The show made for a dependable source of income from 1953 through 1956 and also served to keep him in the public eye. But it did constitute an added drain on his stamina, for while he was in LBH he would take the commuter train to Boston to catch the New York, New Haven & Hartford train to New York and reverse the process after the show, catching the sleeper for Boston at midnight, and then the early Buddliner commuter back to New Hampshire in the morning.

The New York years really began that fall when Mother and Daddy and Isabel moved into their chosen apartment on Fifty-seventh Street. Isabel was at Bryn Mawr College by now and so was not a full-time resident, but Delia and Clarence remained as a permanent part of the household and provided a most welcome continuity. Visiting Marylanders were always welcome. My grandparents, Johnny and I, and our children all enjoyed Fifty-seventh Street hospitality many times and would come home full of what we had done, seen, and heard. The children in particular were blessed by those visits — their world was widened and enlivened by theater, museums, ballet, and fine restaurants, as well as the wonderful evenings of out-loud reading that had made my own childhood so sweet.

But time was flying and changes came fast. In September of 1954, Daddy wrote Vernon,

> You will be interested to hear that Isabel is engaged; a delightful young man of 28 named Freddy Eberstadt who has deserted his father's banking business for television production at NBC; very bright, attractive and worldly, and I think quite equipped to handle Isabel, a task that would be too much for most young men. They are very much in love and we are happy about the whole thing, though dreading a New York wedding.

Between the end of 1954 and the end of 1956, three more grandchildren were added. Frances (Francie) was born in November of 1954, (an engagement that caused me to miss my sister's wedding). Then, in December of 1955, Isabel produced Nicholas (Nicky), Daddy's only

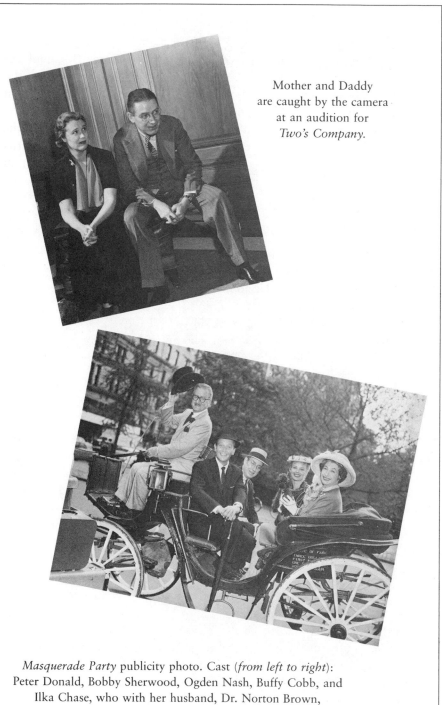

Mother and Daddy
are caught by the camera
at an audition for
Two's Company.

Masquerade Party publicity photo. Cast (*from left to right*):
Peter Donald, Bobby Sherwood, Ogden Nash, Buffy Cobb, and
Ilka Chase, who with her husband, Dr. Norton Brown,
was a dear friend of my parents.

grandson. My Brigid (Biddy) arrived in March of 1956, which completed the Smith contingent, but in November of 1960, Isabel finalized the grandchild roster with Fernanda (Nenna). Nell, because it was "first come, first served," chose the names my parents would answer to in their new roles. They became Mama and Papa — far more genteel sobriquets than her mother's choices a generation earlier.

April 12, 1956

No Petrarch I, but you're my Laura;
I'm Tithonus to your Aurora.
With every passing year I wither,
While you develop more come-hither.
If I reach ninety still alive
You'll still be looking thirty-five,
But don't despise him who adored you —
Whistle, and I will hobble toward you.

Ogden

Nineteen fifty-six saw the last production of a Vernon Duke–Ogden Nash musical. It was put on off-Broadway at the Phoenix Theatre, and made for a delightful evening that incorporated a number of their best songs. Called *The Littlest Revue,* it featured some players who would soon become stars — Joel Grey, Tammy Grimes, and Barbara Cook. Grey's rendition of "Born Too Late" still haunts my dreams. No one could have equalled the subtle beauty of his performance.

By 1957, Daddy was still in the midst of lecturing, but now he was almost always accompanied by Mother. Gone was the desperate loneliness of old. But alas, also gone were the letters that it engendered. However, as luck would have it, she could not join him on a trip scheduled over her birthday, for she had to be in Baltimore to oversee a change in the Maryland family's lives, so the birthday poems came by mail. The change was an important one: Minnie and Boppy moved from their apartment to the house Johnny and I had bought just outside Baltimore. The new house was more than big enough for us all, and had a guest annex that eagerly awaited my parents whenever their New York schedule permitted. So there were many times when the household spanned four generations.

Mother and Nell at Little Boar's Head, summer 1953. Daddy took this snapshot, and it was very special to him. He kept it and another one of Mother in a little leather folding case that he took with him when he was away on trips.

"*The entrance requirements for grampahood are comparatively mild. You only have to live until your child has a child . . .*" Nell and "Papa" at Little Boar's Head, summer 1954.

Early in 1957 Daddy gave me an opportunity to illustrate a children's book that he was working on, *The Christmas That Almost Wasn't*. He sent me the long poem in pieces as he wrote it, some bits from New York, some from his tours. And when the book came out in the fall, he mailed me batches of clippings about it from his clipping service.

It was great fun working with Daddy and I subsequently illustrated two more children's books for him. He was always full of enthusiasm and encouragement, but he never let his role of loving father outweigh his responsibility as honest critic. When he said he liked a drawing, I knew he meant it. Those that did not pass muster, he rejected kindly but firmly. This approach had been a constant from the time I was very little. Isabel and I could always count on his *support* for our efforts, but never the sort of carte-blanche approval that many treatises on "parenting" seem to favor. I think we were very lucky for, from what I've seen through the years, unqualified praise seems to eventually engender more self-doubt than self-worth.

Nineteen fifty-seven did bring one series of letters from Daddy to various members of the family. In late April he and Mother took off on a six-week trip that he spoke of in a letter to Vernon:

> On the 25th of April — and this I can still hardly take in — Frances and I sail on the Ryndam for a combined cruise and business trip. We'll have 18 days on the boat, touching the Azores, Madeira, Casablanca, and Lisbon; debark at Southampton for 2 weeks in London where I'll see my English publishers and agent, then over to Holland for a few days, sailing on the Noordam May 31 and getting home on the 10th of June.
>
> I am really very tired, and sick of living out of suitcases, and the thought of 28 days at sea makes me feel like a child on Christmas Eve, especially as this will be our first trip since 1949.

Daddy reads to Nicky, his only grandson, while Isabel
looks on. This photo was taken for an article written by Isabel
that appeared in *Family Circle* in 1958.
(*Courtesy of* Family Circle *magazine*)

Mankato, Minnesota
April 9, 1957
  for
April 12, 1957

For Frances, As Always

Hammerstein would do all right
If Vernon Duke shot Rodgers,
And Brooklyn would be Brooklyn still
If Los Angeles stole the Dodgers.

Nell will forget her Bobby Toohey,
And Bingley wouldn't miss Lummy,
But I would just be something gooey
If you departed from me.

If ever you ceased to be my pardner
I would be more lard than Lardner
So, darling, let's always be one flesh;
Please resist that man-about — Mara Kesh.

Happy birthday, I adore you.
Ogden

Saul Pough Hotel, Mankato, Minnesota
April 10, 1957

I consider with sorrow
That day after tomorrow
My adoring devotion
Must be purely Neoshan.
If I'd known what it meant
To renounce you for Lent,
I'd have told Colston Leigh
To go climb a tree.
Still, the dollars I earn,
While I sulkily yearn,

As Shean said to Gallagher,
Will buy vineyards in Malaga.
This is small compensation
For birthday celibation,
But I wish you, while wandering forlorn and alone,
Many happy returns, including my own.

I love you, darling.
Ogden

R.M.S. Ryndam
Holland-America Line
April 29, 1957

Dearest Isabel —

The flowers are beautiful and still blooming, the books are ones we had wanted to read, and last night we broke out the Jotto; we understand the game, but not the rules. The weather has not been of the best; only half a day of sunshine so far, and considerable heavy weather, but it hasn't bothered us, and we have walked many miles since leaving port.

The cruise director with his big shiny teeth has not caught us yet, and I fear that in certain sections of the community we are acquiring the reputation of spoilsports, if not snobs. Actually, the passengers, though a mixed lot, are not too bad, and we have met several rather pleasant people.

There are no tables for two — that would violate the cruise tradition of togetherness — so we consider ourselves lucky to be at the captain's table along with a nice quiet little Dutch couple and a loud but likeable Jewish lady who is a sister of the Kriendler boys of "21". The captain himself inspires the utmost confidence as he bears a strong resemblence to Winston Churchill; Mummy suspects he is carrying on with the hostess, a very fetching Dutch lady; he is a splendid man, so I hope Mummy is right.

With this immoral sentiment I close for the present.

Love to you all —
Daddy

R.M.S. Ryndam
Holland-America Line
May 2, 1957

Dearest Isabel —

I think that from now on I shall write to you and Linell alternately and hope that you will send the letters to each other, thus avoiding tedious repetition. Yesterday found us in the Azores after five days of consistent roughness, wind and rain. This time, however, Mummy is proving herself a splendid sailor, so aside from having our opportunities for walking sadly curtailed, we've done very well. A week of salt air has more or less separated the sheep from the wart-hogs, and we have found several pleasant people to have cocktails with while Good-time Elmer and Elmerena pelt the patient stewards with jokes about Dutch courage and Dutch treats.

The Azores are — or our Azore of yesterday is — really extraordinary for landscape and geological strangeness. We drove some 15 miles over steeply rising curvily contorted roads past fences and wind-breaks, some of sod and some woven or plaited like blankets, to the ruin of the old crater, where we could see twin lakes 1500 feet directly below us. Our driver, who spoke and understood no English whatever, took us around the edge of precipices as if a Ferrari were breathing down his neck in the *mille miglia;* we were finally able to slow him down on the way home with primitive gestures, the most primitive and effective of which was the slow waving of a dollar bill. The town — Porta del Garda — most attractive, and, to me, unique.

I feel that Mummy will probably go into greater detail, though she was sadly frustrated in her desire to see all by the seemingly deliberate perversity of the chauffeur, whose obstinate insistence on speeding past everything we wanted to see and decanting us in a museum containing stuffed fish, stuffed snakes, and a two-headed calf so exasperated her that she left a bunch of wild flowers and anise that he had picked for her in the car; he beeped his horn frantically while we were mounting the gangplank to remind her of them, but she was adamant, and understandably so.

Today is clear and calm; tomorrow, Madeira, of which we hear fine tales.

All my love —
Daddy

P.S. Don't forget to forward this to Linell.

R.M.S. Ryndam
Holland-America Line
May 4, 1957

Dearest Linell —

Yesterday Madeira, tomorrow Casablanca and Marrakech. Madeira is a really heavenly spot, marred only by the perpetual imperative solicitations of children, flower vendors, ox-cart drivers, runners for embroidery shops, and innumerable lame, halt and blind. The growth is luxuriant; eucalyptus and mimosa, camellias, azaleas, orchids, oranges, bananas, sugar cane, bamboo wherever you look. The mountain sides are fertile, and neatly terraced, with handsome waterfalls here and there. I see that I left grapes out of the list of crops; of course they are the mainstay of the island, whose economy is based on 1100-gallon casks of Madeira wine. We went ashore by tender at 8:30 and together with our friend Mrs. Gussie Axelrod occupied an 11 year old Austin; the driver a kindly man with a modest knowledge of English. We were willy-nillied into a tour of a winery, given a description of the industry and a drink of Madeira at 9 A.M. which reminded me that we haven't taken communion in too long, then proceeded on a scenic drive that took us up about 3000 feet to lunch at a restaurant on a mountain top. A Portuguese orchestra pleased us by starting out with a lively native number, but immediately switched to Romberg, and ended up with with Hi Ho Hi Ho Its Off To Work We Go and What Lola Wants Lola Gets. We descended the 3000 feet on wicker sleds with wooden runners, partially controlled by two wild men who seemed in a hurry. Mummy opened her eyes twice on the way down and saw some very pretty houses and gardens. The shopping was disappointing unless you wanted to spend hundreds or thousands on the embroidery, which costs about the same as on Fifth Avenue.

The weather was warm and bright except for an occasional light sprinkle, and last night we wore summer clothes for the first time. This morning the Cook people briefed us on Marrakech, warning us against the smells, the sights, the food, the water and the natives. We can hardly wait.

All my love to all of you —
Daddy

P.S. — Please send on to Isabel.

R.M.S. Ryndam
Holland-America Line
May 7, 1957

Dearest Isabel —

We are now in harbor at Malaga, refreshed by 10 hours of sleep after two exhausting days in Casablanca and Marrakech. (Mummy has interrupted to ask me to ask you to airmail Nicky's measurements to her in London together with a tracing of his feet.) In the 4 hour bus trip into the interior of Morocco we went back 2000 years; would not have been surprised to overtake Joseph and Mary at any moment. Much fertile country miserably cultivated by Arabs with wooden plows — usually drawn by a camel and donkey yoked together — the many miles of bad lands almost like our Southwest with mesas and pyramids and other grim geological formations. Marrakech almost completely native, with small European quarter. Hotel comfortable but food abominable; hence:

> I hope I never learn what flesh
> I ate today in Marrakech,
> But after struggling with a jawful
> I though it tasted humpthing awful.

Snake charmers and story-tellers in abundance, narrow crooked passages and tunnels, beggars chanting — a really fascinating experience.

Mr. Thos Cook and Son now summons us for an inspection of Malaga.

All my love —
Daddy

P.S. Please pass on to Linell.

———————

Nineteen fifty-eight marked the first of Daddy's engagements with the surgeon's knife. For one who had never been possessed of a strong constitution, he had often pushed his endurance to the limit, and at times beyond it. When he reached his fifties, the strain began to tell. Many small infirmities plagued him, but one condition began to be a constant companion — an intestinal ailment that never responded for very long to the various treatments given it during its twelve-year tenure. Polyps, regional ileitis, enteritis, Crohn's disease — all these things were diagnosed and treated — three times by surgery — but nothing worked for very long. Years afterward, one doctor suggested to me that perhaps the underlying cause might have been an intestinal spot of the long ago TB that had festered over the years. To a man as fastidious as my father, an ailment that made it necessary to arrange his life around the proximity of the nearest bathroom must have been an almost insufferable burden. But he never complained and continued the hefty schedules of lecture tours until he bowed to doctors' orders in 1965.

He came down to Baltimore in February of 1958 for that first operation and recuperated at our home on Coniston Road. For anyone but Daddy, recuperation there would have been well-nigh impossible. The household bore a strong resemblance to the one in *You Can't Take It with You.* My grandparents had brought a chauffeur/butler and cook with them when they moved in, so the mechanics of living were pretty well attended to, but my girls — at this point two, three, and five — were constantly underfoot, full of questions, or begging to be read to or sung to or played with, and generally a source of confusion. Added to the terrible tots were two German shepherds, two cats, a goat, a pony, and last but not least, an invisible companion of Boppy's — an Indian chief in full war regalia.

At times, Boppy was aware that "the Chief," as we all called him, was not flesh and blood. He would comment wryly, "By George, he looks as real as a Remington, but I know he's not." But at other times, especially if the room was full of twirling children and gamboling dogs, Boppy would say with delight, "Gee-rusalem! Look at that Indian dance! He'll wear the little girls out!" Each night when he retired to bed, the Chief retired with him to his very own tepee — the clothes closet. The fact that he was a devoted companion in all settings was corroborated in a letter Daddy wrote Katherine White that summer from LBH in which he commented, "It's worth it to see our menage — two members over 80 and four under 4. Working conditions are unique. My father-in-law sees Indians in his clothes closet."

The summer households of LBH were becoming the Rugby Road of our children's lives. My girls and Nicky and, later, Nenna were (and still are today) grateful guests in that changeless place. Mother and Daddy took on the children and their parents, staggering the visits to correspond to available beds and vacations, but always welcoming and warm. As had been the case since the 1930s the houses were summer rentals but it was becoming apparent that Daddy's need for the familiar rocky coast and steadfast friends of LBH was growing stronger with each passing year. His health almost always took a turn for the better from the moment he arrived.

The visits of my grandparents to New Hampshire were nearing an end. They spent the summer of 1960 at LBH, but only Minnie made the trip in 1961; Boppy was under full nursing care by that time and unable to travel.

Shortly after Christmas, a cataclysmic event occurred at Coniston Road. All four generations had retired to bed only to be awakened by the night nurse with the news that the stable was in flames. Daddy commented in a letter to Vernon, "We are trying to recover from a ghastly tragedy that hit Linell. On the 4th day of Christmas their stable went up in flames and with it the three beautiful prize show horses she had raised by hand on which all her future hopes were pinned. No insurance and nothing left but debts."

What he didn't pass on to Vernon was the fact that the fire proved to be arson, which made the agonizing loss much harder for me to deal with. I went into something of an emotional tailspin, frantically attempting to puzzle out whom I could have offended or angered to the extent that such a frightful payment was deemed meet and right. While Daddy and Mother had to return to New York on the thirtieth of December, he had become deeply concerned about my state of mind. His letter proved a lifeline that pulled me back to my responsibilities as a wife and mother.

Suppose April 12 Fell on June 6

Thirty years a-coming up,
Coming up, coming up,
Thirty years a-coming up,
My own darling.

Thirty years are not enough,
Not enough, not enough,
Thirty years are not enough,
My own darling.

Thirty years and thirty more,
Thirty more, thirty more,
That's what I am waiting for,
My own darling.

Daddy and me in photo taken for
The Christmas That Almost Wasn't, 1957.
(*Photo by Frederick Eberstadt*)

*"A wide green meadow,
And the bees booming over,
And a little laughing girl with the wind in her face ..."*
Biddy, Francie, and Nell, 1960.
(*Photo by Frederick Eberstadt*)

Girl of everlasting grace,
Lasting grace, lasting grace,
How the years increase their pace
Everywhere but on your face!
Happy birthday!

Ogden, 1961

North Hampton, New Hampshire
August 20, 1961

Dear Mrs. Leonard —

Your generosity leaves me shocked, delighted and grateful; I can only say thank you again, and promise you that your check will be put to good use. — I had a perfect birthday. The weather was the kind we always hope for, and the ocean invitingly warm. The little girls were good as gold, and presented me with an ice bucket, which was equally welcome to Clarence. After dinner, and the cake and the singing of Happy Birthday we saw the full round orange moon rise out of the sea, then Francie and Biddy went nicely to bed and Frances and Nell and I played a game of parcheesi, which I won — as a birthday bonus, I suppose, since it was the first game I have won out of six we have played. Nell proved herself a graceful and good tempered loser, which pleased me.

Biddy is still fascinated by my crooked finger. She assures me that it will soon disappear and a new one will grow, for which I must thank God; she furthermore tells me that my eyebrows will also disappear, but that they too will grow back, and I must again thank God. Nell read us a long fairy story yesterday; she reads extraordinarily well, with such intelligent comprehension and expression; better, I fear, than 90 percent of the adults in our TV-ridden land. (At this point Biddy arrives to tell me that Francie has hit her with a shoe, so you can see that our quiet middle one is standing up for herself).

We were taken night before last to Saunders by Mrs. Ingersoll, along with Mary, Waddy, Betty, and Yanne's football player Princeton son, Henny. Waddy sends his best to Mr. Leonard, whom he refers to as Old '96.

Frances is out cutting roses, and the sea breeze reminds me it is time to take her away from the flowers and get her to the beach.

Holiday Magazine has enthusiastically bought the Christmas poem I
wrote when my stomach ache was at its worst — two letters from the editors to say how much they like it. I love good news, don't you?

Affectionately,
Ogden

December 31, 1961

My very dearest Linell —

You must know that above all things I would wish to be with you now,
but I can't for another three weeks, so I will try here to tell you a few of
my thoughts.

Your arrival on March 26, 1932 made me a proud father. Your courage and fortitude make me even prouder today. Because I love you so
much I am going to run the risk of sounding like Polonius.

Believe me, I realize the full extent of what has happened and all its
implications: I want now from that realization to talk about the future.

I saw Jerry after Petey Gorman's death, spent hours with her during
the shock and agony of the sudden wiping out of a supremely happy
marriage. She was completely inconsolable, all alone, facing a black
empty eternity. Now she has had these many good years with Ray. She
could never find another Petey and I suppose her love for Ray is different
love, but who is to say that it is not as true and rewarding?

No self-reproach, no If onlys, darling. Not only morbid, but worse,
useless; serving only to hamper you in the job of rebuilding. You *must*
accept the finality of a cruel and senseless tragedy to the utmost of your
ability, not let it keep dragging you back into the might-have-been world.

Please think long and carefully before rejecting the various generous
offers of your friends. These are in no sense charity, but a tribute to you
and to Johnny, to your character and his, and a practical and deserved
recognition of the extraordinary talent of the Smiths as horsebreeders. If
they want, as they evidently do, to help you back on your feet, do not re-
pulse them. I have enough confidence in your ability and Johnny's to
know that you would some day be able to repay any present kindness.

Above all, for your sake and the children's do not let this sorrow with-
draw you from them. They need their mother as she has always been,
and will be bewildered and frightened by a mother whose thoughts when

with them are unhappy and elsewhere. Remember that they are uncom-prehending and resilient, not callous.

I rather think that these words are unnecessary, as I have utter faith in you, but I wanted to voice them anyhow before setting forth into the wilderness.

Eat enough, take care of yourself, and obey Phil Wagley and Johnny on the matter of your health.

I love you
Daddy

April 12, 1962

I ought to feel euphoria
Upon this blessed day,
But I am in Peoria,
And you a week away.

TV's phantasmagoria
No consolation lend;
Your birthday in Peoria
I do not wish to spend.

My heart which in Peoria
Upon this day should leap
Lies like the Andrea Doria
A thousand fathoms deep.

Yet were I in Emporia
At this enchanted hour,
In Queens or in Astoria,
My mood would be as sour.

For absence makes a heavy heart,
Too glum to chant a gloria;
When we are even a street apart
The world is all Peoria.

Happy birthday, darling Frances,

I love you.
Ogden

In 1962, another loss while Daddy was on a lecture trip in the South, Boppy died in late March after a mercifully short bout with pneumonia. Minnie traveled to LBH in the summer of 1962 for the last time. The rental house that year was next to one that came up for sale during the summer and so, while Minnie was never to stay at Nine Atlantic Avenue, she knew all about it and had been through it with my parents before they decided to buy it. She was tremendously pleased that after twenty-eight years of playing musical houses, the Nash family could at last put down permanent roots in that much-loved corner of New England.

About the same time Mother and Daddy were buying Nine Atlantic Avenue, Johnny and I were selling Twelve Coniston Road. In a copy of *Everyone but Thee and Me* Daddy wrote, "For Minnie, Linell, Johnny, Nell, Francie and Biddy —"

> Before you move from the old abode
> I send this book to Coniston Road
> With a hey nonnie nonnie and a tra la la
> From Ogden, Daddy and Papa
>   10/12/62

The circumstances of the fire were still a cause for concern, and when Boppy died, feelings of sadness associated with the place were hard to escape. So, in March of 1963, we moved to a small farm in north Baltimore County. While Minnie was almost bedridden by now, she was able to advise on plans for the house and garden. At the time we moved, the surrounding countryside was still "unimproved." The local hunt, which met three days a week, often passed through our valley, the hounds in full cry as they pursued the local fox. Minnie, who had been a fine rider as a girl, enjoyed the sight as well as the antics of the wily fox. When Mother and Father came down to Baltimore on visits, she and the girls would recount to them the joys of watching the fox outwit the earnest hounds by setting a tortuous trail and then doubling back on his own tracks to perch on a little bluff, surveying the confusion he had created. It was a story Daddy thoroughly enjoyed and, since the fox always "won," was an ongoing source of pleasure to him.

For Frances
February 14, 1963

Just five and thirty years ago
I walked alone on earth,
That callous, carefree creature,
A bachelor from birth.
No thrill of premonition,
No tingling of the spine
Foreshadowed the appearance
Of my only valentine.

I had no thought of courtship
At that far-distant date;
One girl was like another,
So why, then, concentrate?
One pearl was like another
To this self-centered swine
Who was surfeited with sameness
And knew no valentine.

Just five and thirty years ago
I danced with mind astray,
And suddenly saw the sameness
Was forever swept away.
I hardly heard the music,
I couldn't taste the wine,
For, lovely as a legend,
I saw my valentine.

Oh, lovely as a legend,
Or a silver birch in spring,
And haunting as the twilight song
That hidden thrushes sing!
How I labored through my fellows
As they stood in penguin line!
How I dodged among the dancers
As I sought my valentine!

The orchestra played waltzes,
Blank faces swirled about;
I have no foot for waltzes,

Ogden Nash publicity photo for
Everyone but Thee and Me,
1962.

So we sat the waltzes out.
Came the tunes of Kern and Gershwin
But I liked the terrace fine;
Till the band played Good Night Ladies
I wooed my valentine.

Just five and thirty years ago
I walked the earth alone,
The shortest five and thirty years
That earth has ever known.
Young love is well-remembered,
But why long for old lang syne
When tonight she is beside me,
My beloved valentine,
My fairest valentine,
My rarest valentine
Through five and thirty precious years
My own true valentine.

In late June 1963 my parents moved to Nine Atlantic Avenue. However, for the first time, LBH was not to be the panacea for Daddy's illness. He had been feeling badly for some time before they set out for New Hampshire and finally, after trying to live with his problems for six weeks, acquiesced to Mother's insistence that he go into the hospital in Boston. He was there for two weeks, coming home to LBH in late August.

In October of 1964, Daddy and Mother sailed for what was supposed to be a delightful six-week business/pleasure trip. In a letter to Vernon in early 1965, he recounted what had befallen him on that junket:

> The week after arriving in London at the beginning of November for a trip which Frances and I had been anticipating and saving up for for seven years, I was taken violently ill, ending in the London clinic with some sort of bug that took 25 pounds off me in 5 days, and left me in a ridiculously weak and wobbley condition from which I am just beginning to recover.

In this letter to Vernon, Daddy also recounted changes that 1965 would bring.

> On doctors' orders I have cancelled 20 lectures that were on my schedule for this year and have been forbidden to undertake any in the future under threat

of having valuable sections of my insides removed. One result of this hint that I should lead a quieter life than I am able to achieve in the smog, traffic and turmoil of New York is that we are selling the New York apartment and moving back to Baltimore where we will rent one, spending about 6 months in Baltimore and 6 months in New Hampshire interspersed with as many visits to New York as may become necessary.

He and Mother chose a townhouse in the new James Rouse development in the Roland Park section of Baltimore, "The Village of Cross Keys." It was constructed on what had been the golf course of the Roland Park Country Club, a course Daddy had often played in his earlier days in Baltimore. They rented the house at first but eventually bought it. It suited them very well. Daddy's description to Vernon:

> Big living-dining room, kitchen, and lavatory downstairs, and upstairs two full bathrooms, and three bedrooms, one of which is my study, and another our guest room for touring midgets. From the living room we look out on a terrace planted with dogwood, azaleas, myrtle, laurel and other exotic flora and then up a hillside covered with fine trees that evoked many a fervent goddam from thwarted golfers in days of yore. A birdbath and plentiful largesse of seed brought us many feathered visitors, cardinals, catbirds, doves, bluejays, song sparrows singing 'Roundabout' and 'Speak Low' and a horde of grackles with their campfollowers. Just enough country, just enough city for my perverse ego, which is fully at home in neither.

Biddy and Francie, who were now at my old school, Calvert, were quite close by and often used to spend the night in the "touring midgets'" bedroom, especially if the winter weather made the twenty-four-mile journey to our farm a hazard.

———————

October 10, 1963

Dearest Linell —

Here's another copy of the Saturday Review Notice, in case you should lose the first one.*

Temperature here today nearly 90, and well over 80 yesterday, so we have had two really superb beach mornings. My color is the cherry-red of a hot old-fashioned stove lid, and this time I know it is not the result of gin and tonic.

We're still tinkering with the house. Chose new living room curtains and some chair materials today, as well as a wall paper border for the bedroom, the rest of which we will paint if the painter ever answers his telephone. The twisty pine just off the front porch was braced today, and the messy plot between us and Waddy loamed and seeded; also the back field mowed. We're becoming very conscientious householders.

Cocktails at the Meyers this evening with Jean Kitzmiller, who is here briefly with Johnny and Jimmy, then dinner with the Higginsons, so we are glamorous socialites too. Friday, to Boston to see the doctor, with faint hopes that he will liberalize my diet. With no greens and no fruit and a constant voracious appetite I am getting a Kate Smith figure, all starch.

Tell the girls we wave at young Borings passing the house; Mary K. has a new puppy, a beagle, and the seller pays us regular daily visits.

I had a letter from Vernon enclosing ecstatic reviews of his "Zenda," a huge success in San Francisco and Los Angeles; comes to N.Y. in November with bright prospects. He is so much better than the current crop of mail-order two-finger composers; it's high time that his luck in vehicles turned.

We're still planning to take off on the 15th and will see you soon thereafter.

All my love —
Daddy

*The enclosed *Saturday Review* item was a book review of my children's book   *Miranda and the Cat* (Little, Brown, 1963). — Ed.

Royal Albion Hotel
Brighton, England
November 19, 1964

Dearest Isabel —

We are here on the third day of an excursion taken for convalescent purposes which has turned out as we would have wished. We are established in a most comfortable room with a window overlooking the channel just 50 yards away, joyfully exposed to the sea sounds and smells so dear to me. We take a mild walk daily and my legs are beginning to work again after 2 weeks in bed. About my illness, I can only say it struck without warning and I was really deathly sick the first 6 days, so much so that I really have no memory of that period — constant vomiting and diarrhoea and opiates administered by the first doctor. A horrible time for Mummy 2500 miles from home, even though our English friends stood by valiantly. When she insisted on a second opinion our original stuffy doctor by design or chance got the man who we were later told is tops in London, who took one look and put me in the London Clinic, where I had superb care complete with warm hearted Irish nurses, and emerged at the end of 8 days tottery and 20 pounds lighter but feeling well and in good spirits. So much for me and my gastro-intestinal life. We are now living from day to day between telephone calls to Baltimore. If all goes well, we follow our original plan and sail on November 27 on the Franconia, due in New York on December 5. I have written to Alan Collins who offered to arrange limousine and as easy customs clearance as possible, so you might keep in touch with him about our arrival. We can only hope and pray about Minnie; I just don't know how we'd set about it if things go wrong — many complications here and I don't want flying for either Mummy or myself, but it might be necessary. — We had a pleasant weekend in Bath just before I was stricken, with a trip to Wells and Glastonbury, and luncheon with the Anthony Powells at Chantry, a charming place in the country, the result of a dinner we were asked to at the Embassy where Mrs. Bruce had said she was going to tell the Powells we were in Bath and then by gosh did so. And we liked the Douglas Fairbanks couple, who asked us for dinner later, but while I was ill. — My reception by the English has been astounding to me — they really know my stuff well and demonstrate a warm affection from the booksellers through to the press. Very good for my always vulnerable self-esteem. We have today purchased and ordered sent to Nicky a set of the Oxford Junior Encyclopedia, which will begin to arrive one volume at a time, as the cost of shipping it as one parcel is prohibitive. There are 10 or 12 volumes, so you may need to lease an extra apartment. At any rate don't give him any of them until they are assembled, which should be before Christmas.

Mummy and I were pleased to hear that you and Freddy are on the way to arriving at some kind of financial steadiness. The rags to riches to rags life is an intolerable one. Mummy has come as close as possible to solving it by arrangement with her trust people, and Sukie at Curtis Brown keeps me in line. It doesn't bring in any more money, but at least we know more or less where we are.

Aunt Gwen has seen you in pants in Life, and we have seen a photograph of Diana Vreeland by Freddy in one of the London papers with his
name more prominent than in Herald Trib credits.

Today is Thursday, we plan to return on Saturday to London and the
Connaught until next Thursday the 26th when we'll go down and spend
the night in Southampton before an early sailing.

It's been a weird trip full of exploded plans, but the final 2 weeks we
are enjoying. No theatre, but there is really nothing on now that we want
to see. I simply relish observing and participating in the many customs
that vary so little yet so much from our own.

All my love to you all —
Daddy

The Connaught London
November 25, 1964

Dearest Linell —

If all continues well this letter will not precede my arrival by many days,
but I could not leave without telling you what a strength your love and
constant thoughtfulness gave to your mother and me in a truly desperate
period. The flowers from you and Johnny brightened my hospital room
and filled it with thoughts of home, and they were still blooming enough
when I departed for me to give them to my favorite of the wonderful
Irish nurses who popped into the room within 60 seconds of my pressing the button and spent the day re-filling my jug with fruit juice and
ice.

The first week of sickness, in the hotel, was the worst. Mummy was
sure I was going to die, and I would rather have. But as soon as dear
sweet Dr. Avery Jones appeared and whisked me to the clinic things began to improve. I have lost 20 pounds — embarrassing to my tailor, who
measured me before I was stricken — and am still woefully weak and
easily tired, but my spirits are high and my appetite not bad. Dr. Avery
Jones doesn't believe much in restricted diets, and recommended any
form of alcohol except beer.

Our stay at Brighton was both beneficial and delightful. Mummy
really needed it even more than I did, and now looks much better.

What a time you have had with Minnie. As you know, our hearts were always with you.

Dearest love —
Daddy

June 25, 1965

Dearest Linell —

The driver, who delivered the car in perfect condition, arrived and fled with the dawn and without letting me know he was here. I therefore enclose a check which will cover his services and trip home. Incidentally, as soon as you can fix a date, I want to send a check for the girls' travel, as their visit is our pleasure.

We are sitting on our hands and biting our fingernails (the neatest trick of the year) waiting for the movers' telegram. I have just talked to the N.Y. office which says it will talk to the Washington office which I suppose will talk to Prime Minister MacMillan. This month's issue of the Consumers Union Report which just arrived has an article on the vanning trust — very discouraging, the customer is obviously at their mercy unless the ICC takes some action. I just hope we get to L.B.H. before Labor Day. Clarence reports glorious weather there.

Daddy

North Hampton, New Hampshire
August 3, 1965

Dearest Isabel —

Everything here is what you would hope; in fact so far, even better. Nicky is on even keel and the sailing is smooth. The only tears of his visit flowed for a minute or two last week when after a merry evening at the Warrens where he grilled hamburgers for the company we had to cancel his plan for sleeping in his pup-tent on the lawn because it had begun to rain. Even then his reason soon took over and he went happily to bed indoors. He and Biddy did sleep out the following night, their second such venture. They claimed to have enjoyed it, but there have been no requests for a repeat. He has taken to the surf like a Polynesian, and seems to achieve the speed of light on his canvas raft. I am delighted with the bredth (breadth?) of his mind and the range of his interests; he is also revealing a latent sense of humor which he often applies to himself. His deportment is perfect, as is his care of the Kangaroo rat. We try to fill him with more meat and greens and fruit than sweets, although he did have his share of Clarence's birthday cake baked by dear sweet Mrs. Knowles.

We have had to postpone his tennis lessons because of a swelling on the tip of his right thumb, the result of something he did to his hand at camp. Dr. Bryer thinks there is a tiny thorn or other foreign object in it. No infection. We are soaking it several times daily in hot water and Epsom salts to bring it to a head; Dr. Bryer has seen him twice and I am taking him again today, as there are indications that it is completing its course. We took him with Biddy to the old York jail the other day; a great success, particularly the stocks and the dungeon. The trip included exploration of the old Colonial graveyard and attempts to decipher the almost indecipherable epitaphs, and ended with a tour of one of the old houses and later, if you will forgive us, ice cream sodas for all.

Katharine Mulry arrived last Friday and is the usual comfort; her presence is most welcome and helpful.

My carbuncle has almost vanished and I am feeling well; just completed a promotion verse for Reader's Digest for a princely sum. It's straight commercial work, but I tried to do it honestly and respectably. We're expecting the Perelmans and Jane and Edgar Ward next week which means two successive evenings of partying; after that, back to the leisurely Little Boar's Head lolling.

Your letter meant much to me in many ways. As partial response, I assure you that Nicky is a joy to us; we love him dearly and are most proud of him, and would gladly keep him with us for years.

Mummy is writing to you, but includes her love here along with mine.

Daddy

P.S. When are we to see Nenna again? We miss her sorely. Do kiss her for me.

———————

Nineteen sixty-five, a year that began happily, ended in sadness when Minnie, who celebrated her ninetieth birthday on Guy Fawkes Day (November 5), died at the year's end. We had one last Christmas with her.

Daddy taking a break from writing. Freddy shot this picture in my
parents' last New York apartment, where as usual Daddy's work area
was decorated in his favorite motif — wall-to-wall books.
(Photo by Frederick Eberstadt)

Daddy's love for Minnie was as deep as any son's. Their thirty-seven-year relationship had been marked by unusual warmth and understanding. He acknowledged his love and respect for her frequently, and often voiced it in the inscriptions of his books. One book, *Many Long Years Ago,* was formally dedicated to her, and he asked her permission to do this in a note that I found carefully tucked inside her copy of the book. Dated July 18, 1945, it ran, "Dear Mrs. Leonard — I hope you won't mind if I use the enclosed as a dedication in the new book. Frances thinks it is all right, and it says what I want to say. I took the children out fishing again yesterday; Frances joined us and slept peacefully . . . love, Ogden."

The dedication he enclosed was indeed used:

> For N.J.L.
> In June of 1931
> She gained a moody, broody son,
> While he acquired with loud hurrah,
> A calm and understanding ma.
> Because she never tried to change him,
> Reform, reprove or rearrange him,
> But gave him only love and wisdom
> And in her kingdom freedom was hisdom
> In '45 he can but purr
> And dedicate this book to her.

And on the flyleaf of the book he had written:

> For N.J.L. —
> If my affection you would gauge
> Just look beyond the title page.

On the flyleaf of an earlier book, *The Face Is Familiar,* he had inscribed:

> "The awe and dread with which the untutored savage contemplates his
> mother-in-law are among the most familiar facts of anthropology." Sir James
> Frazer — *The Golden Bough*

Tut and triple tut, Sir James!
Who do you think you're calling names?
If you'd married a girl from Baltimaw
You'd be mad about your mother-in-law.

> For N.J.L. from O.N.
> with affection untainted by terror.

In her copy of *You Can't Get There from Here* he wrote:

For my beloved N.J.L. —
With years of grateful thoughts.

And after her death, he wrote to Vernon: "Frances' mother died shortly after Christmas. She was in the 91st year of a loving and generous life, a completely unselfish woman; one of the few completely good people I have known."

It was a heartfelt epitaph.

Correspondence from 1966 included the annual birthday poem to Mother and two verses sent to my daughters from Florida, where Daddy and Mother were visiting with friends over Valentine's Day.

To Francie

From the woods St. Valentine
Carried home a pretty vine.
St. Valentine was over-eager,
Now he's a poison-ivy-leaguer,
So Francie, avoid the ivy patch —
I love you, and when you itch I scratch.

Papa

To Brigid

St. Valentine, as I've heard tell,
Would never, never learn to spell.
Because he shared his speller with me,
I send you all my L–U–V.

Papa

For Frances
April 12, 1966

Once, love, there was a language fresh and shining
As sunrise sparkling on a dewy lawn;
The humblest poet, on pride and porridge dining,
Found noble words to shout the joy of dawn.
Then every tongue was young,
Then art
Sprang innocent from the heart,
And then were body and soul
Not separate, but whole.

Too soon the precious heritage was looted
As loutish vandals stormed the treasury;
Gold into plastic gewgaws they transmuted,
Like monkeys playing at inverse alchemy.
Coinage debased, defaced;
The word,
Once helmeted and spurred,
Distorted on the rack
By every fumbling hack.

How aptly you were born in Easter season,
Long-tarnished phrases resume their gleam for you,
Here's honor, and fierce loyalty scorning reason,
And beauty each sculptor year reveals more true.
Dance, dance in renaissance,
Sweet words;
Elizabethan birds
Should sing my love awake
Rather than this harsh music that I make.

                                             Ogden

———————

The following verse constituted a sendoff to my girls on the occasion of a six-week Smith family trip to Europe.

Dear girls, when to the feast you go
Aboard the Michaelangelo
These are the rules of etiquette —
No ketchup on the crêpes Suzette.
Good shipboard manners also bar
Butterscotch sauce on caviar,
And do not ask for currant jelly
On antipasto or vermicelli.
Remember not to make a fuss
When served a tasty octopus;
If met beneath the ocean blue,
He gladly would have eaten you.
You'll find upon occasions gala
Veal scallopini and veal marsala;
Then at the ordinary meal
You'll dine on ordinary veal.
Italians don't do things by halves
When they begin to butcher calves.
If when the ship through tempests labors
You spill your soup upon your neighbors,
Do not apologize or pine,
That is the captain's fault, not thine.
But I hope the trip is calm, not lurchy,
So until August, arrivederci.

Lots of love,
Papa

For Nell
September 16, 1966

Roses are red,
Money is green,
I'm sixty-four
And you are fourteen.
I might send you roses
Sweet-scented and sunny,
But you cannot spend roses
The way you spend money,
So accept this small gift

With your usual poise
And pick out a dress
To bowl over the boys.

> *Love and happy*
> *happy birthday,*
> Papa

Daddy frequently wrote place cards for the dinners my parents gave. This was an example from October 1966:

FRANCES

Hush! Hush! Whisper who dares!
Clarence is answering Frances's prayers.
Hush! Hush! Everyone quiet!
Frances is quitting that god damn diet!

Staying late into the autumn at LBH was a great joy to both my parents. A number of their neighbors were residents so the socializing that Daddy enjoyed so much did not end on Labor Day. Life was quieter but the joy of being there never diminished. Daddy's "rocky coast" was all he had ever hoped it would be.

Nineteen sixty-seven only produced two family letters, but the year was marked by a family disaster in April. Daddy explained it this way in a June letter to Vernon:

> Much has happened since I had to break our engagement in Baltimore. We left for New York almost immediately after I talked to you. Isabel was desperately ill, and for the first ten days we thought we were going to lose her. Some toxic substance in the entire system, but centered in the kidneys. Miracle doctors with miracle machines worked their miracles, though not complete ones. She was released from the hospital after five weeks, but must return two days each week for treatment under the kidney machine. We don't know yet if this must continue for the rest of her life; it's still a toss-up. She is very frail, but faces the prospect with fortitude.

Daddy was truly a marvel during the terrifying first two weeks of her illness. Being with Isabel at that time was a shattering experience to those who loved her because the toxicity caused by lack of kidney function caused her to suffer frightful hallucinations. No one, not even Freddy, was able to comfort her in her terror, and it was really an agonizing thing to watch. Mother and Daddy and I would spell poor Fred from time to time — giving him a chance for a much-needed break — but Daddy's strength was far greater than Mother's or mine during those sessions. He would sit quietly with my tortured sister, talking gently and reassuringly to her when the nightmares took over, never wavering in his steady support. My recollection of that time centers on Daddy's steadfast battle for his daughter. He took on Isabel's dragons in their lair — beating them back with love, and, as she began to emerge from that terrible place of darkness, his constancy helped speed her on her journey back to us. For months she lived with a shunt in her wrist and a weekly date with the machine. And then at last it was over. Sufficient kidney function returned to make dialysis unnecessary. A miracle indeed.

The assassination of President Kennedy in 1963 set the stage for a decade of upheaval that was deeply disturbing to my father. So many things that pervaded the national and international scene were abhorrent to him. He struggled with a curious dichotomy regarding the war protesters. Though he agreed wholeheartedly with the message, he was unsympathetic with the majority of the messengers, deploring the language, appearance, and behavior that they brought to the stage of American life. It contrasted markedly with the broad nobility of the civil-rights movement led by Dr. Martin Luther King, Jr. So in 1968, when King was gunned down, his murder to be followed shortly by that of Robert Kennedy and the debacle of the Chicago Democratic convention, the world as he knew it seemed to be self-destructing. His work suffered; often he had periods of drought that frightened him.

About this time he once said to me, "I wonder if what I write has relevance anymore. In a world gone mad, humor may have been the first casualty of war."

It was a total non sequitur. We were at the racetrack together, and were in the process of handicapping the first race. He moved on to another topic before I had gathered my wits to reply, but he must have been quite desperate to have voiced that thought, for he was never one to share depressions or doubts with his family. Patterning himself on his father, he clearly felt that a man should endure without complaint the doubts, failures, and disasters that came his way, bearing the wounds lightly, and never dwelling on them. He believed that the head of the household was responsible for the morale of the household; he had learned to appreciate the worth of that dogma in his own childhood.

Occasionally in his work one can feel his isolation (e.g., "Listen"), and in the soul-searching world of the 1960s, when the watchword for relationships was "letting it all hang out," he was something of an anachronism. But he achieved his end as far as his family was concerned. By the time Isabel and I were grown, we acknowledged that Daddy couldn't always "fix it" when things went wrong for us, but we knew just as surely that he would be there with sound advice and loving support to help us survive whatever crisis might occur. We were loathe to probe him over his own worries; we had learned that such a course of conversation made him uncomfortable and we sensed, I'm ashamed to admit, that should he have responded with a flood of doubts and fears, it would have been extremely unsettling for us. We had based a lot of our own security on a subliminal perception of his invincibility. But we were certainly aware of his deep concern about the country in 1968. He and Mother traveled to New Hampshire in late winter for the presidential primary, where they cast their votes for Eugene McCarthy. Daddy even involved himself to the extent of writing a campaign birthday poem for the anti-war Senator, thus breaking a rule he had imposed on himself long ago after World War II. The work he had done at that time for the Treasury Department and on war-bond tours did not measure up to his personal standards, and so he had sworn off dealing with the sort of political or patriotic subject that brought his own emotions so strongly to the fore that he lost touch with his innate sense of balance. Composing a poem for the McCarthy for President Committee was stark testimony to the depth of his feelings about the direction of the nation.

He fretted over the Smith family trip to Albuquerque during the summer to attend the Arabian National Championships. I know he did not approve of the undertaking, which entailed a crazy journey across a good part of the warmest sections of the country in a venerable Pontiac station wagon, pulling an occupied horse trailer. It was certainly an experience to remember, especially since it necessitated overnights at "horse" motels that occasionally turned out to be stockyards. But when we returned and were able to recount some of our stranger adventures, we found that Daddy had been everywhere we had been — save, thank heaven, the stockyards — and had a tale for each location that would send us all into hysterics. I had not read his "lecture tour" letters to Mother then, and so heard some of the stories for the first time.

For only the second time in their daughters' lives did my parents spend Christmas away from the family. Daddy had been engaged to appear with the San Francisco Symphony on the twenty-seventh and twenty-eighth of December, where he would be reading his verses to Saint Saens' Carnival of Animals. Since he had never changed his mind about the appropriateness of man's traveling by air, he set about to find a way to make the trip by way of his old love, the train. The state of rail travel in 1968 was not what it had been even a decade earlier. It was soon apparent that the West Coast dates and Christmas at home were incompatible. So, that being the case, Mother and Daddy planned the trip west via the northern Canadian route, traveling down the coast to San Francisco in time for Christmas.

When they returned early in the New Year, Daddy had two extra presents in tow for us — both records. The first was *The Incredible Year,* which played the newsbreaks of 1968: that roller coaster of events just past. The second record was ninety minutes of sounds — railroad sounds — of the country's past: the mournful whistle of the old trains long since gone; steam engines — American ghosts as dogged and hardworking as the westering pioneers they followed, metal ghosts that had helped build a nation. It was Daddy's antidote to *The Incredible Year* and, after my first bewilderment at the contents, I came to find it as relaxing as he did, for I was old enough to remember those sounds from my childhood when Daddy would take us to wave at the trains as they passed nearby crossings either in LBH or in Baltimore. And the engineers and firemen would always wave back at the two little girls as Daddy had known they would.

For Frances
April 12, 1968

My wife
Was a girl from the foaming seas of twilight lore
On a lucent shell by Nereids borne ashore.
Such being her birth,
She found swift joy in the common things of earth.
She exulted in simple scent and sound and sight,
And her unfeigned delight gave me delight.
She carelessly gathered my heart like a daffodil.
She has it still.

My wife
Is a woman who walks with the inborn pride of a queen,
After turbulent decades of marriage still serene.
Through death and birth
She has learned that the world is not all grief, all mirth.
Steadfast beside me when ventures and spirits fail
Her courage flies as brave as a flag in the gale.
I marvel at her loveliness, her grace —
But not to her face.

My wife
Will be an old lady mischievous and flighty,
Will shake her gold-headed cane in the face of God Almighty.
She will be revered,
Be pampered, be boasted of, be adored and feared.
She will love a surprise, and a dry martini as well,
She will still be the girl who was borne ashore on a shell,
And I'll shout, as the ivy on my stone advances,
Go to it, Frances!

Ogden

For Frances
February 14, 1969

For your lover's shoulders round
What comparison may be found?
When you storm I feel like this (
A single sad parenthesis,
But when you brighten, then am I
More like a rainbow in the sky,
That archèd and effulgent sign
Seen only after storm and shine.
In you the elements combine,
My weather and my valentine.

Ogden

———

The spring of 1969 was full of excitement and anticipation, for the family was to meet together in Ireland at a marvelous place Isabel and

Freddy had rented for June and July. Mother and Daddy were going first to England and Scotland, leaving the end of May on the Holland-American line and eventually coming to Ireland in early July to stay for two weeks with the Eberstadts before sailing for home on the twenty-third from Cobh. Johnny and I and the two younger girls were supposed to fly over to Ireland toward the end of June for a two-week visit; only Nell would be missing since she had been signed up for a student tour of France.

But two days before our parents were supposed to sail, Isabel called me. She had been to the doctor about an irritating mole on her instep; it had been biopsied and the diagnosis was cancer. Surgery was set for the following week, and it included not only carving up her foot but also removing the lymph nodes in her groin. She did not want Mother and Daddy to be told because she knew they would cancel their long-awaited trip. She was determined to get to Ireland herself, unlikely as that might seem. We decided that I would go over on June 20 with my girls and Nenna, to be joined later by Johnny, and later still by Nicky. Isabel and Fred would come as soon as she could leave the hospital. It seemed a real scenario of positive thinking to me, but I knew Isabel. Like Daddy, she was frail, but also like Daddy, she was an immovable object once she had made up her mind. I felt that to argue would imply concern that the operation would not go well — besides, I knew better than to try to match wits with my sister. She had always been able to talk rings around me in any argument from the time we were tiny.

And it all turned out as she had planned. She did indeed reach Ireland and we were together for ten glorious days in July.

R.M.S. Nieuw Amsterdam
Holland-America Line
June 6, 1969

Dearest Isabel —

We are happy today, our 38th anniversary, after a relaxing trip across a billiard table sea. We have liked the ship, which is well, as we shall be returning on her; solid, stolid, heavy old-fashioned elegance; meals and service not deluxe but more than adequate. Our only gripe is at meals. We are seated at a table next to one occupied by a German glamor girl and her pretty 3 year old daughter. The mother is competently maternal at luncheon, then at dinner slinks in in a clinging evening gown looking like an adventuress and international spy. (She does speak 3 languages.) Our little waiter whom we share with her is about 18 and moons over her exactly like a Willie Baxter or Noble Dill with the result that we get almost nothing to eat until her delicate appetite has been satisfied. Mummy has restrained her ire, but barely. Fellow passengers mostly Dutch, but some Irish, bound for Cobh. Among these, the delightful Charles (Con) Cremin, Permanent Irish Ambassador to the U.N., with his wife. They are spending 2 months at home in Kerry, which he tells me is not too far from Glin (he seems to know all about Fitzgerald), and will return on this same ship with the Warrens and us. He has promised me some introductions in Dublin, which should be helpful. Tomorrow may be difficult. We are due in Southampton about noon, but the captain tells us that we shan't get ashore before 8 P.M. because it is Saturday and the dockers won't and can't work while the football matches are in progress — it's in the union contract.

You gave us such an auspicious send-off, and we think of you often and deeply. With luck we shall talk to you on Sunday.

> *Meanwhile all love from us both.*
> Daddy

Stafford Hotel
St. James's Place
London, England
June 8, 1969

Dearest Isabel —

I am sorry if Mummy and I were over-emotional last night; the news reached us at the end of an arduous and vexing day which I shall presently describe to you. Your letter set forth the situation clearly, and this morning we talked to Linell, who gave us what amounted to a word by word repetition of Phil Wagley's view of the situation. As a result we are less jittery today; in fact, considerably reassured. Without being foolishly and irresponsibly optimistic, I think we can be most hopeful about the outcome, both immediate and eventual, of the nasty ordeal. I can't tell you, darling, how much I admire your fortitude; my pride in you, which was already great, has grown to almost ludicrous size, the way Nicky kept growing.

Because of one thing and another we didn't dock at Southampton until 7:30 P.M. after slowly gliding past the Isle of Wight on a superb early summer evening. Then three quarters of an hour standing in line in the smoking room for British Immigration; another three quarters waiting for the luggage to come ashore, still another waiting for customs inspection — during which Mummy did *not* tell the official that I carried 4 packs of Luckies and half a bottle of Dewar's over my quota — and finally a porter for our 9 pieces of luggage. We shared a compartment on the train with a German who teaches German literature at the U. of Pennsylvania and his wife, he a genial and interesting man, and all went well until we reached Waterloo Station, where we eventually got a porter, but found ourselves at the tail end of queue waiting for taxis, which were almost as rare as at Penn Station. After half an hour of helpless standing in a cold wind I finally used my head and called the hotel, and in 10 minutes we were rescued by the night porter cheering on the driver of the most adorable taxi I have ever beheld. An even warmer welcome when we reached the hotel well after midnight, and we were shown to an elegant small suite from which we shortly talked to you.

I am happy to tell you that we got safely off the ship without your mother's having slapped the face of the Rhine maiden, her Rhine kind or the idiot waiter. A near thing, that, but we made it. Tell Nicky, while we speak of Germans, that on the final day the ship's newspaper was printed only in German and Dutch; no English version. I took a whack at the German — there were momentous dispatches from Saigon, Bonn, Washington, etc., but the only one I was able to decipher informed me that an *Engländerin* aged 48 had, 8 days after her silver wedding, given birth to a 6-pfund mädchen. I suppose it was the one cheerful item of the day. We attended part of a service at St. Paul's this morning, then drove back along the embankment and so to lunch and a nap. Tonight we dine with the Nick Bentleys and André Deutsch, tomorrow we learn our itinerary from the travel agent. A kind telephone invitation, thanks to the Higginsons, from the Earl of Lindsay, who wants us for a weekend at his place in Fife. He was a classmate at Groton of my old friend Stuart Stone and others, left at end of 5th form when he inherited. More as more happens.

All my love —
Daddy

Stafford Hotel
St. James's Place
London, England
June 10, 1969

Dearest Isabel —

Simply to tell you that you will shortly receive a delicate little *art nou-
veau* pin that we saw today in the Burlington Arcade and couldn't
resist — it bears your birthstone and carries our love on wings.

You'll be amazed to learn that we are not to be drummed out of our
cozy suite tomorrow and stored in the luggage room for the night but
may stay on until our scheduled departure; also that the Stafford has suddenly discovered that we can be accommodated here on July 9, 10 & 11
instead of going to something called the St. James. The fact that this
change of mind coincided with my TV appearance on the Eamon An-
drews show last night and interviewers from the Times and the Standard
today is purely coincidental. — But I am amused by the fact that I am
better known and more highly regarded in London than in New York. —
Mummy and I have done some shopping, more tomorrow.

Dearest love —
Daddy

Roxburghe Hotel
Charlotte Square
Edinburgh, Scotland
June 19, 1969

Dearest Isabel —

We had a glorious 2-hour run by train from Newcastle, much of it along
edge of North Sea, sparkling blue as the Mediterranean in today's fine
weather. Even saw the Holy Isle with its castle in the distance. Green hills
to our left, beaches and rocks to our right. Sheep everywhere, also cows
of every color except purple. We are in a splendid old hotel on a lovely
square. Arrived in time for a good lunch, talked to Linell in Baltimore,
then walked to Cook's to cash check and inquire about guided bus tour
of city which we hope to take tomorrow afternoon. All British hotels fur-
nish marvelous towels but never a wash cloth. Do all the natives carry
sponges in bags? We have a back-brush here. Porter who carried up 7

bags and performed other services refused pound — "Far too much, sir. Service is included in your bill" — reluctantly accepted half a crown. We are waiting now for our call to you to come through, late plan to go to a little outside city for dinner at restaurant recommended by Postgate, best of British food guides. — Later. No, not that one, it's fully booked to-night and tomorrow, but a third good one will let us in. And we have just talked to you, a great pleasure. — The porter also says "Aye". — A message informed me that P —— S —— C —— (try to say that name fast) will telephone in the morning from Chipping Campden (which I fear I spelled without the "p" when I wrote you). He was once on the Balti-more Sun, married to daughter of editor, drunk at Christmas party, told Aunt Eleanor she had no business to be on paper, everyone hated her. Sorry when sober. Great friend of Anne Duffy. Divorced, re-married, lives here (he's ½ English), has written a book or two and contributes to *Punch*. I assume that he may want to do something for us when we are in his neighborhood around July 3 — perhaps red, white and blue cake on July 4? I'll tell you when I know; we are happy to scrounge from anyone.

We shall now go forth into a glorious evening (8:05 P.M.) with the sun far from ready to set, walk around the green square with its many shade trees, and ingurgitate a gourmet dinner.

All love —
Daddy

Roxburghe Hotel
Charlotte Square
Edinburgh, Scotland
June 20, 1969

Dearest Isabel —

I left you in suspense last night as we were preparing to go out to dinner. Walking and following directions we came within 25 yards of our restau-rant but didn't know it — asked the way from a kindly native whose ad-vice led us to climb back up the steep hill we had just descended, walk a long block to the left, go down another steep hill, walk another long block to the left and *voila!* There it was, 25 yards from where we had been 15 minutes earlier. Restaurant excellent, most attractively decorated, and only 3 other couples dining. After dinner we walked up hill again and around Charlotte Square, on which our hotel is situated. Woke today to insistent drenching rain. Perhaps because of this perpetual precipitation the British don't need to drink water; I do know that it takes great effort to have any served at table. I had come abroad hoping to taper off on smoking, but seem instead involuntarily to be giving up water. We did some desultory shopping this morning, got back sopping, dried off during luncheon, then set out, again in persistent rain, on a Cook's guided bus tour of the high points — and high they were. The Castle, perched far on top of an abrupt minor mountain, then an endless climb on foot over cobblestones and up winding steps. Luckily my leg muscles had been resuscitated by turns around the promenade dock of the ship and further foot work in London, Canterbury, York, and climbing the stiles of Northumberland to reach Roman ruins, so I made it to the top of everything, much to Mummy's astonishment. The view of the city spectacular, as was that of the Scottish Crown Jewels. The best part of the tour was Holyrood Palace, truly exquisite, with an extra treat for my gruesome mind — to walk into the very closet off Mary's bedroom where Darnley and friends murdered Rizzio. The effect of this almost but not completely spoiled by a guide who never stopped talking and had an endless routine of bad jokes which even his rich Scottish accent could not make palatable. Matter of fact, the only acceptable guide I can remember having been led by was the lady in Williamsburg. The bus tour decided one thing for us. We were scheduled to go by chauffeur driven car from here to Pitlochry on Sunday at a cost of £ 30. I had seen that we could also reach Pitlochry on a conducted bus tour for 22 shillings apiece. We had been contemplating practicing this considerable economy until being subjected both to the cramped bus seats and the yammering of our leader this afternoon, and now it's the hell with the extra expense. — I write this by the window and the sun has just burst through, so we can at least start on foot to our next restaurant adventure, this time with the exact location of our target firmly fixed in my mind, as I marked it down this morning as we sloshed past it. Of course we came expecting, and reasonably prepared for, capricious weather. I must say that I enjoy it all, drink history and tradition where I cannot drink water; and am, in a word, having a glorious time which I think can only be topped when we are reunited in Ireland.

All love,
Daddy

Roxburghe Hotel
Charlotte Square
Edinburgh, Scotland
June 21, 1969

Dearest Isabel —

Today has so far been a glorious one in every way, starting with the weather, cool and sunny. A little shopping this morning, then Mummy went to the hairdresser and I to the barber. A walk in search of Lucky Strikes turned out to be approximately a mile longer than necessary, thanks again to kindly pedestrians, taxi drivers and policemen, all of whose ideas differed as to the route to Queensferry Street. I was rather pleased than not, since the detour (or diversion) led me past many charming squares, circles and crescents. I next remembered that a pleasant Scot named MacEwan whom we had met at St. Mary's in the Mountains had spoken of a place called Prestonfield House, a short distance from town, an old inn mentioned by Dr. Johnson as a stopping place on his return journey from the Hebrides. We went, and found it utterly delightful, everything in period and in good taste. We had the best meal yet, white bait for me and Jaffa orange cup for Mummy to begin, then guinea with excellent sauce, along with a perfect chablis, finishing with foamy meringues. We then strolled on the lawn admiring the flowers and the peacock and his girl until the simultaneous arrival of our taxi and a Rolls containing the bride and groom for whom a large marquee had been set up. All in all, a truly happy venture. The British can't add up pounds, shillings and pence any faster or more accurately than I can, and when they have to make change the money is always in the next room. — You will shortly receive 15 paperback Georgette Heyers; you have probably read many of them, just discard what you don't want. We are hoping to hear from Linell in Ireland in a couple of hours if she isn't still sleeping after the flight. Then off to sample another restaurant, this one in Leith, which adjoins Edinburgh and where we trust that the police will dismiss us.* The fish and shellfish recommended. Then off by car for Pitlochry in the morning. 7 P.M. and Linell has just telephoned, all well and delighted with Glin.

All love,
Daddy

---

*A favorite family tongue twister:
"The Leith police dismissith us." — Ed.

Oban
June 27, 1969

Dearest Isabel —

We have now almost had our fill of the highlands. A beautiful but interminable drive from Inverness today — I'd guess 1 air mile to 6 ground miles, what with the narrow twisting roads. Walter Scott grandeur all around us — Loch into loch, Ben topping Ben, glen undercutting glen. Two submarines, one red, one yellow, preparing to plumb the deeps of Loch Ness in search of the thing. Good driver, looked rather like Gilbert Highet, but with less Scot accent — luncheon at quite primitive inn where we had to walk through heavy rain shower to and from the bar, which was isolated from the dining room. Engaged in conversation with lone elderly lady full of local lore and still angry with the Campbells. — Most unpopular locally, Cameron and MacDonald country — and got full details of Glencoe massacre. We got here about 4 P.M., 5 hours drive to cover 120 miles. Oban is incomparable as to situation, on waters that I shall find the name of when I consult the map — our room, facing west, looks out over them, clumped with a group of islands. The view is all this hotel has to offer, our room otherwise is miserable, small and cluttered, hand-basin in the bedroom and dark cubby hole, unventilated, containing tub and W.C. Food at dinner execrable. Odd rag-bag of fellow patrons. In a word, 3rd rate British seaside resort. But our spirits are high in this lowspot. We pray for fine weather tomorrow, when we take the 9 hour boat trip to the isles of Staffa and Iona. I have a tenuous sentimental attachment to Iona, home of Saint Columba, because when I was at St. Georges in the pre–John Nicholas Brown chapel days, we had to walk 3 miles to and the same 3 miles back from a church called St. Columba's for our Sunday morning worship. We talked to Linell earlier this evening, Johnny had got there and all seemed merry as a marriage bell.

We are so happy that you will soon leave the hospital, and await the outcome of the clash of wills over what you do next. Much as we hope for you to get to Ireland we don't want you to do anything rash. Do think twice before you decide.

All love,
Daddy

Oban
June 29, 1969

Dearest Isabel —

Before I describe Sunday in Oban I must report on Saturday night in Oban. We made the mistake at dinner of taking the chef's suggestion, *dindonroti* (Scotch for roast turkey) and later moved sluggishly into the telly lounge only to find that the program was an old film of Jimmy Cagney as George M. Cohan singing I'm a Yankee Doodle Dandy and It's a Grand Old Flag to an audience of frozen-faced valetudinarians. Your American parents slipped away before being identified as such. Now we come to Sunday in Oban. It is now 1:30 in the afternoon and we have had Sunday in Oban. The porter, who I think speaks only Gaelic, forgot to reserve the Sunday papers for us, so the only ones that came in were snatched up by the resident cormorants. (Note: after lunch, the porter sold us half of a second hand London Sunday Times for a shilling.) Earlier we inquired of the porter, the usually absent young lady at the reception desk, *and* the headwaiter, where to find St. John's Cathedral. None of them had ever heard of it (Scottish Episcopalian in communion with the Anglican church, said the poster). It turned out to be immediately behind the hotel — luckily, as we walked to it in a light rain and returned through a cloudburst. A long but pleasing service, everything chanted or sung but with the congregation pitching in with or without talent. The service alone took 55 minutes, and from what I had read of Scotland I feared a 55 minute sermon, but it was exactly 8 minutes, eloquent and to the point. — Still raining. We shall now nap, and if it clears, or at least if the rain slackens, we hope to walk around the harbor. The porter looks like Alderman Ptolemy Tortoise; he huffs and puffs and pants from his continuous efforts to frustrate at least two members of the clientele. — BULLETIN — I have just telephoned Glasgow and been assured that a car will be here in the morning to carry us away from this house of Usher. What will the Trossachs hold for us? You shall hear in due time.

All love —
Daddy

The Trossachs Hotel
Trossachs, Perthshire, Scotland
June 30, 1969

Dearest Isabel —

At longest last we are out of Oban. It was pouring rain when we awoke, slackened enough so that we could pack car. From then on, all was pure bliss — double bliss, in fact, first because of our release from the charnel house, and second because the drive down was so beautiful, running water everywhere, thin ribbons winding down the hillsides, rushing streams in the glens pouring into lochs, and the clouds and mist giving way to timid sunshine. Excellent driver. The trip took only 3 hours, just long enough, and we are now in a roomy suite of a delightful hotel run by courteous and accommodating people. It is on the banks of one of the smaller lochs with a field full of white horses intervening. Loch Katrine is but a short distance away, but I fear too far for us to walk. We have only this afternoon to explore in — we leave at 8:45 tomorrow morning for a 12-hour train journey to Winchester — and I think we will rest a bit and content ourselves with the placid scenery immediately in front of us. I only wish that we had had 3 days here instead of Limbo-by-the-sea. When we were almost here we passed a shop with a sign saying OPEN and for one dreadful moment I thought it said OBAN and we were doomed to circle forever, always ending up at the Great Western Hotel. Heard first Scotch joke today, you might as well undergo it too. Scotchman reaches heaven's gates, greeted by St. Peter. "What's your name?" "Jock MacGregor." "From Scotland?" "Aye." "Sorry, Jock, you'll have to go to hell. We can't serve porridge for one." Our driver, who contributed the anecdote with understandable diffidence, had the strongest burr we have yet encountered. We also had our first close-up of the shaggy Highland cattle; a herd was blocking the road, and gave way with great reluctance. This is MacGregor country, proud of the fact that it was a MacGregor who was the greatest cattle thief of them all.

No rain since this morning. Not much sun, but a sort of mild clear gray. And oh, the joy of not being in Oban! A simple pleasure, but one we cherish deeply.

We look forward to talking to you in half an hour.

All love,
Daddy

Cotswold House
Chipping Campden, England
July 4, 1969

Dearest Isabel —

The hither from yon of yesterday left no opportunity for letter-writing. A full day, and an interesting one. Nice Englishwoman named Mrs. Williams drove us. First to Salisbury Cathedral — beautifully proportioned, with a sky-high spire, and surrounded by wide lawns so you can get the full effect from any point. A mistake to enter it, however, for it is like an empty barn. — Next we climbed the hill and minced our way across a sort of duck board specially designed, I think, for the stride of ducks, that spanned a deep moat which led us to Old Sarum, once an Iron Age fort, later site of the first cathedral. Then to Wilton House, seat of the Earls of Pembroke, a truly luxurious palace crowded with art and furnishings of sufficient quality and quantity to fill several museums. Unfortunately we were immediately clutched in the talons of a Teutonic governess-type gauleitress who was inexorable in her insistence of telling you all you didn't want to know and nothing of what you did. After lunch in Marlborough we stopped at the church in Burford, full of Crusaders and touching inscriptions. — Then on through the Cotswolds, beautifully rolling, to this hotel. Our room is bright and comfortable, with the one disadvantage that it is at the top of 2 steep flights of stairs and there is no lift. Didn't seem to discourage the boy who carried up our 7 bags, and we have so far survived very well. A pretty old town, once a great wool center; the high street lined with low stone houses. — Off on tour with Mrs. Williams this morning. First Stratford, Shakespeare's birth place, house in which he died, etc., much as expected, but with gorgeous gardens. We did particularly like the church he attended and in which he lies beneath the famous inscription along with several members of his family. We lunched at what had been an old mill on the River Leam, then on to Coventry for a quick look at the Cathedral. I hadn't realized that part of the walls of the original cathedral are still standing. They are right beside the new one, which is indeed unique. Highly imaginative, but I kept thinking that it was the joint creation of Roxy and Frank Lloyd Wright — there is a strong suggestion of picture-palace. But the windows over the entrance are great — religious figures etched into clear glass; and an Epstein group on the outside is fine. Home through a series of charming thatched roof villages; with a glimpse of

Warwick Castle in the distance. We have decided to rest from gazing to-morrow, perhaps stroll the streets here for a while, and generally relax. We have a dinner engagement tomorrow night and must be mentally bright and chipper; we can't physically; because there are no facilities here for pressing, cleaning, or laundry. — Where road work is in progress a sign reads "Loose Chippings." As we are in the midst of Chipping Campden and Chipping Norton I thought at first it was another village; just another American who wants a glass of water at table. But I now understand their money better than they do.

All love —
Daddy

Studley Priory
Horton-cum-Studley
(9 miles from anywhere, including Oxford)
July 6, 1969

Dearest Isabel —

At the end of our lazy yesterday, P —— C —— picked us up in a bulky Buick with Maryland plates (left-hand drive, of course) which he guided with skill through tortuous lanes and eventually through the narrow gate posts of the thatched cottage, where we joined his wife and the Rubin-steins (he my agent at A. P. Watt). A good dinner despite too many kinds of wine; some pleasant talk, and back to the hotel at 10:45 — at which unseemly hour we had to admit ourselves with a latch key because they lock up at 10:30. C —— rather mellower than of old, most hospitable, happy with new wife and children. His first wife, the Baltimore one, well established in marriage to member of government here. — Hilary and Helga offered to drive us today, so this morning I released Mrs. Williams from the chore. This worked out beautifully — in the first place, we have become devoted to the Rubinsteins, both individually and as a couple. Charming, interesting, thoughtful. In our departure from Cotswold House we were maliciously delighted because the manager himself had to carry down our 7 bags because the Boy was occupied in delivering the Sunday papers to the peerage. After an easy trip to Oxford, Hilary drove us around the university, then took us for a tour of his old college, Mer-ton, which vies with New College for the honor of being the earliest founded. He had wanted to show us the medieval library, but it was closed. Just as we were leaving we encountered the Fellow in charge, an old friend of Hilary's so we turned around and he opened it up for us. All the old bookstalls and scholar's benches and some unique early man-uscripts, plus some good stories about a recent Professor Garrod who took broken pieces of glass from the chapel windows and jigsawed them into intelligible wholes (not whales) to replace library windows that had been destroyed. Final fillip, 20 minutes in the Max Beerbohm room. Lunch in a converted boat house on the Cherwell. Pouring rain did not discourage the punting enthusiasts, of whom we had a fine view — best floor show in years, with spectacular climax when pole stuck in mud and punt kept on, leaving punter clinging; slipped into river and swam ashore, pipe in mouth.

Studley Priory a priory indeed — old, stone, rambling, obviously haunted. We may have the abbot's chamber, vast, plaster and timber, floor waving and surging like floor of fun-house. No telephone. Switch of bedside lamp came off when pulled, as did knob on great front door.

Daddy

July 7

P.S. Your letter of approximately July 1 finally caught up with us this morning and gave us happiness.

––––––––––

Life divided between Cross Keys and LBH suited Daddy very well. He and Mother delighted in feeding the birds on their patio during the win-ter, and one of his first poems of 1970 was an anguished cry to the man-agement of the village regarding avian safety. He gave me my own copy of it since I had occasionally chased the marauders for him if they ap-peared when I was visiting.

In March, Daddy and Mother took what would be their last trip abroad together. They sailed aboard the *QE II* in a party of six, the two other couples being close friends from LBH. Daddy's letters home kept us abreast of their news, which unfortunately included a broken wrist for Mother.

The inclusion of Tenby toward the end of the trip must have served as something of a pilgrimage for Daddy. Grandfather's last years had been occupied by tracing the Nash family back to its roots in Wales, though, of course, neither his health nor his purse allowed him to visit the spot from which the original Nash had set sail for the colonies. So my parents' visit to the old town marked more than a mere sight-seeing expedition. Daddy was able to complete the quest his father had begun nearly half a century before.

In June, Daddy gave the commencement address at Farmington. Nell was thrilled when she learned the school had invited him and quite taken aback when he inquired if she would object. Poor Daddy! He was so used to his daughters' rejoinders to similar requests. Isabel and I, both as children and then adolescents, had always lived in mortal terror of being noticed in any way — even obliquely — and our automatic response to a parental performance was "Oh, Daddy, please don't. We would just *die!*" So he must have been thrilled at his granddaughter's enthusiasm. At long last Daddy delivered an address at a descendant's school.

His text that hot June day brought the accustomed laughter that he had courted so successfully in his years of lecturing, but he mixed some serious stuff in with the lighthearted froth. The girls listened quietly when, in defining American humor, he said,

I have a theory that American humor of today — or, rather, of yesterday and tomorrow, because you will find all too little of it today in young or old — American humor is a unique blend of three ingredients: one of these, a sort of logical illogical playfulness, started with Lewis Carroll, crossed the Atlantic to Canada where Stephen Leacock toyed happily with it, and came to the United States where Robert Benchley and his contemporaries gave it citizenship. The second, more full-blooded, originated with the tall tales, the sly understatement and uproarious overstatement of the pioneers. When this reached its peak with Mark Twain, it was nobly carried on by a truly worthy successor, James Thurber. The third arrived with our Jewish immigrants, tired, sad, and gently cynical after generations of oppression. These three streams, I believe, converge to form the vast Mississippi of American humor, in which you'd do well to refresh yourselves from time to time.

After graduation, Nell and her best friend from school, a charming English girl, Sarah Firth, spent the summer driving across the country in a trusty VW Beetle. Daddy's concern showed in his summer letter to Isabel. He had already voiced his misgivings to me. But his disapproval didn't prevent him from alerting his West Coast friends of the girls' plans, and they were royally entertained when they reached the coast. The whole trip was an unmitigated success and they returned home full of the

"How confusing the beams from memory's lamp are;
One day a bachelor, the next a grampa . . ."
Daddy with his youngest grandchild, Nenna, in 1965.
(*Photo by Frederick Eberstadt*)

Ogden Nash, who in his lectures
often referred to himself as a
college dropout, was in his
later years awarded many
honorary degrees.
This photo was taken
at one such event.

things they had seen and done, but Daddy's forethought in arranging things for them in California made for the most lasting memories.

Complaint to the Management
of Cross Keys — February 13, 1970

I wish to scotch the rumor that
I am an enemy of the cat.
I guess that no one on this globe
Is less of an aleurophobe,
In spite of which I hate the feline
That for my warblers makes a bee-line,
Whose owner turns it loose to prey
On nuthatch, cardinal, junco, jay,
Whose ancient hunting urge is stirred
By sight of dove and mocking bird,
Who spurns its Puss-in-Boots to speed
To where I've scattered sunflower seed.
Three cats there are which mar the scene
At number 30 Olmsted Green;
One gray, one black, one black and white,
All insolence and appetite.
Like witches at Walpurgis' party
To them "Scat!" simply means "Eat hearty!"
Here cats walk wild, but dogs on leashes.
Are cats a special privileged species?

HMS Queen Elizabeth 2
March 26, 1970

Dear Linell —

We had intended to telephone you a birthday wish, but find that it can't be done when in port — which we are. Have been since 8 this morning. Shall be until 2.30 A.M. tomorrow. The port, St. Thomas. Temperature 90°. The day sunny and windy. We went ashore by launch and just wandered through the streets and alleys of the town and into and out of shops. Before lunch I made modest purchases, 2 pair of casual shoes and

3 ditto shirts, but after 2 Planters Punches really went mad on a warm weather wardrobe; I shall sweep into Little Boar's Head like a rajah. My excuse is that this is a free port, and my garments from Haiti and Thailand cost about half of what they'd be at home. Your mother contented herself with a hat and shirt for the beach; we plan to visit one in Barbados.

This is a handsome ship, but so streamlined and super-modern as to have no character. Everything on a giant scale. Fine service, food moderately good. We have 2 other traveling companions besides the Higginsons and Bryers — Mr. and Mrs. Philip Nash, he having retired as a master at Groton 7 years ago. The first New England Nashes I have met; I'm glad to say we like them. They brought with them as far as St. Thomas one daughter, one son, one daughter-in-law and 3 grandsons, all of whom leave the ship here and fly back to Florida for the rest of the spring vacation. Their daughter Peggy, now Gifford, was at M.P.S. with you and Isabel; an attractive young woman.

Only one deck for walking, the boat deck, but it doesn't go all the way around and is too windy for walking anyhow. Everything else is flush with the side, large windows for fine observation. Our table in dining room is practically in the ocean; the same thing in the bars and various vast public rooms.

Catherine Collins gave a fine party Sunday night. Cocktails at the apartment of an architect named Walter Cain, then dinner at Périgord, just across the street through a drenching rain.

Two shipboard movies so far. The Lion in Winter, which I thought tedious, repetitive and nasty, and the Russians are Coming, preposterous and delightful. Other entertainment, 2 evenings of Bingo with no luck.

The Smith flowers are still brightening our cabin, and we miss you all.

Love,
Daddy

Hotel Vendôme
Paris, France
April 7, 1970

Dear Linell —

It is exhilarating to be back in Paris after 21 years. We got here yesterday in time for luncheon — a fine one especially appreciated after the pseudo-French meals on the QE2. The hotel old-fashioned, intimate and comfortable — also, if I have not misread the rates, quite reasonable. We left Le Havre in a slashing rain, ran through more rain and some sun on journey up and were greeted by sleet in Paris, but the weather cleared in time for us to have an hour of strolling, window-shopping and eaves-dropping on the passers-by before dinner. — We were enchanted by Lisbon and those parts of Portugal we could see during our 8.30 A.M.–7.30 P.M. stop; promise ourselves to return for a longer stay. — We miss you all, but at least are glad not to have to put up with Elizabeth during the basketball playoffs. — It is now 10 A.M. and we shall start our rounds of the city —shopping list for moment headed by oranges for breakfast, books, and map, and unvarnished toilet paper. Only English books in French shop across street 100% pornographic.

> *All our love —*
> Daddy

Hotel Vendôme
Paris, France
April 10, 1970

Dear Linell —

We take off in an hour for London via Calais and Dover if your mother is still ambulatory. She had her second fall of the trip 10 minutes ago in one of the arcades. This time she protected her face, but one of her ankles is somewhat sprained. — Otherwise our Paris visit has been a fine success. One night with the Bryers to see the new Anouilh play, "Les Poissons Rouges," beautifully staged but rather mysterious happenings in the mind of an author who at the age of 8 had *fait pis-pis* in the fishbowl of his grandmother and can't forget it. — All museums closed by strike (une grève) of the guards, but we have done much walking and some driving to good effect, and eaten well in several good restaurants. Yesterday at *La Pérouse* your mother had guinea and I had wild boar, both well appreciated. We also had an extra pleasant meal at *Le Vert Gallant*, where we took you and Isabel and I embarrassed everyone by complaining about the canned pineapples. Today the first of full sunshine, the others have been on the sullen side, not too disagreeable, but far from poor Vernon's idealized picture. — Dr. Bryer has just thoughtfully presented me with the published version of the Anouilh, so now we can perhaps discern what those lines were that had the audience convulsed with laughter. The only one I understood was that if everyone were a gynecologist there would be fewer crimes of passion.

We look forward eagerly to getting your news in London, particularly of Johnny's mother. We feel quite isolated.

All my love —
Daddy

P.S. Correction — it's the wrist, not the ankle that is sprained. In the first fall, on shipboard, she bruised her nose, cut her lip and gashed her shin. All healed now.

Stafford Hotel
St. James's Place
London, England
April 13, 1970

Dear Linell —

A sweet birthday cable from Nell put the icing on the cake of our talks with you. — Your red and black bag has been a godsend. — I have learned how to get a lady into a girdle and attach garters — at least, I have nearly learned. — Now that the pain has gone your mother manages to make do very well, although she is denied use of half her wardrobe because plaster won't go through sleeve.

We have been moved into room we had last year, much nicer than one we arrived to. — Quite steady rain until this evening. We are now promised 3 clear days. — Hour and half in National Gallery yesterday afternoon, following morning service at the Abbey. — Looks like good theatre here, we plan to see about 5 plays. — Also several trips outside London with Higginsons. — Radio here just marvelous. Also, newspapers full of odd items like enclosed.

All love —
Daddy

Stafford Hotel
London, England
April 21, 1970

Dearest Isabel and later, Linell —

We hope all is well with you, have had no word since telephone call. However, mails seem to have gone mad — air mail letter from Linell received yesterday took 10 days to get here. We are pleasantly surprised at the speed with which Mummy has adapted to her handicap. She manages to do almost everything unaided, and my services as maid are no longer in much demand. The chief nuisance is clothes, as she can't get the cast through many of the sleeves. We had a delightful day yesterday, went by train to Liss in Hampshire to visit Peter and Iona Opie, authorities on origins of Mother Goose, children's songs and games, etc., with whom I have had a pleasant correspondence for some years. We found them charming. He is quite small and highly nervous, doesn't drive car but never leaves off directions and warnings. She a pretty woman, considerably younger. House literally built around books, shelves even running through middle of living room. In one upstairs room a marvelous collection of toys dating from the 18th century. After an excellent luncheon, cooked by her, they took us to Selborne, seat of the naturalist Gilbert White. Fine 12th century church, robin in churchyard. We were lucky in weather, like a fine October day. The rail service is great; if this be the result of State operation, I'll take it over Henry Large any day. We shall test it further on Friday, as we have planned a 3-day excursion to Wales, returning on Monday. I want to see Tenby, St. Davids and in general the region from which the Nashes set sail in 1720. Still constantly impressed by universal courtesy and patience, visualize with horror these narrow winding streets filled with N.Y. taxi drivers. Any one of them refusing to yield or wait a moment would tie up the entire city. But you still have to bring your own wash cloth. —

April 22 — Pen planned delayed birthday party for Katherine last night. At last moment she felt too unwell to come along, so Mummy and I and Pen and his friend B. J. (Quackie) Harrison started off in chauffeured Daimler large enough to house the royal family. First to Hurley, beyond Windsor, to see and have drinks at the Olde Bell, a 14th century inn which had housed some of the guests at Peter and Connie's wedding in '61. Not quaint, just honest, most attractive. — Then on again through heavy rain another 20 miles to Sonning-on-Thames for dinner at the French Horn, I should guess the most elaborate and expensive of riverside restaurants. Landscaped, waterscaped and illuminated. Duck turned on spit as we watched. We had been joined here by Captain Jumbo Edwards and wife, he old friend of Pen, rowing coach at Oxford, whom we met several times at L.B.H. — No rain yet this morning but gray sky threatens. We don't worry, as we are now fairly impervious to weather.

Note to Isabel — please send this letter on to Linell.

All our love to all of you.
Daddy

Postcard to Miss Frances Smith
from Tenby, Wales
April 21, 1970

This is what we see from
our window, although no
flowers as yet. It was
around here that your 5 times
great-grandfather, John Nash,
lived until sailing for America
in 1720. A pretty town, we
walked through much of it
this morning in rain. Now
sun is out and I wish I had
brought swim trunks.

All our love —
Papa

Stafford Hotel
St. James's Place
London, England
Friday
May 1, 1970

Dear Linell —

I write this at the close of our 6th consecutive rainless day, in fact the temperature is in the 60's. We are trying to finish as much as possible of our packing, as we are being ousted from our lovely room at noon tomorrow and the boat train doesn't leave until 7 P.M. We shall take the Higginsons to the Garrick Club for luncheon. Last night and the night before we gave dinner parties, the first to my London agent and his wife, both of whom we love, and the second, including the Higginsons, for Bob and Babs Lusty, old friends, he a top publisher who would like to take me over. Both events at fine and unusual restaurants, most successful. Last Tuesday on our return from Wales the Lustys had given a party for us in a private room at the Garrick, at which I sat next to Mrs. Harold Wilson, wife of the Prime Minister; found her charming. She has a book of poetry coming soon, so I've sent her one of mine with a special inscription in verse. Also present, John Betjeman, a poet I enjoy and admire.

Now for our inevitable demands on you. We should be at the Gotham early afternoon of Thursday the 7th and will telephone you. Dining with Kay Reynal at 7.15. Luncheon we hope with Isabel either Thursday or Friday. Dentist Friday 10 and 10.30. We'll take an afternoon train but I can't say which, since the time table would have changed with DST and we wouldn't be able to get our 9 or 10 pieces of luggage on a metroliner, must find an old-fashioned train. Would love to be met, but if inconvenient will get limousine. Now — will you see if Agnes can come on Wed., Thurs. or Friday to make beds, put out towels, etc. Ask Elizabeth if she can come on Monday. Ask yourself if you can put in milk, oranges, eggs, bacon, enough to start us. And be sure there is water in the ice trays. And we hope that you and Johnny and the girls can Elkridge with us for Sunday luncheon.

Your mother has bought almost nothing for herself and has not allowed me to buy anything for her — my only birthday present so far has been a taxi ride to St. George's Hospital and a rather dismal dinner at the Café Royal, but I shall return looking like a bird of paradise. — Both Higginsons have been ill, but we have maintained good health, barring a broken bone or two. Our trip has truly been all we could have hoped for.

Love from us both to all.
Daddy

Sheraton-Plaza Hotel
Boston, Massachusetts
May 18, 1970

For Frances,

> The twelfth of April came, and then it went,
> And horsemen carried sad news from Aix to Ghent.
> From kitchen-maid to king, from priest to peasant,
> The rumor flew, She won't select a present!
> I tempted her with everything in view
> From the Place Vendome to Bond Street, Old and New,
> With gem and gewgaw, print and watch and wig,
> With various kinds of exotic thingmajig.
> At her constant evasion, she might see something later.
> I felt as lost as Chloe or Judge Crater.
> Frustrated after seven weeks, and frantic,
> I choose this gift completely unromantic.
> You spurned all others, so why should I be excuseful?
> It's not elegant, but at least you'll find it useful.
> It represents those things I wanted to give.
> Happy birthday, darling.
>   I love you while I live.

Ogden

North Hampton, New Hampshire
July 8, 1970

Dearest Isabel,

What has the current issue of the local papers to report? Francie and Biddy have returned to Baltimore, leaving a horrid grandchild gap which we count on you to fill in August and September. Linell and Nell plan to come to us on August 17 for a while but even then there is room for Nicky and Nenna; at any other time, of course, for all four of you. Last night Nell reported in from St. Louis. She and Sarah will visit a classmate in Los Angeles, than go to Page in Santa Cruz; Ted and Ruth have invited them to stay at their place in Sausalito. We try not to think about the trip too much. Kay Reynal comes to us this weekend; we are having dinners for her on Friday and Saturday and taking her to a Higginson fishhouse do on Sunday; not an overdose of hospitality, I hope. No Saunders at present. Bail Tucker, Dorothy's husband and the cook, laid up with nervous exhaustion, so no lobster dinners for the next 10 days or so. Recent weather glorious. Very hot inland, but our blessèd sea breeze here, perfect for beach.

After 6 month dry spell induced by disgusted contemplation of the triviality of my stuff in today's world I have concluded that trivia are also a part of life and got back to work. Four verses in the past week — more than there are magazines to print them. I still can't decide whether I work because I feel well or feel well because I work.

I have agreed to do a job with André and the Philharmonic next June, an entirely new venture called "Marriage Lines" after the book. Will consist of readings of my verse concerned with marriage and its concomitants along with music from classics on same theme. Might be fun.

Your mother flourishes, picking peas and cutting flowers daily. In the evening when the TV is impossible we are reading Trollope. I read the Mavis Gallant book; truly the most boringly unloveable heroine in years. Halfway through the Arlen book, find it truly moving.

We miss you all and count on your coming to us fairly soon rather than skipping off to Austria, Italy, or Tonga. The summer goes by too fast.

All love —
Daddy

October 19, 1970

Dear Biddy —

You write such good letters that we always enjoy getting them. We are so interested in what you are doing at home and at school, and you keep us well up to date. — Up here the weather man has finally decided that summer is over and a little frost would be a good thing. The red and yellow leaves have fallen down and my red and yellow trousers have gone upstairs. I ate the last of the tomatoes today and the cabbages in the garden have crumbled, but the price of lobsters is down and clams are plentiful. Last week we went to Boston with Mr. and Mrs. Higginson and saw a musical comedy about Noah and the Ark. Danny Kaye was Noah.

We thought the play went on for 600 years. Part of the time Noah was a juvenile delinquent of 90. Mrs. Noah died before he did. I don't blame her. — I wrote a short verse today:

> Said the slothful tree toad
> To the three-toed sloth,
> Is it true that you are lazy
>   enough for us both?
> I don't even bother to
>   scratch when mosquitoed,
> Said the three-toed sloth
>   to the slothful tree toad.

> *All my love,*
> Papa

In December Daddy and Mother gave a dinner for Nell before her presentation at the Bachelors Cotillon. The dinner was held at The Elkridge Club — the scene of many important occasions in the life of our family, beginning with the famous November dinner dance in 1928. But this night, another poem of Daddy's tugged at my thoughts:

> When I remember bygone days
> I think how evening follows morn;
> So many I loved were not yet dead,
> So many I love were not yet born.

He called it "The Middle"; he wrote it when he was forty. The bittersweet words echoed in my mind as I thought of "absent friends."

By 1971, Daddy had a work in progress with Milton Rosenstock, his old friend from the days of *Two's Company*. He was looking forward to its production off-Broadway in late March. He was also finishing up his book *The Old Dog Barks Backward*. The second half of 1970 and the first two months of 1971 were unusually productive ones for him, despite his infirmities.

Verse at Dinner for
My Granddaughter, Nell Smith
before the Bachelors
Cotillon at the Lyric
Baltimore   December 4, 1970

TALE OF TWO DEBUTANTES

Exactly twenty years ago tonight
I was a rumpled mass of black and white.
With this same vicious collar did I grapple
As it made cider of my Adam's apple.
This same white tie drooped listless, limp and dying,
Dappled with thumbprints from an hour of tying.
And this, the very identical shirt, I vow,
Kept bulging then just as it is bulging now.
You'd think that through the years it had grown mellower.
It didn't. Only contrarier and yellower.
Two such discomforts faced but did not daunt
The prideful father of his first debutante.
I didn't dream, though t'was as clear as Poland water,
That this debutante daughter would have a debutante
    daughter.
                    So —
Two decades later, here again am I
Victim of selfsame collar, shirt and tie
Plus some expansion of the waist and hip
That makes the trousers hard to button — or zip.
This time I'm not the prideful sire, but rather,
Proudest of all, this debutante's grandfather.
What phrase is apt from my slim Latin store?
'Tis *Mater pulchra, filia pulchrior,*
Which means, referring to face and grace and torso,
Mother is beautiful, her daughter even more so.
Dear Nell, this saying, with all respect to you
Is, like most sayings, not exactly true.
But if you haven't yet out-shone your mother
You're still some lengths ahead of any other.
You're all that any grandfather could want,
The season's most enchanting debutante.
Here's health and love and joy to you, dear Nell.

Off to the Lyric, child,
and give them hell!

For Frances

That you should guide me when I steer,
Why should it cause surprise?
You've been my heart this forty year,
And now you are my eyes.

And when the mocking bird perverse
Upon the fence appears
I cannot hear his impudent curse
Unless you are my ears.

Upon this Christmas day I vow
Both ear and eye do show
Your face and voice even lovelier now
Than forty years ago.

Ogden, 1970

Baltimore, Maryland
February 28, 1971

Dearest Isabel —

We are much heartened by news of your improved health, hope that more of same treatment will bring Nenna back to par. I wish we could be with you, but you will see from the schedule below that time is against us.

March 4	X-rays (part of check-up, so far so good)
March 9	Dentist
March 15	Dentist
March 19	Dentist
March 25	Dentist
March 28	Tentative date for opening of my venture with Rosenstock; should go to NY for few days of rehearsal if possible
April 2	Dentist
April 7	Reading at Poetry Forum in Pittsburgh

All of them a nuisance, but must be maintained. — Friday night we took the Smiths to see Nureyev and the Australian ballet, quite a fascinating evening despite the fact that the ballerinas were heavy-footed and Comrade N. made only a brief if brilliant appearance in the third and last ballet around 11 P.M. The second one featured an affair between a lyre-bird and a lady and clearly demonstrated how Leda and the swan went about it, something I have often wondered about. That, with the 2 Pinter plays, should bring Biddy's sex education course up to date.

Our weather has been good for the last week. Our mocking birds, cardinals and warblers are singing gleefully and we have seen a blue jay dance his courtship dance, which he seems to do on a pogo stick.

Elizabeth was out for 2 weeks with the flu with the result that Mummy and I concocted some fabulous dishes, varying from triumph to disaster and always with Mary Kitchen Roast Beef Hash to fall back on. — Prompted by mention of Elizabeth, I have just telephoned Clarence, find he has recovered from the flu, now up and around, x-rays show chest clear.

I now at the cost of $30 own one tenth of one eleventh of a race horse in partnership with a group from the Sunpapers. Linell still waiting for her 19 year old mare to give birth. Two of the horses she sold are doing well on the track, one ran at Hialeah 3 lengths ahead of a field with Phipps and Whitney horses. But I worry about her over-all operation. She looks well, and the girls are happy.

We miss you, and send love
to all.
Daddy

That horse, Gain or Loss, was to become the grandam of the 1987–88 2 million dollar winner, Lost Code. Daddy would have enjoyed that. Of the appointments, only the first was kept however; time was indeed against us all. A problem was found in the March 4 X-ray, and surgery was recommended. He entered the hospital on March 12, but before he went, he completed two poems, making a total of eighteen for the year by that date as compared to the twenty-six in 1934 and twenty-seven in 1935, his two most productive years. He had somehow freed himself from the gloom of the 1960s, and against all odds been able to work once more.

He may have had some presentiment of what was to come, for he wrote many old friends and far-flung family members in the week between diagnosis and surgery, but all went well at first. The operation turned up nothing serious, and we rejoiced, but prematurely. Suddenly things began to turn sour and, while he fought the odds gamely and cheerfully, his body was giving out. It took death almost two months to defeat this frail and gentle man. After his hospitalization in 1966 he had written:

> Enter, breath;
> Breath, slip out;
> Blood, be channeled,
> And wind about.
> O, blesséd breath and blood which strive
> To keep this body of mine alive!
> O gallant breath and blood
> Which choose
> To wage the battle
> They must lose!

The battle was lost on Wednesday, May 19, shortly after 3 P.M. Mother and Isabel and I were with him. The afternoon was almost painfully beautiful, the essence of spring.

We sat beside the bed, half numb with grief, well-nigh oblivious to the blue and gold and green of the day. He couldn't leave us — he mustn't! But he did. No fuss, no trouble; he died as gently as he had lived.

We drove home to Olmsted Green in silence; each a prisoner of her own thoughts. The shadows were lengthening in the courtyard where the birds picked last bites of sunflower seed before nightfall. In the twilight, a solitary monarch butterfly fluttered near the sliding-glass doors. "How odd," I thought absently as I followed Mother and Isabel into the kitchen. Mother took a bottle of champagne from the refrigerator, set out three glasses, and filled them, slowly and carefully. Everything seemed almost dreamlike as we carried our glasses back to the living room. The butterfly was still there, hovering near the glass.

We raised our glasses, our eyes misty with visions past. "To Ogden!" said Mother, and we drank. The butterfly fluttered once more, a shadow now in the glorious May evening, then suddenly soared skyward and was gone.

(*Photo by Frederick Eberstadt*)

Epilogue

DADDY was buried from St. Andrew's By-the-Sea, the little Victorian summer chapel on whose vestry he had served and where his granddaughter Brigid had been christened. It was opened specially for the day of the funeral. The minister who held the service was one of the family's oldest and dearest friends in LBH. At the end of the service he read a poem Daddy had written many summers ago:

> I didn't go to church today,
> I trust The Lord to understand.
> The surf was swirling blue and white,
> The children swirling on the sand.
> He knows, He knows how brief my stay,
> How brief this spell of summer weather,
> He knows when I am said and done
> We'll have a plenty of time together.